Drupal™ User's Guide

Drupal™ User's Guide

Building and Administering a Successful Drupal-Powered Web Site

Emma Jane Hogbin

PRENTICE
HALL

Upper Saddle River, NJ · Boston · Indianapolis · San Francisco
New York · Toronto · Montreal · London · Munich · Paris · Madrid
Capetown · Sydney · Tokyo · Singapore · Mexico City

Many of the designations used by manufacturers and sellers to distinguish their products are claimed as trademarks. Where those designations appear in this book, and the publisher was aware of a trademark claim, the designations have been printed with initial capital letters or in all capitals.

Drupal is a registered trademark of Dries Buytaert.

The author and publisher have taken care in the preparation of this book, but make no expressed or implied warranty of any kind and assume no responsibility for errors or omissions. No liability is assumed for incidental or consequential damages in connection with or arising out of the use of the information or programs contained herein.

The publisher offers excellent discounts on this book when ordered in quantity for bulk purchases or special sales, which may include electronic versions and/or custom covers and content particular to your business, training goals, marketing focus, and branding interests. For more information, please contact:

> U.S. Corporate and Government Sales
> (800) 382-3419
> corpsales@pearsontechgroup.com

For sales outside the United States please contact:

> International Sales
> international@pearson.com

Visit us on the Web: informit.com/ph

Library of Congress Cataloging-in-Publication Data

Hogbin, Emma Jane.
    Drupal user's guide : building and administering a successful Drupal-powered web site / Emma Jane Hogbin.
        p.   cm.
    Includes index.
    ISBN 978-0-13-704129-9 (pbk. : alk. paper)
    1. Drupal (Computer file) 2. Web site development. 3. Web sites—Design. I. Title.
    TK5105.8885.D78H695 2011
    006.7'8—dc23

                                                                        2011025848

ISBN-13: 978-0-13-704129-9
ISBN-10:   0-13-704129-2
Text printed in the United States on recycled paper at RR Donnelley in Crawfordsville, Indiana.
First printing, September 2011

Editor-in-Chief
Mark Taub

Executive Editor
Debra Williams Cauley

Managing Editor
John Fuller

Project Editor
Anna Popick

Copy Editor
Kim Wimpsett

Indexer
Jack Lewis

Proofreader
Linda Begley

Technical Reviewers
Michael J. Ross
Simon Hobbs

Publishing Coordinator
Kim Boedigheimer

Cover Designer
Chuti Prasertsith

Compositor
The CIP Group

For my mother, Maryann, who asked for the manual to her Web site.

Contents

Preface

In the late 1990s I began my career in Web development by making simple Web pages while studying at college. My degree in science and the environment combined with my summer jobs of Web site building landed me a job as a project manager at a firm making Web sites for environmental organizations. The in-house programmer would sometimes tell me that things "couldn't be done," and being the stubborn sort of person that I am, I began to learn programming. We were always working on a shoestring budget, and free software was absolutely essential to our toolkit.

A few years later I branched out and created my own content management system—mine was going to feature a multilingual discussion board for college students learning a second language. (To this day, this is probably one of *the hardest* problems to solve.) Before writing a line of code, I downloaded all the different free content management systems that were available at the time. Drupal had the most sophisticated translation interface for multilingual Web sites. I ripped out the parts I thought were useful and spent two years working on my own little project. I thought I was doing a splendid job. And then I went back to check on Drupal. The work I'd done in two years was an embarrassment compared to how Drupal had grown. With only a slight hesitation I threw out my work and started building Web sites with Drupal.

What made Drupal so much more successful than my own CMS? Drupal is an open source software package that is free to download, modify, and use. People who build modules and themes for Drupal are encouraged to contribute them back to the pool of add-ons. The software license used by Drupal (GPL) ensures that the code you download will always be free for you to alter in any way that suits your needs. But you don't have to be a programmer to take advantage of this (and there's no *requirement* to give back to the Drupal community). If this seems a bit weird to you, think of it as a potluck or a church dinner—when everyone brings a dish of food to share, a complete meal is made.

The more community contributions have been made into the community, the less programming is required to build a robust site in Drupal. "There's a module for that!" is a common expression, and it's all too true. It's rare that my Web sites need custom programming these days. Most of the time, it's click-to-configure site building.

A few years ago I realized something really important: I don't *love* maintaining Web sites. What I *love* to do is empower people to manage their own online presence with the least amount of anxiety possible. This has shifted my work again. Where I was once a programmer and then a site builder, I am now primarily a trainer and technical author. The book you are reading right now is the book I've been working on for nearly a decade. It's the planning workshops I've given to small businesses that are getting ready to build (or rebuild) their Web sites. It's the "how to maintain your site" instructions that I've created for clients. And it's the case studies from my training program, Site Building Extravaganza.

I hope you find this book useful as you build your own site with Drupal.

About This Book

In a nerdy *Star Wars*–esque fashion, I think of this book as the prequel to my first book, *Front End Drupal*. It assumes you want to build a Web site without having to learn any code. It is structured to help you jump right in and start building your own Web sites. If you are new to Web site building, you may find it useful to start at the first chapter and work through to the end of the book. If you are a little more experienced with site building, you can use this book as a reference and jump around to suit your needs. Wherever possible, the topics are cross-referenced. Don't feel that you need to read every single word in this book. Skip the parts that you don't need (or you're not ready for). Learning Drupal shouldn't be stressful, and I promise not to quiz you on whether you read about such-and-such before proceeding to so-and-so. When you need to have specific skills, I'll let you know what the prerequisites are and where you can find them within the book or online.

Part I: Quick Start

The first four chapters of the book get you up and running with your first Drupal Web site. Chapter 1 introduces you to the kinds of Web sites that are built with Drupal. Chapter 2 covers the installation of Drupal on OS X and Linux-based Web servers.

Chapter 3 covers the new administrative interface for Drupal 7. In Chapter 4 you will build your first basic site with core modules.

Part II: Planning

With the basic understanding of the key Drupal concepts, we'll take a step back and do some planning. Chapter 5 steps you through the basics of creating SMART goals. Chapter 6 focuses on the people your site will be serving. Chapter 7 walks you through a content audit (assuming you have some content that you know you want to put into your site). Chapter 8 gives you the shortcuts you'll need to choose great themes for your site.

Part III: Case Studies

Two in-depth case studies show you how Drupal modules fit together to make complete sites. In the first site build, discussed in Chapter 9, you will learn, step by step, how to create a community site with a private discussion area. In the second example site, discussed in Chapter 10, you will create a business directory. These are two of the most common types of sites I've built over the years for community groups and business associations.

Part IV: Build Anything

This part of the book provides you with the foundation to build any Web site using Drupal. Chapter 11 covers important information about core and contributed modules. Chapter 12 shows you how to use, extend, and create Web forms to capture and display any kind of content you can imagine. In Chapter 13 you will learn how to create lists of content—from navigation to tags to the very popular Views module, this chapter explains the Drupalisms so many experienced site builders take for granted. The wrap-up chapter in this section, Chapter 14, includes short recipes that point you to the best combination of modules needed to build any type of Web site.

Part V: Extending Drupal

There are a few more topics that aren't about site building but are nonetheless critical to a successful Web site. Chapter 15 covers the basics of creating your own Drupal themes. Chapter 16 teaches you the ins-and-outs of search engine optimization. Chapter 17 covers the importance of accessibility with tips on improving the experience of your site visitors.

Acknowledgments

My thanks to those who offered their feedback as the book progressed (in alphabetical order by first name): Ben Finklea, Diana Montalion Dupuis, Diane Gilleland, Jeff Eaton, Katherine Kahl, Lynda Chiotti, Michael J. Ross, Mike Gifford, Rain Breaw, Simon Hobbs, Todd Nienkerk, and Wayne Atkinson. Any mistakes left in the book are entirely my own fault.

To the chaos crew: Thanks for your support and friendship and that other thing I can't put in a book but that starts with the same first three letters. Amy, Amye, Chris, Earl, Greg, Lynette, James, Jeff, and Stephanie, you are fantastic human beings, and don't let anyone ever tell you otherwise.

To all of my students: You are wonderful. Your questions are wonderful. You help me clarify what I am trying to say. Thank you.

To the team at Pearson Education: Sorry about the election. I promise it wasn't my intention to delay the book . . . again. Debra, the Lagavulin's on me next time.

Thank you, James and Maryann, for your support and gentle reminders that I need to eat and sleep (and write).

Thanks to Angela "webchick" Byron for shepherding the community through the release of Drupal 7. Thanks to Dries Buytaert for inventing Drupal. Thanks to the programmers who maintain modules, designers and themers who made beautiful designs for Drupal, the security team for keeping our Web sites safe, and the infrastructure team for keeping Drupal.org (the Web site) up and running. Thanks to everyone who provides bug reports and patches and documentation. You are the Drupal community, and without you there would be no Drupal and no reason for this book to exist.

About the Author

Emma Jane Hogbin makes Drupal easier through her books, videos, classes, and conference presentations. Emma's first book, *Front End Drupal*, is recognized in the industry as the most important book for Drupal designers. She has been teaching Internet technologies since 2002 and has been building Web sites since the 1990s. She is a frequent speaker at technical conferences, and she also likes single malt whiskey. These two things are probably not related. As a highly sought-after speaker and trainer, Emma has taught Drupal in France, Belgium, Hungary, Canada, New Zealand, England, and across the United States. Emma has also worked as a technical college instructor at Humber College and Seneca College and has worked on curriculum development for Humber College and the Ubuntu Linux distribution.

Emma encourages nontraditional participation in technology through craft and believes that everyone is capable of mastering the tools that surround them. She is a recipient of the Google Diversity award. To help engage new ways of participating in technology, she open sourced one of her knitting patterns so that you can make your very own Drupal socks (www.emmajane.net/craft/drupal).

Part I

Quick Start

Chapter 1

Introduction to Drupal

Congratulations on choosing Drupal (or at least choosing this book, which is about Drupal). If this is the first time you've built a Web site, you might be a little bit nervous. It'll be okay! This book will walk you through the step-by-step instructions you need to create and maintain your first Web site. In this chapter, you will learn about the following.

- What Drupal is
- Online content management
- Different types of Web sites you can build

Let's get started.

About Drupal

Drupal is an open source content management system (CMS) that is free to download, modify, and use. It was first released to the public by Dries Buytaert in 2001. The name Drupal, pronounced "drew-pull," is derived from the Dutch word *druppel*, which means "drop."

Drupal has been installed by thousands of people around the world to create Web sites that are used by millions of people every day. By choosing to use Drupal, you are accessing an award-winning platform and its vibrant contributor community. The community Web site, `http://drupal.org`, includes free support forums and the code (and documentation) you'll need to build just about every type of Web site imaginable.

> **Create Your Free User Account on the Drupal Web Site**
> Be sure to take advantage of the free support that's available on the Drupal community Web site. You can sign up for your account at `http://drupal.org/user/register`. Once you've created your account, head over to the support forums at `http://drupal.org/forum`.

Some Drupal sites are built with very large budgets and custom code. Drupal developers often create contracts with their clients so that the code they produce is put under a special public license, the GNU Public License (`www.gnu.org/licenses/gpl.html`), which allows others to share and build on their work. This sharing sometimes makes competitors into collaborators. For example, a voting system commissioned by Sony Music Entertainment, Inc. was made freely available through the Drupal Web site. Then Sony's competitor, Warner Bros., started using the code too. Warner Bros. made a few changes to the code that it contributed back to the freely available version of the software. These changes benefited Sony too. You can use that very same voting system on your Web site too (`http://drupal.org/project/fivestar`).

There is no obligation for open source programmers to share their custom code freely with the general public; however, when they do share, they have access to a much larger pool of software testers and potentially developers as well. This sharing is one of the big reasons why programmers choose to work on open source software projects. Don't worry, though! This doesn't mean you too need to have a programmer on staff to make a Web site. Open source software is almost like having your own team of international software developers—for free. Unlike having your own staff, though, open source developers who are donating their time aren't accountable to you, so if there's something really specific that you need, you will either need to learn how to make the changes or hire someone to help you.

Drupal isn't a piece of software in the typical definition of the word. Instead of being a single executable program, it is a combination of a Web server, a database server, two scripting languages, a markup language, and a formatting language. Fortunately, you don't need to learn all of these different things—you just need to learn Drupal's administrative interface to create content for your Web site.

Online Content Management

In 1995 I built my first Web page. I used a text editor to edit HTML pages. Then I used a special program to upload each file to a Web server at my friend's school (there were no student Web page accounts for my department). It was pretty magical. The next summer I got a job teaching professors how to make course Web pages. Five years later I was making database and Web forms that my co-workers used to create their own Web pages without having to know any code. Skip ahead five more years. I was now downloading the code that *other people* had built so that I could quickly create Web sites for my clients. And now I teach people how to build Web sites using Drupal.

The Web has grown a lot, and you would need to know an epiphany of information if you wanted to have the equivalent level of domain expertise that I had back in 1995; however, by the end of this book, you will be building sophisticated Web sites in half the time of what it would have taken me five years ago. You can do it by leveraging the power of Drupal and its community of contributors.

Unlike the days of yesteryear, most of the popular sites built today are structured so that site administrators can create pages and manage content *online.* There is no special desktop software needed to create a Web page using Drupal. You need just a computer, an Internet connection, and a Web browser.

> **Drupal Is Committed to Web Site Security**
> Just because your Web site is managed through the Web doesn't mean that any-
> one can edit your pages. Drupal is very committed to security and will protect
> your Web site so that only you can edit it. You can read more about the security
> team at http://drupal.org/security-team.

How Pages Are Built

When a visitor comes to your Web site, a series of actions is kicked into gear. Figure 1.1 shows the sequence of how a Web page is built and delivered to the site visitor. The basic sequence is as follows.

- The URL a visitor requests is translated by the Web server into a file on the Web server.
- In Drupal's case, this file initiates a self-sustained process that retrieves content from the database and assembles a Web page. This is known as the *bootstrap* process.

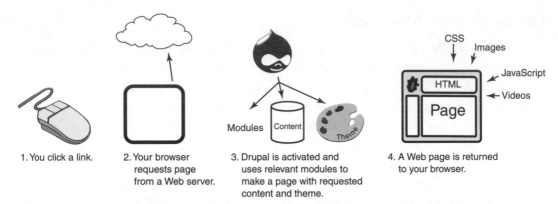

1. You click a link.   2. Your browser requests page from a Web server.   3. Drupal is activated and uses relevant modules to make a page with requested content and theme.   4. A Web page is returned to your browser.

FIGURE 1.1 The Web server converts a visitor's request for a specific URL into a complete Web page that the Web browser software displays.

- Drupal uses the URL to retrieve the correct content from the database. Using the configuration options set by the Webmaster, Drupal dumps this content into pages that have been built using *modules* and designed by *themes*.
- Once it's assembled, the Web page is returned to the Web site visitor.
- The Web page will have references to images, style sheets, and interactive scripts. Once the Web browser has the page that Drupal built, it will return to the server to request all of these additional resources.
- Finally, the whole thing is displayed as a Web page that you can see.

And all of this happens in a fraction of a second.

Before it is installed, Drupal is just a series of text files written in the programming language PHP. You could open every part in a text editor and look inside (not including the images, which are binary files). When you install Drupal, a relationship is created between these text files and a database on your Web server. The database will store your content and most of the configuration information for your site.

Within the package of Drupal files there is also a special theme directory that contains design files for your Web site. These are also text files, but they are written in PHP, HTML, CSS, and JavaScript. Packages of design files are referred to as *themes*. When building a page, Drupal combines these files as shown in Figure 1.2.

The good news is that your biggest responsibility in maintaining the site will include *only* writing text via a form in a Web browser and uploading images. Drupal will take care of (almost) everything else.

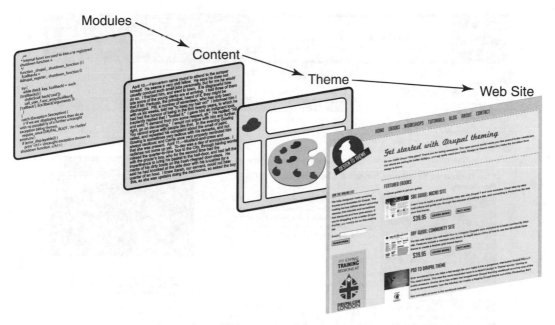

FIGURE 1.2 Content is stored in a database, and theme files are combined to style the content according to your site's design.

Types of Web Sites

Several examples of different kinds of Web sites are provided in this chapter to give you an idea of the kinds of Web sites Drupal can build. This section is not an exhaustive list—it is meant to give you an overview of the types of Drupal sites commonly found on the Internet today.

Reported News

News sites have a very simple model: Collect stories and share them with others. This might be either a traditional "news" company or perhaps a community Web site that is reporting its past events. The news may be collected by professional journalists or community members. Community-contributed content is often referred to as user-generated content (UGC). On community-driven sites, it is not typically necessary for visitors to contribute stories (and often only a small percentage of visitors do create content). The biggest distinguishing feature of a news site, therefore, is that visitors are consuming time-sensitive information.

An example of a community site built in Drupal is NowPublic (www.nowpublic.com), shown in Figure 1.3. This news site allows amateur reporters and concerned citizens to

FIGURE 1.3 NowPublic promotes citizen journalism.

upload their news stories. The community then votes on which stories should appear on the front page of the Web site.

Digital Collections

A digital collection is a collection of things centered around a theme. It may be photographs, rich media clips (such as audio or video clips), essays, or just about anything else you can "collect." These types of sites are commonly used by museums and archives to share their information with a wider public. In some cases, the sites provide access to high-resolution scans of fragile pieces typically or videos from regions of the world that are physically inaccessible to the public. Samples of these types of sites include the

Gutenberg Galaxy (texts of books available in the public domain) and the video library on Archive.org. Digital collections are ultimately page after page of things.

The Founders and Survivors Project (`www.foundersandsurvivors.org`) is an example of a digital collection built with Drupal. This online database stores information about the convicts transported to the colony of Van Diemen's Land (now Tasmania) in Australia. The Founders and Survivors Web site aggregates data from a variety of archival sources that have been transcribed to XML or imported directly into Drupal. Members of the public are encouraged to add their relevant family information to the archive project. Figure 1.4 shows the community nature of the collection, and Figure 1.5 shows a sample of the data form used to collect information about the convicts.

FIGURE 1.4 The Founders and Survivors project page

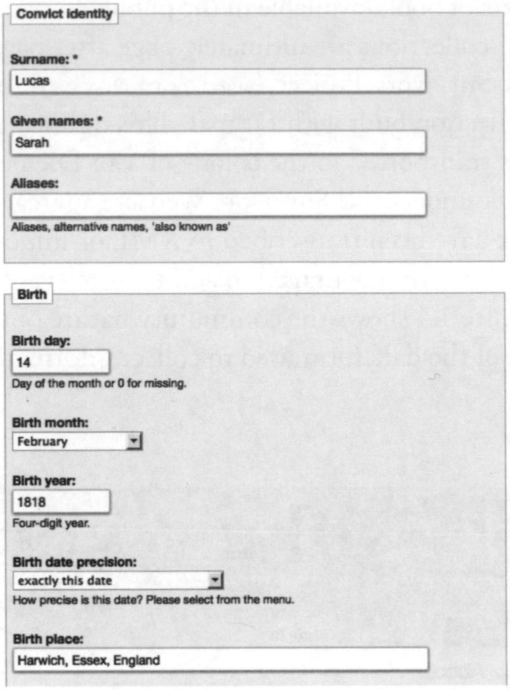

FIGURE 1.5 Data form used to collect information about the convicts

Instructional

In the two previous examples (news and digital collections), information was provided to the visitor with no additional structure. In an instructional site, there may be news and digital collection qualities; however, visitors will also be guided through the contents of the site with the expectation of gaining new skills and competencies. An instructional site will offer some kind of framework to its visitors that links content together. Site content may include videos, text-based tutorials, activities, and an evaluation scheme of some kind. Not all components are required for a Web site to be instructional in nature. For example, the Drupal Dojo (`http://drupaldojo.com`) offers free lessons to new developers via an online conference system. Sessions are recorded and made available to the public after each session (Figure 1.6).

Self-Promotion and Identity

These aren't just for celebrities and media icons. Self-promotion sites allow businesses to promote themselves and their company without being commerce centered. For

FIGURE 1.6 Home page of the Drupal Dojo Web site

example, if your shop currently has a few photos of products and a blog, you have essentially the same type of site as media mogul Seth Godin (http://sethgodin.typepad .com/). Your site promotes your ideas, your ethics, and your products or services without the capacity for sales. The content that you offer on this site will be technically and socially different from a commerce site whose aim is generating sales. Self-promotion sites will sometimes evolve to the point where ancillary products are available for sale. These may include T-shirts or books based on the author's experiences.

Self-promotion sites may promote a person, place, or just about anything. These sites may include a portfolio of an artist's work or case studies that describe how your company has helped its clients. Although information about fees may be included in a self-promotion site, the most wanted action from visitors is not to click a "buy here" button. This style of Web site is perfect for artists who focus on custom work and

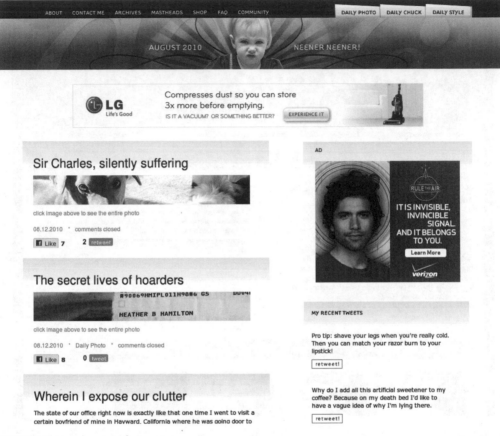

FIGURE 1.7 Home page of www.dooce.com

businesses that need a "brochureware" site (high on gloss but low on content). In many cases, it will be a fine line between this category and many of the others (including news, digital collections, and commerce sites).

An Internet-famous self-promotion site is Heather Armstrong's site, Dooce (www .dooce.com). Advertising on her blog is now the family's sole source of income. The site, very simply, is her life story. Figure 1.7 shows the home page of her site.

Portals and Aggregators

A portal is a jumping-off point that redirects the user from your Web site to another Web site. This format was very popular in the early days of the Web but has fallen out of style with the invention of site syndication through Really Simple Syndication

(RSS). The caliber of search engine results has also been part of the decline in portals. Where the Open Directory Project once fed human-categorized Web sites as the base content for search engines, improved web crawlers and search algorithms have made this time-consuming task (almost) irrelevant. Now, instead of sending visitors to other sites, the goal of most sites is to keep visitors right where they are.

Portals remain a valid format for some sites but under a slightly different incarnation. What was once a list of links to other sites has now become a collection of aggregated bits of content from those sites that used to just be links. Within the free software community, we often see "planets" where content from member contributors are gathered into a single place for reading. Often the full story is not available, and the reader must go to the original site to read the complete story.

Drupal's contributor community portal is available from `http://drupal.org/ planet`, as shown in Figure 1.8.

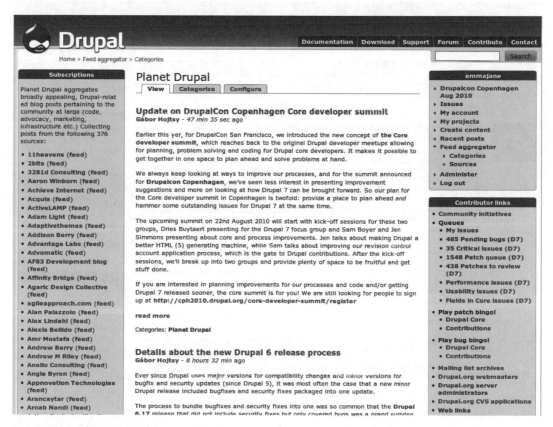

FIGURE 1.8 Planet Drupal aggregates news stories from community members.

Community Sites

Ever heard of Facebook? I bet you have! (No, it's not built in Drupal.) Membership sites are changing the way we share information online today. Unlike the user-generated content in news sites, the content generated in a membership site is often all about you (or me). Membership may be free, with revenue coming from advertising or ancillary product sales. Or membership may be paid (online classes and business coaching are also examples of membership sites). In a membership site, the focus is on *internal* conversations that do not necessarily relate to the world outside. Unlike the "Reported News" section's example, the goal is not to create citizen journalists but rather to promote and foster a sense of belonging and community. An example of this type of site is Drupal's own Groups site (http://groups.drupal.org), as shown in Figure 1.9.

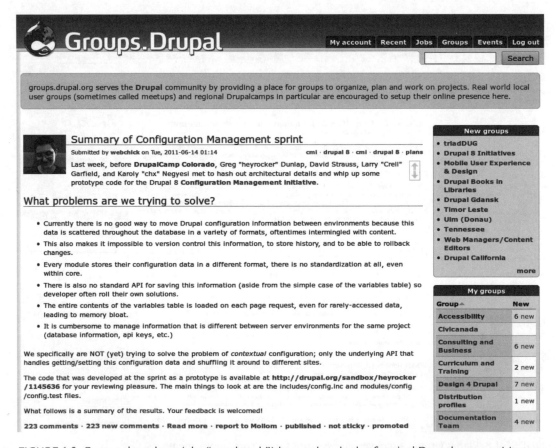

FIGURE 1.9 Groups.drupal.org (aka "gee dee oh") houses hundreds of topical Drupal communities.

Commerce Sites

As the name implies, these sites are designed with one core purpose: to make money. They will typically take the form of a product shopping cart with an entry form for your credit card at the end. The Web site may be focused on a single business or provide support for a large network of independent salespeople. To some extent, this model is similar to print-on-demand companies such as Lulu.com and Zazzle where the parent company offers the service and the community provides the customization that can be bought as a product.

The sample site for this type of site is Jenny Hart's Sublime Stitching (`http://sublimestitching.com`) shop (Figure 1.10). From her store you can order her entire

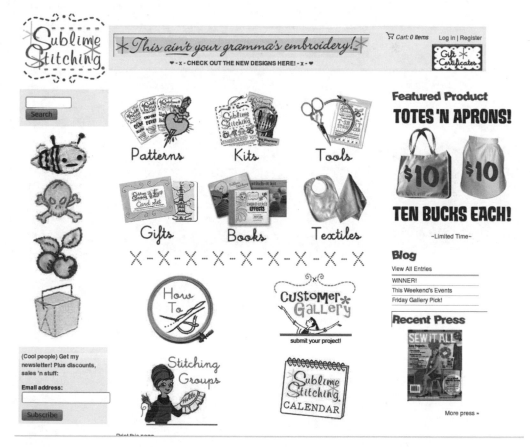

FIGURE 1.10 Sublime Stitching will sell you everything you need to create fabulous embroidery embellishments.

product line of embroidery templates and everything you need to put those designs onto fabric.

Summary

In this gentle introduction to Drupal, you learned a little about Drupal, open source software, and the kinds of Web sites that can be built using Drupal. Let's jump in and find out the basics of how Drupal works.

Chapter 2

Installing Drupal

This chapter outlines the requirements for selecting an appropriate hosting company and gives you step-by-step instructions on how to install Drupal. If Drupal has already been installed for you, please skip ahead to the next chapter.

Hosting Your Web Site on the Internet

Although Drupal is free, having a Web site is not. There are several parts to being online and having a Web site.

- Your personal or business Internet connection
- Annual domain name registration fee
- Web site hosting
- Web site development and maintenance (which you will learn in this book)

If you expect a large proportion of your marketing to happen via e-mail, you will also want to hire an e-mail service provider (ESP) that specializes in newsletter delivery.

Internet Service Providers (ISPs)

An Internet service provider (ISP) will connect your computer to the Internet. This is the service you will use to check your e-mail and surf the Web. Your ISP may offer you a small amount of Web space with your Internet connection for free, and they may have a discount on web hosting for customers who already use one of their services. "Free" hosting packages typically come with an address like www.bmts.com/~gingerpress and are not suitable for Drupal.

Web Site Hosting

You will need somewhere to install Drupal so that others on the Internet can view your Web site. Expect to pay $10 to $50 per month for Web site hosting and a mailing list. Most companies that offer Web site hosting will have a range of packages with different options.

Features included in hosting packages can vary. Specific requirements for installing Drupal are listed later in this chapter. When comparing hosting companies, look for the following options.

- Unlimited data storage
- Unlimited data transfer
- Unlimited databases
- PHP scripting language version 5.2 or greater
- File and database backups
- Free technical support

Additional nice-to-haves include the following.

- Web site statistics (you can also use an add-on free package such as Google Analytics)
- One-click install of Drupal
- Environmentally friendly/carbon-neutral hosting

There are few hosting companies with unlimited *anything*. That's okay. You don't really need unlimited capacity, but you do need to be with a company that will treat you reasonably when your zombie-brain cookies are featured on *Martha Stewart Living*.

If you are not very technical and you are hoping to build your own Web site, be sure to look carefully at the support your hosting company provides. Find answers to the following questions.

- When is technical support available (24/7 or 8 to 5)?
- How do you get in touch with technical support? Do you phone them, or do you fill out an online form to start a support ticket?
- Is there a limit on the number of support questions you can ask per month?

Read your contract carefully before signing up.

Domain Name Registration

If you want to have your own "dot com," you will need to register a domain name. This name is the address that people will use when they visit your Web site. You should expect to pay no more than $15 per year for a common top-level domain name such as .com, .net, or .org. This fee grants you the right to use the domain name for your Web site in the same way as a business license gives you permission to operate a business with a specific name.

Domain name registration can often be performed by your Web hosting company, and annual Web site hosting plans often include one free domain name registration. Ask your hosting company for more information. Some hosting companies will charge a small setup fee to register a domain name for you. Be sure to ask ahead of time if there is a setup fee. If someone else is doing the setup, make sure to have your name and contact information included on the registration to secure your ownership rights.

Uploading Files to Your Web Hosting Account

An FTP client is essential for installing Drupal if you are not using a one-click installation of Drupal from your hosting provider's control panel. A File Transfer Protocol (FTP) client allows you to move files from your own computer to a Web server. I recommend FileZilla. It is a free program that can be used on Windows, OS X, and Linux. You can download it from `http://filezilla-project.org/download.php`. If you already have an FTP client (such as Fetch, WinSCP, CoreFTP, and so on), you are welcome to use it instead. Depending on how your server is configured, you may need an FTP client to add extra modules or themes later in this book.

Installing Drupal

Your nerd factor will determine which of the following installation guides you need to use.

If you want to make a Web site on the Internet that other people can see too, proceed to the section "Hosted Installation." If you want to install Drupal on your own computer, you will want to start with Appendix B, Preparing Your Development Environment, and then proceed to the instructions for the hosted installation in this section. Finally, if you'd rather listen to Rick Astley sing "Never gonna give you up" than install Drupal, proceed to the section "One-Click Installation."

One-Click Installation

One-click installs are special software programs configured by a hosting provider that install Drupal for you. They are not available from every hosting provider, and they do have some disadvantages: They might be modified slightly from the default Drupal installation. For the most part, you shouldn't notice the differences; however, there may be additional modules installed that are not described as part of the base install in this book. The biggest advantage of a one-click install is that it's easy! You won't need to worry about the minimum system requirements or making a database or any of that froo-f'rah technojumble. Ask your hosting provider if they offer a one-click install of Drupal.

If you want to create a practice Drupal Web site without having to mess around with the installation process, try the following providers first.

- **Drupal Gardens** (www.drupalgardens.com). This site allows you to quickly create a Drupal site. You can choose from several designs and get a feel for how Drupal works with no risk.
- **WebEnabled** (www.webenabled.com). I use this service to create test Web sites for clients and students. Through its control panel, you can easily install Drupal in a practice area and then "launch" the site to another server when you're ready for the public to visit it. Their technical support is top-notch.

Each one-click install process is a little bit different. Ask your hosting company to help you through the installation process if you have questions.

Hosted Installation

So, you've opted to install Drupal yourself? What a great choice you've made! To proceed with your installation of Drupal, you will need to do the following.

- Ensure your Web server meets the minimum requirements to install Drupal.
- Create a database for your Drupal site and know its host name, user name, and password.
- Install an FTP client on your computer.
- Use an FTP client to upload Drupal's files to the correct folder on your Web server.

Each of these points is covered in greater detail in subsequent sections.

Minimum Server Requirements

The following are required to run Drupal.

- Apache 2 or greater running on Windows, Mac OS X, or Linux. IIS is also supported when correctly configured.
- MySQL 5.0.15 or greater (requires the PDO database extension for PHP; see the "PHP" section) *or* Postgres 8.3 or greater. Instructions on configuring Drupal with Postgres are not covered in this book.
- PHP 5.2.*x*. At the time this book was written, there were still some bugs for PHP 5.3.
- *Minimum* PHP memory allocation of 64MB and support for the GD Image Library enabled. Most shared hosting providers set the memory allocation to 16MB by default; be sure to check you have enough memory allocated to PHP before starting the installation.

> **PHP Memory Errors**
> Insufficient memory allocated to PHP may give one of two errors: "Fatal error: Allowed memory size of n bytes exhausted" or a blank page (the White Screen of Death). Troubleshooting tips are available from the Drupal Installation Guide (http://drupal.org/documentation/install/troubleshoot).

The detailed list of current requirements is available at http://drupal.org/requirements.

Creating a Database for Drupal

Drupal stores your content and its configuration settings in a database. Although there are a few alternatives, most Drupal installations use MySQL databases. You will need to create a new database for your Drupal installation. There are several ways to do this. On your hosting provider, you may need to use one of the following methods.

- **phpMyAdmin.** This is a configuration tool for MySQL databases that is available on most hosting platforms.
- **Command line.** On Linux or Unix-based systems you can also create a database without the use of a graphical/Web-based interface.
- **Hosting provider's administrative panel.** Many hosting providers offer either a standardized control panel, such as cPanel and Plesk, or a customized control panel unique to that company.

Instructions are provided for the first two options—if your hosting provider offers their own administrative tool for databases, they should be able to provide you with instructions on how to create a database. Follow their instructions and then proceed with the next section, "Preparing the Drupal Files for Installation." You need only one database, though, so don't follow both sets of instructions!

Creating a Database with phpMyAdmin

To create a database using phpMyAdmin, complete the following steps.

1. Log in to the phpMyAdmin administrative Web interface. Ask your hosting provider for the login information if it's not obvious from their introductory e-mail or their control panel interface.

   If you are the administrative user, complete the following steps; otherwise, proceed to step 6 to create a new database.

2. Click the link Privileges and then the link Add a new User.

3. Enter a user name and password for your new Drupal database.

4. In the Host field, select "localhost" unless your hosting provider has instructed you to use something else. Setting an explicit host helps prevent malicious people from accessing your database inappropriately.

5. Click Create to save your new user.

6. Return to the main configuration screen for phpMyAdmin by clicking the logo in the top-left corner of the screen (Figure 2.1).

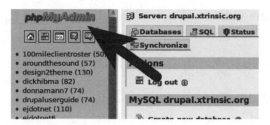

FIGURE 2.1 Return to the main phpMyAdmin configuration screen by using the logo link.

7. Locate the form field "Create new database" (Figure 2.2). The words after "MySQL" will match your database server name.

8. Complete the form fields as displayed in Figure 2.2. Use a relevant database name (all one word, no spaces). Leave the first drop-down as Collation and the "MySQL connection collation" drop-down as utf8_unicode_ci.

9. Click the button Create to create your database.

10. Write down the name of the database, its username, and its password. You will need this information to complete your Drupal installation. Take note of the server name as well. It will either be "localhost" or something else.

Your database has been created. You are ready to proceed with the next section, "Preparing the Drupal Files for Installation."

Creating a Database from the Command Line

To create a database using the command line, complete the following steps from the command line of your server.

1. Create the new database for your site (substitute a relevant database name and adjust the user name for your account):

```
$ mysqladmin -u root -p create databasename
```

2. When prompted, enter the root password for your MySQL account.

FIGURE 2.2 Locate the form to create a new database.

3. Open the command-line utility for MySQL (you will be prompted for a password):

```
$ mysql -u root -p
```

4. Using the MySQL utility, set the permissions for your database with the following command (adjust the database name, user name, and password):

```
> GRANT SELECT, INSERT, UPDATE, DELETE, CREATE, DROP, INDEX, ALTER, LOCK
TABLES, CREATE TEMPORARY TABLES ON 'databasename'.* TO
'username'@'localhost' IDENTIFIED BY 'password';
```

5. Jot down the name of the database, its username, and its password. You will need this information to complete your Drupal installation. Your host name will be "localhost."

6. To activate your new database, enter the following command from within the MySQL command-line utility:

```
> FLUSH PRIVILEGES;
```

7. Close the command-line utility by typing the command exit.

The database has been created. You are ready to proceed with the next section.

Preparing the Drupal Files for Installation

To install Drupal, you will need to download the source package from the Drupal Web site and then put the files onto your Web server.

Complete the following steps to prepare Drupal's files for installation.

1. **Download Drupal.** Go to http://drupal.org/download and locate the latest Drupal 7 release. Click the release number. The Drupal software package will be downloaded to your computer. Note the location where the files are being downloaded to (often this is your desktop).

2. **Unpack the downloaded archive file.** Usually it is sufficient to double-click the package that was downloaded from the Drupal.org Web site.

3. **Connect to your Web server using an FTP program.** If you are using FileZilla, open the Site Manager (located under the File menu). Enter your logon information for your Web server and then click Connect. Ensure the host, user, and password are entered. Figure 2.3 shows a sample connection screen.

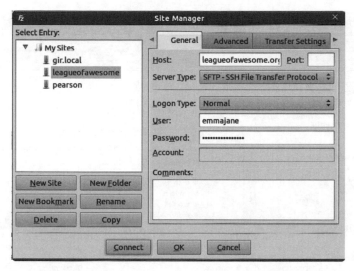

FIGURE 2.3 The FileZilla Site Manager. You will need the host, user, and password information for your Web server.

4. **Within your FTP program, navigate to the Web folder on your server.**
   Once connected, the right panel of your FTP program displays the files on your Web server (Figure 2.4). Locate the public Web folder. It is typically labeled something like htdocs, www, or public_html. Double-click this folder name to open it.

5. **Upload the files to the appropriate directory on your Web server.** On your local computer, open the Drupal folder that you unpacked in step 2 and select all the files. Then drag these files into the pane on the right of your FTP program to upload the files. Be sure to copy the hidden file .htaccess too. It is in the main Drupal folder.

You should now be ready to install Drupal.

Drupal's Install Wizard

The Drupal install wizard will lead you through a series of screens that prompt you for information about your database and that help you create a maintenance account.

1. In a Web browser, navigate to the URL that holds your Drupal files, such as http://mywebsite.com/drupal or just http://mywebsite.com. Drupal will automatically recognize that you want to install Drupal. Your first step

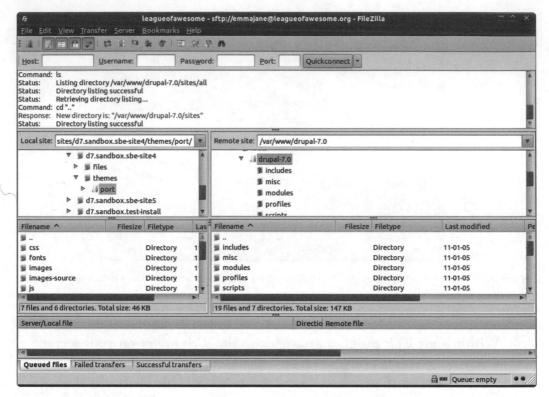

FIGURE 2.4 The FTP program FileZilla. The main window is divided into your computer (left side) and the Web server (right side).

is to choose the install profile you would like to use (Figure 2.5). If this is the first time you have installed Drupal, leave the selection at Standard and click "Save and continue" to proceed.

2. By default there is only one language option available for Drupal: English. If you want to install Drupal in a different language, click the link "Learn how to install Drupal in other languages." Otherwise, click "Save and continue" to proceed to the next step.

3. On the third configuration screen, you will be prompted for your database information (Figure 2.6). Enter your database name, database user name, and its password. If your database host name is something other than localhost, click the advanced link and complete the inset image portion of the form in Figure 2.6.

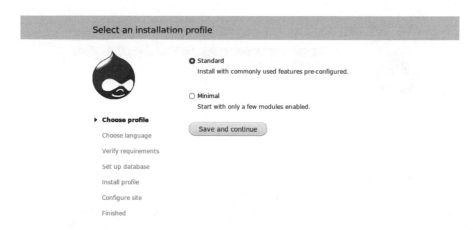

FIGURE 2.5 The Standard install profile is appropriate for novice Drupal administrators.

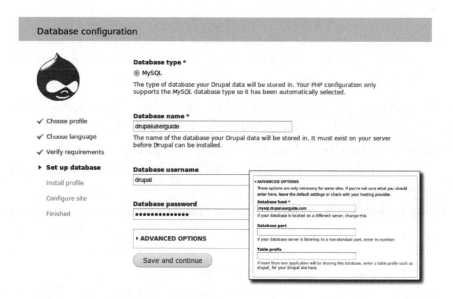

FIGURE 2.6 The installation wizard will prompt you for your database user name and password.

4. With your database information entered, click "Save and continue" to install Drupal. Figure 2.7 shows the status bar that will appear as your Drupal installation is automatically configured. Depending on the speed of your Web server, this may take up to 30 seconds. Do not close the browser window. Wait patiently while Drupal installs itself.

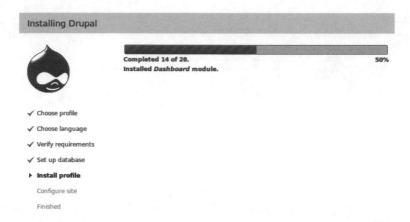

FIGURE 2.7 Drupal will install and configure itself with the settings you have chosen.

5. Once Drupal is installed, you will need to create a site maintenance account and configure some basic administrative settings. Figure 2.8 shows the site configuration screen. Complete each section using the most appropriate options for your Web site.

- **Site name.** This will be displayed in the header of your Web site. Use your business name if you are creating a business Web site.

- **Site e-mail address.** This address will be used any time e-mail is sent from your Drupal site, including password resets and automated notifications. It must be a real address.

- **Site maintenance account.** This includes the user name, e-mail address, and password. This account must be used for site updates and is all-powerful. By default the site e-mail address is used for this account. You can change this to a different address if you would like.

- **Server settings.** These settings are not required, but they will be used to timestamp your blog entries and other content creations.

- **Update notifications.** These settings allow Drupal to check in with the mother ship and send you an e-mail whenever a security release or new version of your installed modules are available. Leave these settings as is unless you are running a development Web site that is not exposed to the Internet.

These settings can all be changed from the administrative area after Drupal is installed.

FIGURE 2.8 Configure your new Drupal Web site.

Drupal is now installed and configured for basic use. You will be redirected to the front page of your Web site (as shown in Figure 2.9).

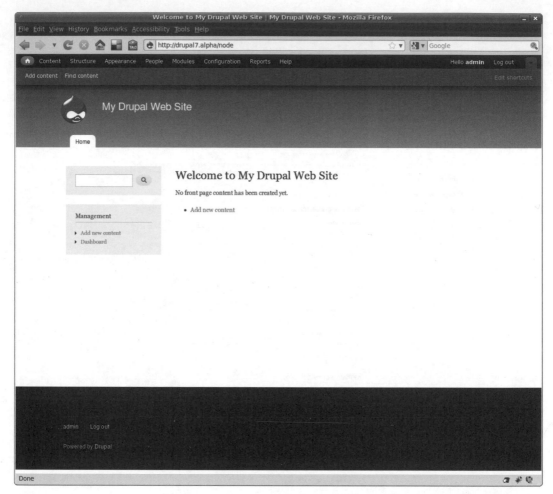

FIGURE 2.9 Drupal is installed, and you are now looking at the front page of your new Web site. Congratulations!

Troubleshooting

You will know whether you have prepared your server correctly if you are able to complete Drupal's install wizard without any errors.

> **Error Messages Are Useful**
> Don't be afraid of error messages. They are very useful. If you come across an error you don't know how to resolve, copy the error message and paste it into a search engine. Chances are good someone else has had a similar error and has posted a solution to it online.

The most common error I run into when trying to install Drupal has to do with incorrect permissions on files and folders. This can prevent Drupal from creating the configuration files it needs to complete the installation. Figure 2.10 shows a sample error screen that is directly related to permission problems on the server.

To correct the permission error, proceed with the following steps.

1. Using your FTP program, locate the folder `sites/default` on your Web server.

2. Select the `default` folder for configuration. In FileZilla this is done by right-clicking the folder in the pane on the right and choosing "File permissions" from the context-sensitive menu (Figure 2.11).

3. Modify the settings so that the folder is read-write-executable by your Web server.

Figure 2.12 shows the adjusted permissions using FileZilla.

When you think you've made all the necessary changes, go back to the Web interface and click the link "proceed with installation" at the bottom of the screen in Figure 2.10.

Web server	Apache/2.2.16 (Ubuntu)
PHP	5.3.3-1ubuntu9.3
PHP register globals	Disabled
PHP extensions	Enabled
Database support	Enabled
PHP memory limit	128M

❌ **File system**

The directory *sites/default/files* does not exist. An automated attempt to create this directory failed, possibly due to a permissions problem. To proceed with the installation, either create the directory and modify its permissions manually or ensure that the installer has the permissions to create it automatically. For more information, see INSTALL.txt or the online handbook.

Unicode library	PHP Mbstring Extension

❌ **Default settings file**   The default settings file does not exist.

The Drupal installer requires that the *./sites/default/default.settings.php* file not be modified in any way from the original download.

❌ **Settings file**   The settings file does not exist.

The Drupal installer requires that you create a settings file as part of the installation process. Copy the *./sites/default/default.settings.php* file to *./sites/default*. More details about installing Drupal are available in INSTALL.txt.

Check the error messages and proceed with the installation.

FIGURE 2.10 Configuration errors caused by incorrect file permissions on the Web server

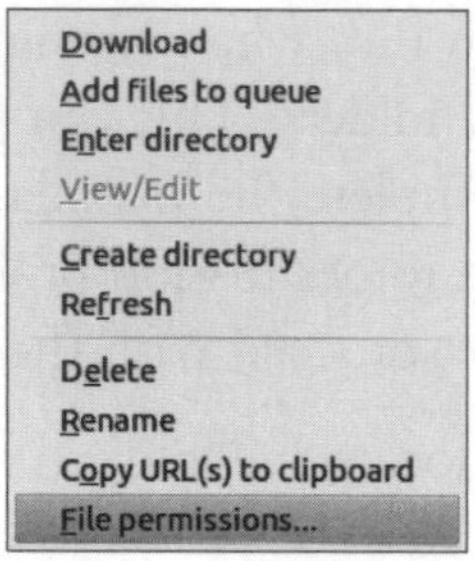

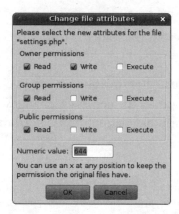

FIGURE 2.11 From the context-sensitive menu, select "File permissions."

FIGURE 2.12 Permissions correctly adjusted using the FTP client FileZilla

If you have corrected all errors, you will be directed to the next stage of the installation (in this case, database configuration).

Additional troubleshooting tips are available from the Drupal Installation Guide (`http://drupal.org/documentation/install/troubleshoot`).

Summary

Assuming you completed each of the steps outlined in this chapter, you should now have a Web site available to the public on the Internet. (You installed Drupal! Go you!)

Chapter 3

Drupal Administration

With Drupal installed, it's now time to turn to the administration area of your new Web site. Throughout the remaining chapters of this book, you will learn how to use Drupal's powerful configuration options. This chapter gives you an overview of different parts of the administrative section. If you want to dig into the administration of your Web site now, read on. If you are happy to let the book reveal Drupal's administrative interface on an as-needed basis, skip ahead to the next chapter.

Overview

In every Drupal installation there is both a public version of your Web site and a private, administrative area. Once you've entered your user name and administrative password, you will have access to the screens described in this chapter.

Drupal focuses on the ability to edit configuration options in place. It uses both a public theme (design) and an administrative theme that you will use when editing content. Once you've logged into your site, you will see a set of toolbars appear across the top of your site. These toolbars are visible only to site visitors who are logged in and have been granted permission to view the toolbar. Figure 3.1 shows the administrative toolbar visible throughout your site.

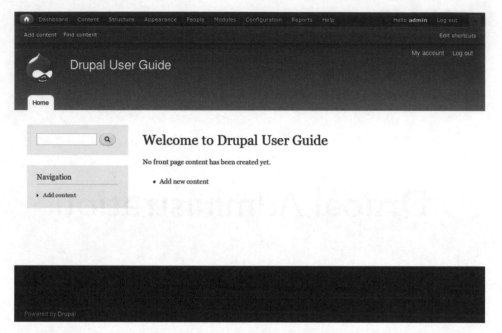

FIGURE 3.1 The Drupal administrative toolbar is visible to authorized users at the top of all pages.

There are four parts to the administrative interface.

- The **toolbar** is visible across the very top of your Web site. It lists the main sections of the administrative area and provides a link to your account and an option to log out of the Web site. It cannot be customized.

- **Shortcuts** are available directly beneath the toolbar. This is a list of links within your Web site that you would like to have available. You can use the default administrative links or create a personal set of shortcuts.

- The **dashboard** provides you with a summary of what's happening on your Web site. You can configure it to display any available blocks for your Web site.

- The **overlay** allows you to edit content, administer modules, and do just about any other administrative task without leaving your current page.

Figure 3.2 shows each of these four components.

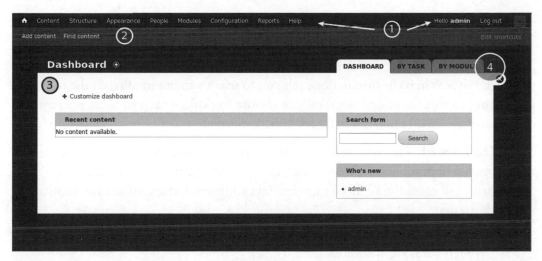

FIGURE 3.2 The numbered areas represent the toolbar (1), shortcuts (2), dashboard (3), and overlay (4), which is the white screen with black background that appears "over" the Drupal contents.

Administrative Overlay

An overlay is a screen that sits overtop another. The administrative overlay allows administrative changes to be made to the site without losing the context of the current page. The addition of the overlay means you can easily cancel any administrative changes and return to the page you were previously viewing. The overlay is also used when creating new content.

Administering Drupal Without the Overlay

The entire administrative theme is also available without the overlay. This book will use screen shots featuring the administration theme Seven with the overlay turned *on*; however, you can choose to disable the overlay by completing the following steps.

1. From the administrative toolbar, click the link Modules.
2. Scroll to the Core section and locate the Overlay module. Unselect the check box beside the Overlay module.
3. Scroll to the bottom and click "Save configuration."

The overlay will now be completely disabled.

Administrative Toolbar

The administrative toolbar provides links to the nine main sections within the administrative area of the site. Throughout this book you will use these links to configure your Web site. When the instructions tell you to select a menu item from the toolbar, it is referring to this list of options. You can choose to explore each of these options now or wait for the menu contents to be revealed as needed.

- **Dashboard.** This new feature is highly customizable. It starts with the following components: "Recent content," "Search form," and "Who's new." You can customize the dashboard to include additional, relevant administrative shortcuts.

- **Content.** Administer content you have created and comments that visitors have left on your Web site.

- **Structure.** To administer menus, content types, and blocks (the stuff that shows up in sidebars), you will use the Structure menu.

- **Appearance.** Don't like the way your site looks? Learn how to change how it looks in Chapter 4 and Chapter 15.

- **People.** Most basic Web sites are managed by a single person. When your team grows larger or if you have a community site where you have multiple participants, you will spend a lot of time in this area of the administrative section.

- **Modules.** Drupal itself is a pluggable architectural framework. It allows you to plug in new functionality. Chapter 11 covers core and contributed modules.

- **Configuration.** Remember how I promised that you would be able to change any of the settings you chose during the installation? If you want to do that, this is the menu item you'll need.

- **Reports.** Drupal comes with some basic reporting tools. From this menu option you can view reports, site errors, and available updates.

- **Help.** Need I say more? Sometimes we all need a little more help. Go here to find out more about modules in your system and some of the interface components in Drupal.

The menu items Configuration, Reports, and Help are covered later in this chapter.

Administrative Shortcuts

Ever notice there are some things you do more than anything else in your Web site? The administrative shortcut menu (located directly beneath the toolbar) allows you to easily add shortcuts of *your choice* to the administrative interface.

At any time you can add items to the shortcut menu by navigating to an administrative page you would like to add to the shortcut menu and clicking the plus (+) sign beside the page title, Default, as shown in Figure 3.3. Once added, the symbol will change to a minus (−) sign. To remove an item from the shortcut menu, click the − sign.

To configure all shortcuts, click the link toward the top right of your screen labeled "Edit shortcuts." An administrative overlay will appear, as shown in Figure 3.3. From here you can add, modify, and delete shortcuts. To add a new shortcut, click the link "Add shortcut." A new screen will appear. Add the name and Drupal path for the shortcut you want to add.

By default Drupal provides a global shortcut menu that is available to administrative users. You can create additional shortcut menus that are available to some, or all, users. By default, authenticated users are not allowed to view or edit the shortcut menu.

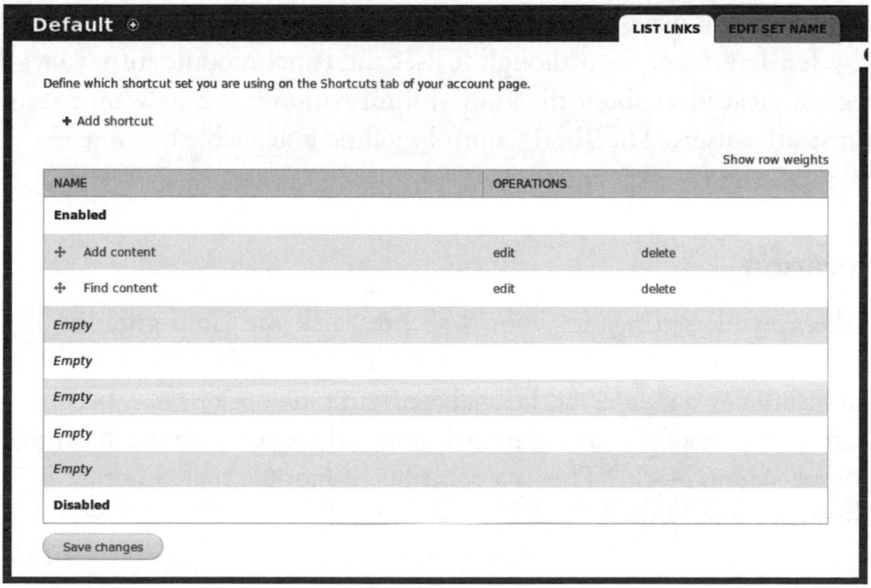

FIGURE 3.3 Configuration screen for the Default shortcut menu

Hiding the Shortcuts

If you want, you can hide the shortcut menu. On the far right of the menu is a little arrow pointing down. To hide the shortcut menu, click the arrow, and the shortcuts will snap out of view. To reveal the shortcut menu, click the arrow again, and the menu will snap back into view.

Dashboard

Drupal allows you to completely customize the main administration page using blocks. In addition to the blocks created by modules, a new block is created for each new menu you create.

> **Drupal Blocks**
> A Drupal *block* is equivalent to what other content management systems some-times call a *widget*. It is a small unit of functionality prepared by a module and can be displayed anywhere on your site. Common blocks include search, user login, and recent comments.

Your administrative dashboard should be customized to include information that is useful to you. See Figure 3.4 for an example of a simple dashboard.

For inspiration on what to put into your dashboard, check out the Total Control module by Jen Lampton. Even though it uses the Panel module for layout, the project page gives great ideas about the kind of information you may want to summarize for administrative users. The Total Control module is available from `http://drupal.org/project/total_control`.

Configuration

To alter the sitewide settings for your Web site, click the Configuration link in the administrative toolbar. You will be presented with an extended version of Figure 3.5.

As you install new modules, additional configuration options may become available on this screen. For example, in Figure 3.5, under the User Interface heading, there is a link labeled "Menu block." This is a contributed module that is not available in the default installation of Drupal.

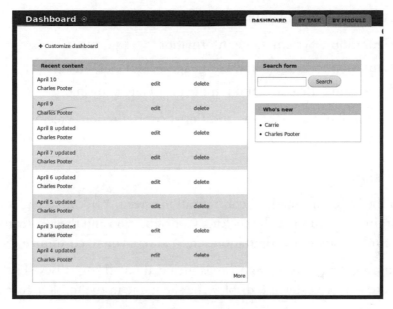

FIGURE 3.4 A simple administrative dashboard includes commonly used links as well as a summary of recent content.

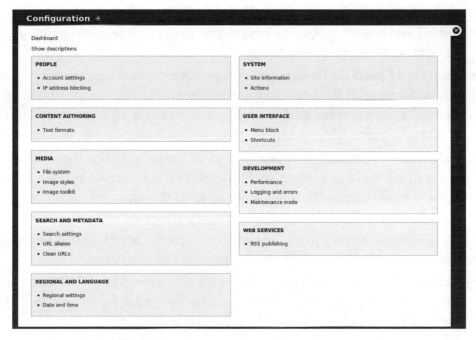

FIGURE 3.5 The Configuration administrative screen with descriptions hidden

At this point, you should familiarize yourself with three configuration screens:

- Configuration > System > Site information
- Configuration > Regional and Language > Regional settings
- Configuration > Regional and Language > Date and time

You will learn about more of the additional configuration screens as you progress through the chapters in this book.

Site Information

Navigate to the "Site information" configuration screen. You can access it at any time from the administrative toolbar by clicking Configuration and then "Site information."

The "Site information" configuration screen allows you to customize the following.

- **Site name.** The name of your site is included on all page titles. The theme for your site will typically also display the site name in the top-left corner of each Web page.

- **Slogan.** This sets a subtitle for your site. Depending on your theme, this will display beside or beneath the site name. The slogan does not typically appear in the page title.

- **E-mail address.** This is used by system messages such as automated e-mails sent during the registration process.

- **Number of posts on front page.** This number controls the number of items that will appear on the front page of the Web site. Additional posts will be grouped by this number too. For example, if you have 20 posts and "Number of posts on front page" is set to 10, there will be 2 pages of 10 posts each.

- **Default front page.** By default this is set to "node," which will publish new content that has been marked as "Promoted to front page." These are Drupal terms you will learn more about as we progress through the book.

- **Default 403 (access denied) page.** When site visitors do not have sufficient permissions to access a page, they will see a generic "access denied" message. This setting allows you to customize the page that is displayed.

- **Default 404 (not found) page.** When site visitors arrive at a URL on your site that does not exist, they will see a generic "page not found" message. This setting allows you to customize the page that is displayed.

Additional display options, such as the site logo and colors, are adjusted from within the theme. You will learn more about these settings in Chapter 15.

Date, Time, and Regional Settings

Now that we're in the space age, your Web server may not be in the same time zone as you. Fortunately, Drupal allows you to perform a little time travel and set the right time for your Web site.

To configure these settings, navigate to Configuration > Regional settings, where you will then be able to adjust the following.

- Default country
- First day of the week
- Default time zone

You can also allow users to set their own time zones. This setting is relevant only to multiuser and high-traffic sites.

In addition to setting the time zone, you can also customize how dates display on your site. To configure these settings, navigate to Configuration > Date and time. Figure 3.6 shows the default settings for time formats. Most themes will use the Medium format Date type for date stamps that appear on posts. Support for custom date types is not necessarily supported by all modules that display dates. If you need to adjust the formatting of dates on your site, you are better off assigning a custom Date format to one of the existing date types.

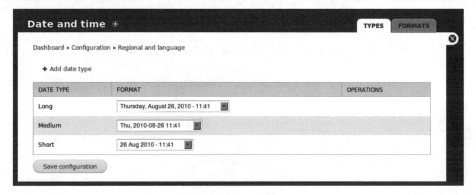

FIGURE 3.6 Default Date types and their formats. Three options are available by default: Long, Medium, and Short. Multiple formats are available for each type.

If you want to remove the time from displaying on your blog posts, you can write a custom date format using the following steps.

1. From the "Date and time" configuration screen, click the tab Formats on the top right of the overlay.

2. Click the link "Add format."

3. In the resulting form (Figure 3.7), add the PHP date constants for the format you want to create. A sample will be displayed to the right of the form field. See Table 3.1 for a list of commonly used formats.

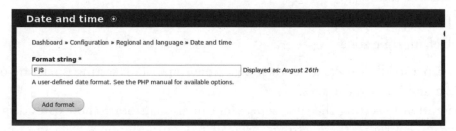

FIGURE 3.7 Creating a new date format for use on your site. The letters *F*, *j*, and *S* will display as the month and date (year and time are both omitted from this sample date format).

TABLE 3.1 Date Formats

Format Character	Description	Sample Output
d	Day of the month with leading zeros.	01 to 31
j	Day of the month without the leading zeros.	1 to 31
S	English ordinal suffix for the day of the month. Sample output is shown as *jS*.	1st, 2nd
D	Three-letter textual representation of the day of the week.	Mon, Tue
l (lowercase L)	Full textual representation of the day of the week.	Monday, Tuesday
m	Numeric representation of the month with leading zeros.	01 to 12
n	Numeric representation of the month without leading zeros.	1 to 12
M	Three-letter textual representation of the month.	Jan, Feb
F	Full textual representation of the month.	January
y	Two-digit representation of the year.	99 or 10
Y	Four-digit representation of the year.	1999 or 2010

4. Click "Add format" when you have entered the desired date output. On the top right of the overlay, click Types.

5. Next to the appropriate date type, choose your new format from the drop-down box. Click "Save configuration." Your new date format will be applied immediately throughout the site.

You can also add punctuation to your format.

- *F j 'y* would display as August 26 '10.
- *Y-d-m* would display as 2010-08-26.
- *F jS, Y* would display as August 26th, 2010.
- *l F jS, Y* would display as Thursday August 26th, 2010.

A complete date format reference, including time formats, is available online at `http://php.net/manual/en/function.date.php`.

Administrative Reports

Drupal provides some basic reports that you should familiarize yourself with. These reports will let you know about the health of your Drupal installation (Figure 3.8). You should get into the habit of checking these reports to ensure your Drupal installation has all the latest security patches applied. Unlike the announcements song from camp, these reports are actually useful. No bull. (You know the song, right? With the bologna and the cow? No? A very excellent guide is available at `www.youtube.com/watch?v=ML2NHsexzb0`.)

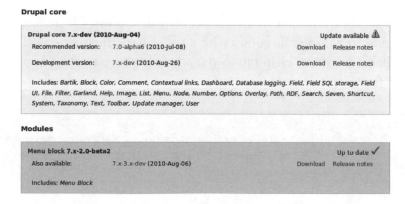

FIGURE 3.8 Available updates report screen. Drupal core is out of date; Menu block is up to date.

From the Reports tab in the administrative toolbar you can access the following information.

- **Status report.** This summarizes the health of your Drupal files including protection of specific files and required PHP modules. If something new that you've installed isn't working, look here.

- **Available updates.** This informs you when Drupal and contributed modules are out of date. This report can be configured from the Settings tab at the top right of the administrative overlay. Figure 3.8 provides an example of Drupal core that is out of date, as well as an up-to-date module.

- **Recent log entries.** These are recent actions taken on your site, such as new pages added, user logins, pages updated, and user-created pages.

- **Field list.** This is an overview of fields on all entity types. You will generate new fields when you create and modify content types in Chapter 12.

- **Top "access denied" errors.** These are URLs commonly visited by nonauthenticated users. Entries are added to this report when someone tries to visit a page that exists but is not within their level of security clearance.

- **Top "page not found" errors.** These are URLs commonly visited that do not have a corresponding Drupal page.

- **Top search phrases.** This is a list of phrases that people are searching for in your site. This report will be of use only if the Search module is enabled for all site visitors.

Help

Every Drupal module comes with a basic set of instructions. Or perhaps that should read every *good* Drupal module comes with a set of basic instructions. These instructions are available from the Help tab in the administrative toolbar. Figure 3.9 shows the help page for the Node module.

> **What Is a Node?**
> *Node* is the word used by Drupal to refer to pieces of content that have been created by the Node module. Nodes are typically displayed one at a time on a Web page or in lists of many nodes, as on the front page of your Web site.

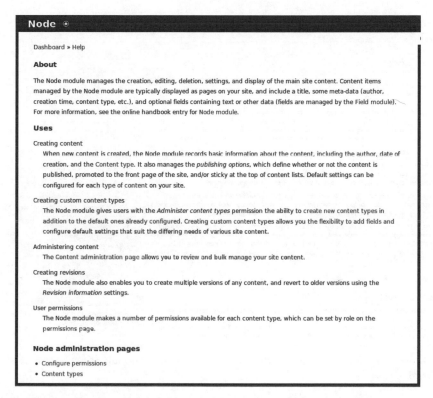

FIGURE 3.9 Help page for the core module Node

As you can see, there are three sections: About, Uses, and links to relevant administration pages.

The help pages are intentionally sparse. Where possible, they link to relevant pages within the relevant handbook page on Drupal.org where community members can update and enhance the instructions. Figure 3.10 shows the corresponding online handbook page for the Node module (`http://drupal.org/handbook/modules/node`). Note the related content on the left side of the screen shot.

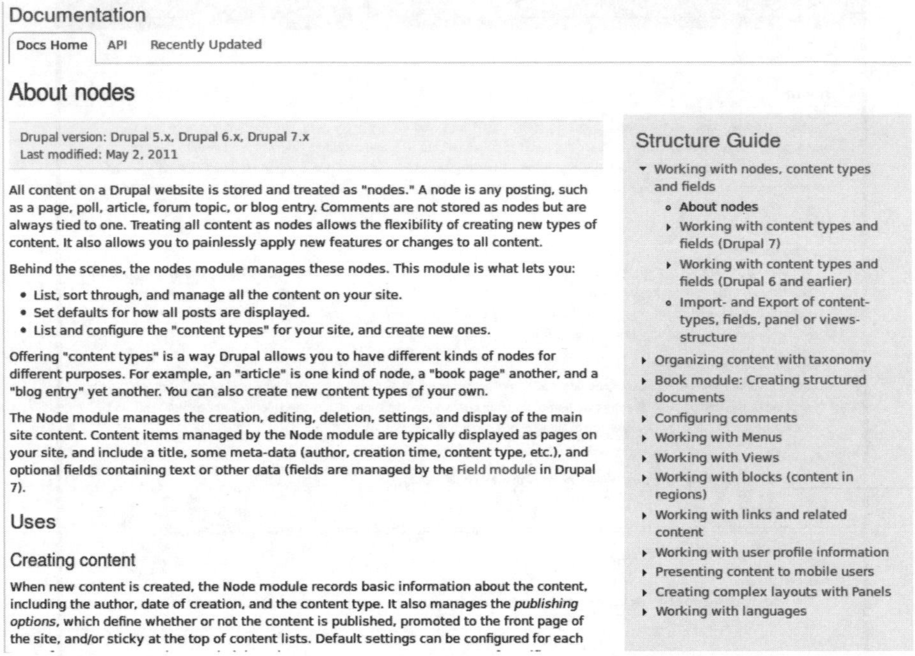

Documentation

Docs Home | API | Recently Updated

About nodes

Drupal version: Drupal 5.x, Drupal 6.x, Drupal 7.x
Last modified: May 2, 2011

All content on a Drupal website is stored and treated as "nodes." A node is any posting, such as a page, poll, article, forum topic, or blog entry. Comments are not stored as nodes but are always tied to one. Treating all content as nodes allows the flexibility of creating new types of content. It also allows you to painlessly apply new features or changes to all content.

Behind the scenes, the nodes module manages these nodes. This module is what lets you:

- List, sort through, and manage all the content on your site.
- Set defaults for how all posts are displayed.
- List and configure the "content types" for your site, and create new ones.

Offering "content types" is a way Drupal allows you to have different kinds of nodes for different purposes. For example, an "article" is one kind of node, a "book page" another, and a "blog entry" yet another. You can also create new content types of your own.

The Node module manages the creation, editing, deletion, settings, and display of the main site content. Content items managed by the Node module are typically displayed as pages on your site, and include a title, some meta-data (author, creation time, content type, etc.), and optional fields containing text or other data (fields are managed by the Field module in Drupal 7).

Uses

Creating content

When new content is created, the Node module records basic information about the content, including the author, date of creation, and the content type. It also manages the *publishing options*, which define whether or not the content is published, promoted to the front page of the site, and/or sticky at the top of content lists. Default settings can be configured for each

Structure Guide

- ▾ Working with nodes, content types and fields
  - ○ **About nodes**
  - ▸ Working with content types and fields (Drupal 7)
  - ▸ Working with content types and fields (Drupal 6 and earlier)
  - ○ Import- and Export of content-types, fields, panel or views-structure
- ▸ Organizing content with taxonomy
- ▸ Book module: Creating structured documents
- ▸ Configuring comments
- ▸ Working with Menus
- ▸ Working with Views
- ▸ Working with blocks (content in regions)
- ▸ Working with links and related content
- ▸ Working with user profile information
- ▸ Presenting content to mobile users
- ▸ Creating complex layouts with Panels
- ▸ Working with languages

FIGURE 3.10 You can find the online handbook page for the Node module at `http://drupal.org/handbook/modules/node`.

Summary

Was that a shiny chapter or what? All that power right at your fingertips. I know you're impatiently waiting to assert power over your new Web site, so I'll quickly summarize what was covered in this chapter so that you can start building your new Web site. In this chapter, you learned the following.

- How to use and customize the shortcut menu
- Key configuration screens for your site
- How to customize settings for your site
- How to find helpful summaries about installed modules
- What information is available from the basic reporting tools provided by Drupal

Chapter 4

Site Recipe: Micro Web Site

Now that Drupal is installed, it's time to get the party started! For this site recipe, you will learn how to build a personal Web site featuring a single-user blog. The site features the capabilities of Drupal's core modules. You will learn how to create content, create a navigation system for your Web site, and configure relevant site settings. You will also become familiar with Drupal's administrative interface.

Web Site Basics

From the moment you install Drupal, you are invited to add content to your new Web site. Drupal provides you with two types of content by default: Article and Basic page. The first, Article, is appropriate for bloglike entries on your site. The second, Basic page, is appropriate for pages that are not time-sensitive and that are more "persistent." An example of a Basic page is an About page.

Your new site will have the following custom features (Figure 4.1).

- Blog-style front page news
- Site logo
- Categories
- About page

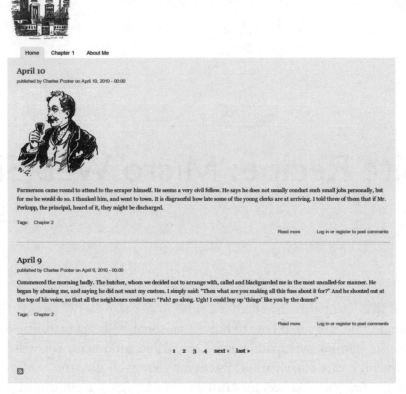

FIGURE 4.1 The front page of the site you will build in this chapter includes many features that can be built using Drupal's core modules.

In this chapter, you will learn the basics of following key concepts as you build each feature.

- Creating new *nodes* using two different *content types*
- Categorizing your articles with the *taxonomy* system
- Creating sidebar content with *blocks* and *regions*
- Adding links to key pages with *menus*

Each time you create new content in Drupal, you are creating a new *node*. A node can be a simple page with text and images on it, but it could also be a completely customized content type that you have created to store your entomological collection of bug photographs. *Node* refers to a single instance of content, whereas a *content type* (sometimes called a *node type*) refers to the specific data structure that is used to create lots of nodes.

These concepts will be expanded on in future chapters as you learn how to build more sophisticated Web sites.

Basic Pages

Most of the pages you create on your Web site will probably be Basic pages. Basic pages have the following antifeatures:

- Are not published to the front page of your Web site
- Do not allow visitors to post comments
- Do not have tagging enabled
- Do not have an image upload widget
- Are not date-stamped

In other words, a Basic page is just a basic page.

Use the following steps to add an About Me page to your Web site. In the next section, you will alter this page's features to add this page to your Main menu.

1. From the shortcut menu, click the link "Add content." An overlay will appear prompting you to choose between Article and Basic page.
2. Click "Basic page."
3. Enter a title and body for your page.
4. Scroll to the bottom and click Save.

Your new page has been created, but there is no link to it yet. It is essentially an orphaned page.

> **It's Easy to Fix Mistakes**
> Don't be afraid to make changes to your Web site. This isn't the print world where you'll be stuck with 10,000 copies of a brochure with the wrong spelling of "Niagara" Falls. You can change your Web pages as fast as you can click-type-click. No more waiting around for a Webmaster to return your phone call. You can easily and immediately fix your own Web site!

Linking to Basic Pages from the Main Menu

The page you created in the previous section has been abandoned. It is lost in your site with nothing linking to it. This makes the page very sad and lonely (and might possibly also make you afraid and angry that you can't find your very first Drupal Web page). Don't worry. You don't need to call the Drupal search-and-rescue team just yet. What you need to do is create a link to your page so that others can find it. In Chapter 13 you will learn several ways to create lists of content. For now, you will add a link to your page to the Main menu for your site.

Use the following steps to find your lost page and add a menu item so that others can find it too.

1. Navigate to the editing screen for the node to which you want to add a Main menu link. You can do this by clicking the Edit tab on the actual node (Figure 4.2) or by clicking the "Find content" shortcut link and then clicking the "edit" link next to the page you want to edit (Figure 4.3).

2. Scroll to the bottom of the screen and select the check box "Provide a menu link." Figure 4.4 shows the configuration screen that appears.

3. Enter the display title of the menu link. By default the page title is used.

4. The setting "Parent item" allows you to choose *which* menu you would like to put the page into. It is appropriate to leave this as "Main menu."

5. Weight allows you to change the order of the menu items relative to one another. To move the menu item up, choose a smaller (or negative) number. Leave the default value for now to see where the menu item falls.

6. Scroll to the bottom of the screen and click the button labeled Save.

FIGURE 4.2 Any node can be edited by navigating to the node and clicking the tab Edit.

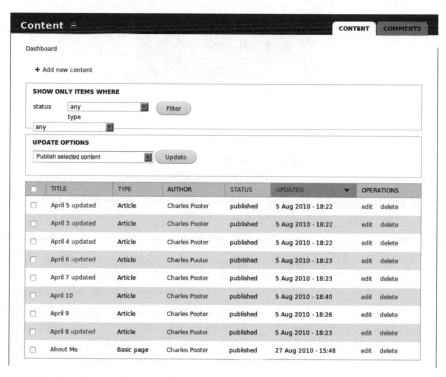

FIGURE 4.3 Using the shortcut bar "Find content" in the administrative toolbar, you can find and edit any node in your Web site.

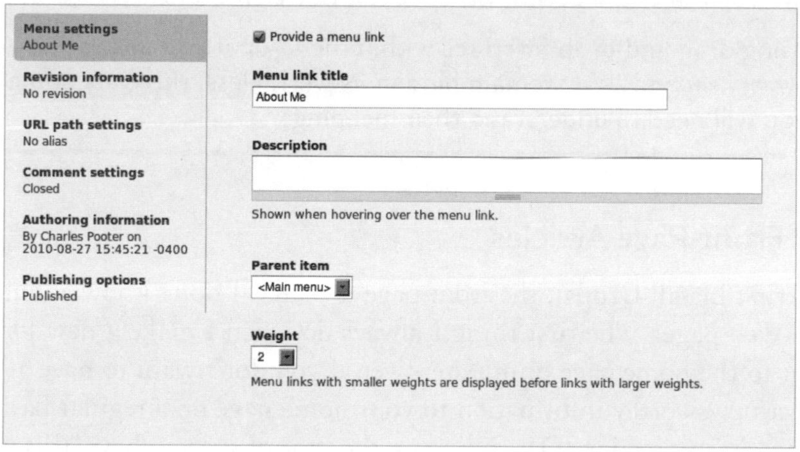

FIGURE 4.4 Any node in your Web site may be placed in the Main menu by customizing the link options in the node-editing screen.

FIGURE 4.5 Two Main menu links are now available.

Your page will now be listed in the Main menu (Figure 4.5). In the default theme, Bartik, the Main menu is located at the top left of the page. You can use these instructions for any content type including articles and any custom content types you create.

Understanding Parent Items and Weight

Both menus and tags may rely on hierarchies for their organization. When items are organized within a hierarchical sorting system, Drupal uses the term *parent item* to define which taxonomy term or menu item is closer to the top of the "family tree." When you are placing an item into a menu, for example, you must decide under which "parent" the specific menu item should be placed.

The *weight* of an item refers to the order of the item relative to all other items in that group. With the Drupal core, the metaphor is that "Heavy items sink." Think of a balloon floating away with its negative weight, and think of the Titanic sinking to the bottom of the ocean with its positive weight.

When using drag-and-drop interface within the Drupal administration area, the terms *parent item* and *weight* remain hidden. Nevertheless, there are some screens where you will need to understand their meanings.

Creating Front-Page Articles

When you first install Drupal, the front page is blank! I don't know about you, but I hate blank Web pages. The first thing I always do when I make a new Drupal site is add content to the home page of my site. Even if you don't want to have a "blog," you can still post newsworthy information to your home page on a regular basis using the steps outlined in this section. Depending on the type of site you have, this may include promotional information about upcoming events or summaries of things that have already passed.

> **Update Your Home Page at Least Twice a Month**
> Web sites that rank well in search engines refresh their home page content on a regular basis. You will learn a lot more about search engine optimization in Chapter 16.

To create a new front-page story, you will use the content type Article. This content type has the following features.

- Summary posted to the front page of the Web site
- Comments enabled
- Option to upload an image to be displayed with the article
- User name of the article author as well as the time it was originally published
- Tags enabled, allowing you to categorize articles

Figure 4.6 shows the basic form you will use to create an new article on your Web site. Figure 4.7 shows a newly created article with a featured image.

Creating Your First Article

You need to be aware of four areas on the article editing screen.

- **Title and Body.** This is the content of your article.
- **Image.** This is an optional field used to add an image to your article.
- **Tags.** This is an optional field used to add keywords to your article. These keywords can be used to categorize similar articles.
- **Additional configuration settings.** For now you can ignore these settings. They will be covered later.

To create an article, complete the following steps.

1. From the shortcut menu, click the link "Add content." An overlay will appear prompting you to choose between Article and Basic page.
2. Click Article. An editing form will appear as in the previously displayed Figure 4.6.
3. Enter a title and body content.
4. Enter keywords about your article in the section labeled Tags. This step is optional.

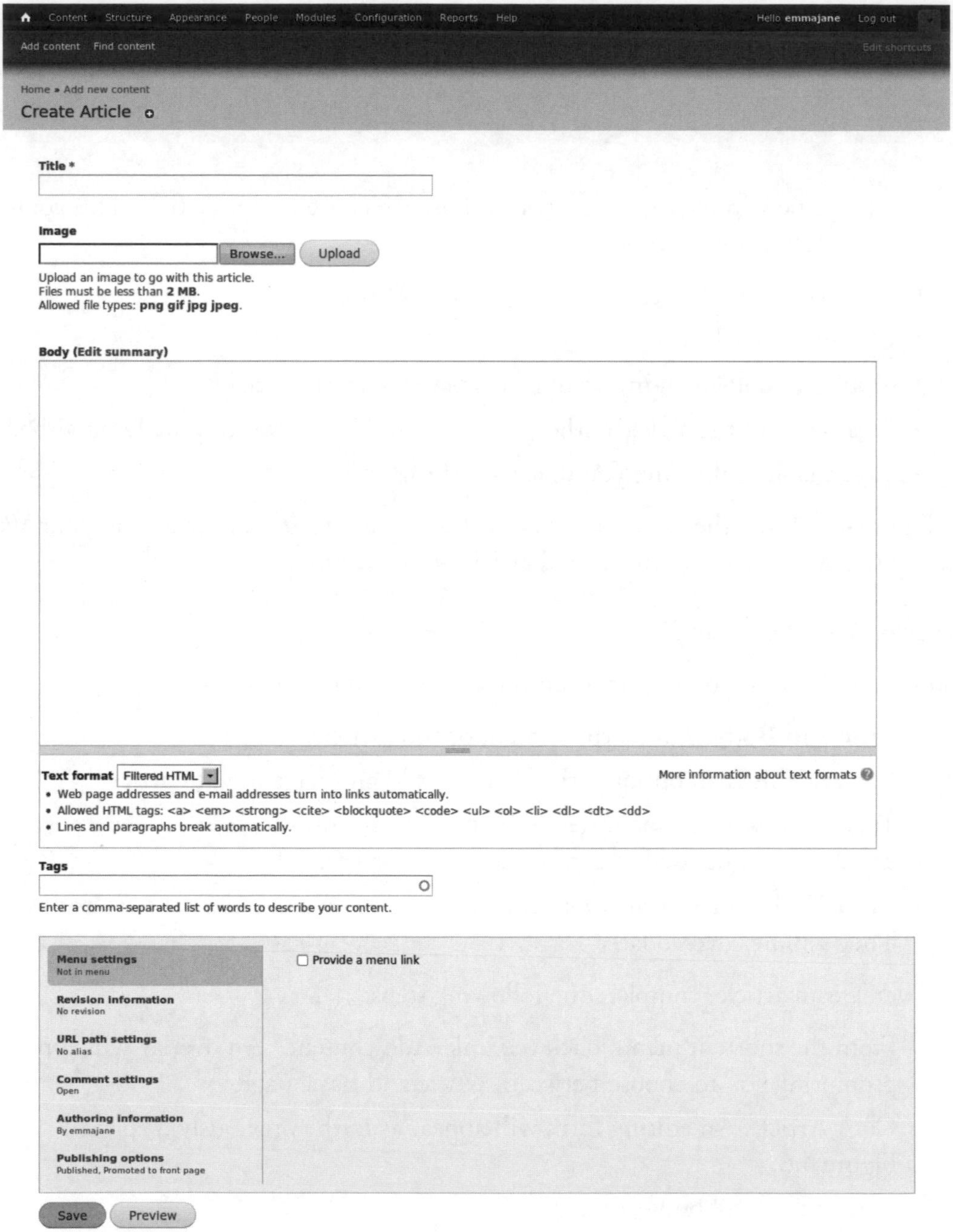

FIGURE 4.6 The form used to create a new article

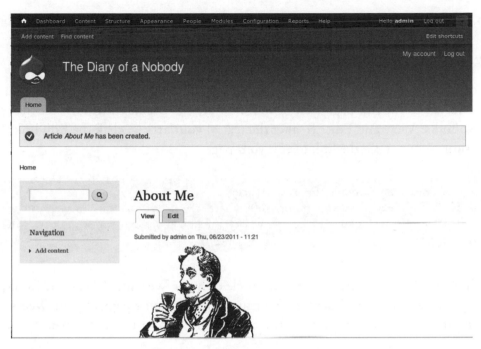

FIGURE 4.7 A node created from the content type Article

5. Upload an image. This step is optional. Click the button labeled Browse. Select the image you want to upload from your computer in the pop-up screen. Click Upload. A new field will appear: "Alternate text." Enter a short description of your image. This text is used by search engines and adaptive technology. The image will be automatically resized but needs to be smaller in megabytes than the limit listed. Figure 4.8 shows the editing screen after having successfully uploaded an image.

FIGURE 4.8 A successfully uploaded image showing a thumbnail and complete alternate text

6. For your first article, you do not need to change any defaults listed at the bottom of the screen. You can scroll past this section.

7. Scroll to the bottom and click Save.

Your article will be added automatically to the front page of the Web site. You will be redirected to the full-page view of your new article. Beside the title of the new page are two links: View and Edit. To alter the text of your article, click the Edit link. Web site visitors will not see the link to edit your page.

> **Customize the Summary for Your Article**
> By default Drupal selects the first 600 characters to use as the summary for the article. To create a custom summary, click the link "Edit summary" and enter your own text.

That's all there is to creating a new article on your Web site. Check the front page to see your new content displayed. You can get to the home page of your Web site by clicking the house icon in the top-left corner of the administrative toolbar.

Front-Page Content

Each time you add a new article to your Web site, it will be added to the top of the list of articles on the front page. This is because the node has been assigned a property of "Promoted to front page." You can change this setting per-node using the following steps.

1. Edit the node you want to change.

2. Scroll to the bottom of the edit screen and click "Publishing options."

3. Select or deselect the check box for "Promoted to front page," depending on what you want to do.

4. Scroll to the bottom of the page and click Save.

Your node will now be removed from, or added to, the front page, depending on the settings you used.

When you have more than 10 articles, a *pager* will appear at the bottom of the home page. A pager is a collection of links that breaks a very long list into smaller sections. For example, a list of 100 items with 10 items per page would yield 10 pages of results. Pagers typically have links for "next" and "previous" pages as well. Figure 4.9 shows a pager.

FIGURE 4.9 A pager allows Web site visitors to navigate through a very long list of items.

If you would like more, or fewer, items to appear on the home page of your Web site, you must complete the following steps.

1. On the administrative toolbar, click Configuration.
2. Click "Site information."
3. Scroll down to the section "Number of posts on front page." Adjust this number to suit your needs.
4. Scroll to the bottom and click "Save configuration."

This number will also be used by the pager to divide the remaining front-page items into pages. In other words, if you change this number to 1, the pager will display only one item per page.

In-Site Searching

By default the Drupal search module is enabled and allows you to search content in your site; however, it is not publicly available. You will need to adjust the permissions for this module to allow all site visitors to search content on your site. Complete the following steps to enable searching for everyone.

1. On the administrative toolbar, click People.
2. At the top right, click the tab Permissions.
3. Scroll to the heading Search.
4. Along the row "Use search," enable all the check boxes.
5. Scroll to the bottom of the page and click "Save permissions."

Chapter 16 covers additional information on making your site search engine friendly.

RSS Settings

Visitors to the home page of your Web site will be able to subscribe to your blog using an RSS reader, such as Bloglines (www.bloglines.com/) or Google Reader (www.google.com/reader), with no additional work on your part. By default the full text of the most recent ten articles will appear in a subscriber's reader. To customize these settings and add a description, use the following instructions.

1. Use the administrative toolbar to navigate to Configuration > Web services > RSS publishing.
2. Enter a description for your Web site.
3. Adjust the number of items to include in each feed. The default setting of 10 is appropriate.
4. Adjust the feed content to suit the content of the feed. In most cases, it is appropriate to leave the default setting "Full text." The other two options are "Titles only" and "Titles plus summary."
5. Scroll to the bottom of the screen and click "Save configuration."

Your new settings will now appear in your Web site's feed. Figure 4.10 shows an RSS feed rendered in the browser Firefox. Note the custom description at the top of the page.

The sample content used in Figure 4.10 is from *The Diary of a Nobody* by George Grossmith and Weedon Grossmith (`www.gutenberg.org/dirs/etext97/dnbdy10h.htm`). The diary was written in the late 1800s and is a fictitious account of the life of Mr. Charles Pooter, a middle-aged, self-important city clerk. Sounds sort of like a modern blog, yes?

Customizing Your Site's Design

Blue is nice. The Drupal mascot, Druplicon, is great. But the default theme says something about Drupal, not about you. Let's start by making your site reflect you. With a few quick changes to your site, you can turn the default theme into one that reflects who you are. Customizing the design of your site will be covered in much greater detail in Chapter 15.

Adjusting the Colors

You may want to adjust the main colors of your Web site. Use the following steps to recolor the default theme, Bartik. (I suppose I could insert screen shots here, but this is a black-and-white book and . . . well . . . you'd just get the same thing but in two shades of gray. It seems like a waste of ink, so I ask you to use your imagination instead.)

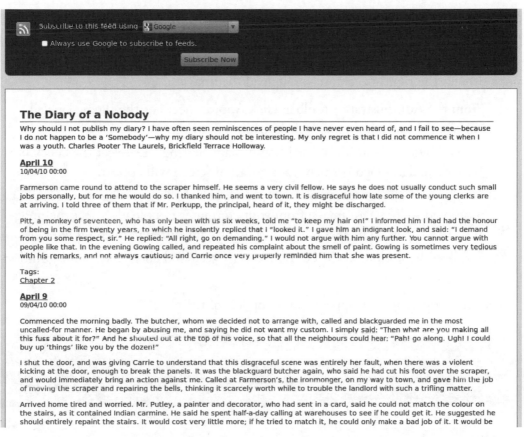

FIGURE 4.10 Your site publishes an RSS feed of all the content promoted to the front page of the site.

1. From the administrative toolbar, click Appearance.

2. For the theme labeled "default theme," click the link Settings.

3. Adjust each of the colors according to your needs. Several color sets are available for you to pick from. These color sets are high-contrast and accessible to all Web site visitors.

4. When you are happy with the preview, scroll to the bottom of the configuration screen and click "Save configuration."

Your site has been magically recolored. I promise.

Adding a Site Logo

The default logo is the Drupal mascot, Druplicon. To replace this icon with your own image, complete the subsequent steps. Your new logo will not be resized by Drupal, so make sure it's the right size before you upload the image.

1. From the Administrative toolbar, click Appearance. For the theme labeled "Bartik 7.0 (default theme)," click the link Settings.

2. Scroll down to the section titled Logo Image Settings. Deselect the check box "Use the default logo." A new configuration screen will appear.

3. To upload an image from your computer, click the button Browse. You will be prompted to locate an image from your computer to upload. Select the image and click Open. (The text may differ slightly for different Web browsers.)

4. Scroll to the bottom of the configuration screen and click "Save configuration settings."

Your new logo will now appear in the top left of the page.

> **Change Your Shortcut "Favicon" Too**
> By default the Druplicon will also appear as your site's shortcut icon. You can change this to a different image from this configuration screen or choose to omit it by deselecting the check box "Shortcut icon."

Summary

That was an action-packed chapter! In this chapter, you made a basic Web site. How cool is that? Assuming you completed each of the steps outlined in this chapter, you should now have the following.

- A Web site available to the public on the Internet
- An understanding of how to use and customize the administration components to navigate Drupal
- An article with an image
- A page with a menu item

Part II

Planning

Chapter 5

Site Goals

The Web was originally created as an interlinked set of text pages. Like a choose-your-own adventure book, you could navigate the pages of the Web by clicking forward and back through the network of information. Over the past decade (or two), the way we interact with the Web has fundamentally changed. We now treat many Web sites as pieces of software with their own rules. What was once an experience of reading a dictionary or a literary work has become more like playing a game of Risk or Monopoly. There are both technical and social rules that govern our interactions online. Hypertext, the building blocks of the original Web pages in the 1990s, is information-oriented; good software, however, is task-based. Businesses can no longer throw a bunch of stuff onto a Web site and expect customers to appear from the Internet ready to buy products and services. Customers want you to read their mind and deliver a reasonable experience that matches their expectations. But not all Web sites need to sell products to be successful.

You can achieve "success" only if you can first define it. Maybe you are looking for new customers, or maybe you are trying to increase the average amount of sales per customer. Or if you have a community-based site, you may simply be looking for more people to be involved in a project (rousing energy for community-based projects can be more difficult than closing a sale!). Everything that you do to your site should be to either fix an existing problem or improve your client's experience with the site (and therefore with your business). Solutions are not always easy to quantify. By deciding *how* you will measure success before implementing changes, you will be able to determine whether your changes were effective. In this chapter, you will build your definition of success for your new Drupal Web site.

This is a planning chapter designed to guide you through the steps of defining what success means for your site.

Defining and Designing Success

In planning a site, you will need to define several types of tasks.

- **Project objectives** are your primary reasons why are you building the Web site.
- **User needs** are the motivations of each individual visiting your Web site. The user needs also define what site visitors want to do on your Web site.
- **Features and data** are the verbs and nouns needed to make your site a success including all of the things a site visitor can read, see, or do on your site.
- **Information design** structures how content is stored within the site.
- **Interaction design** defines how people navigate from one piece of information, or task, to another.
- **Interface design** is the layout of information on the individual pages on your Web site.
- **Visual design** defines the specific colors, fonts, and imagery used on the site.

In this chapter, you will define your project's objectives. In Chapter 6, you will focus on the people who will be visiting your site and their interaction with the Web site. In Chapter 7, you will identify and categorize information (*information design*). In Chapter 8, you will create the visual design for your Web site.

SMART Site Goals

Right now I want you to take the time to write out what visitors will be able to *do* on your site. Make a list of everything a visitor can do. Make sure each item is actionable. If *you* don't know what a visitor is supposed to do, how are they supposed to know? If there's no action item for a page, the action will probably be to close the browser window and visit another Web site.

If you already have a Web site started, look through each of the pages and ask yourself, "What is the most desirable action a visitor can take on this page?" The answer may be one of the following.

- Add a product to a shopping cart.
- Choose a new category to proceed to the next page.
- Add a comment to a blog post.
- Print and use a tasty food recipe.
- Create a user account.
- Download a free e-book.

Customer experience includes the technical limitations of your Web site visitors. Are you working on an intranet that has to support older Web browsers? Does your Web site need to be available in multiple languages? Will it be used by people who travel a lot and use mobile devices to connect to your site? Answers to these questions will affect how you build your site and the additional features that you may need to add to the site to create a successful user experience. Add to your list any technical limitations that you know about now. Technology changes all the time, so make sure this list stays up to date.

Don't keep your goals a secret, and definitely don't try to memorize your goals. Write them down and display them in a prominent place in your office. Remember what you are trying to achieve and work toward it.

> **Use an Online Editor to Collaborate on Shared Documents**
> Google Docs (http://docs.google.com) is an easy way to share an editable version of a file with many team members. You will need to create a free account with Google to use this service.

If you're in the Web business, SMART is your key to sanity and success. Each of the letters in SMART represents an important component in creating effective goals. A SMART goal is the following.

- Specific
- Measurable
- Attainable
- Relevant
- Timed

You may have seen variations on some of these letters, but the essence will be the same: If you can't define success, you can't achieve it.

How does all of this relate to building a Web site? The goals you set will help you determine what metrics you need to keep. The earlier you start collecting information about how visitors are using your site, the more data you will have when it's time to do your analysis.

Specific Goals

By setting a specific goal, you'll have a better chance of knowing that the goal has been obtained. Specific goals for your Web site may include the following.

- Increase incoming traffic from Google organic search results for the keyword combination *pinot noir new zealand* by 5 percent from the previous month.

- Decrease the number of support questions asked in the public support forum in the first month after launch by 5 percent compared to the number of questions asked after the last product release.

- Sell 100 percent of remaining T-shirts from the 2010 promotional campaign before January 1, 2011.

- Rank higher than the Wool Company for the keyword combination *merino possum yarn* in Google's search engine for the month of May.

Measurable Goals

You will need to be able to measure the success of your goals. Measuring success will also help keep you motivated over a longer period of time. For example, if you've completed the first phase of development, give yourself a gold star! And then move onto the next phase. Each of the goals defined can be easily tested so long as you have collected the necessary information. Measuring progress also means you need to know where you currently stand in the market. Measurable goals often have numbers associated with them.

- **How much** volume of sales, activity on discussion boards, advertising click-throughs, and monthly readership do you have?
- **How fast** does your site load?
- **How good** are your customer service ratings?

You will need to start with a baseline to determine whether your business is improving or getting worse. Your baseline metrics should be related to the goals you defined previously. It is very easy to collect traffic data for your Web site.

> **If You Have a Web Site, You Probably Have Web Stats**
> If you already have a Web site, you are probably already collecting data. This may be in the form of unprocessed log files from your Web server, or it may have already been processed by an application such as AWStats or Webalizer. Ask your hosting provider what data is being collected for your site.

The following are some of the trends you can watch for on your Web site.

- An increased number of visitors to your site
- An increased amount of traffic in a new area of your Web site
- An increased number of sales (possibly with the same number of visitors)
- An increase of ad sales or advertising revenue
- An increased percentage of buyers compared to browsers
- An increased number in repeat customers or repeat visitors
- The number of active, registered users for your online community
- An increased number of phone calls inquiring about new (or different) products and services
- A *decreased* number of support phone calls
- The number of people who visited your Web site directly from an e-mail or other marketing campaign
- The number of people signing up for your online newsletter
- The number of orders received through the Web site

To be able to analyze the Web traffic data you have collected, you must have specific questions that you want to evaluate. Take a look at your Web statistics, and ask yourself the following questions.

- What are the most popular pages in your site? How can this content be enriched?
- What are the most popular entry pages from search engines?
- What are the most popular exit pages? Can you do anything to keep visitors on your site longer?

In some cases, Web traffic data will not have the answer for you. You will need to set up new types of tests and keep records on interactions with your customers to see how you are doing with your goals.

If you don't have Web site stats, there are other ways of taking baseline measurements.

- How often do you get phone calls? Start a call log to monitor when a person called and at what stage of the sale cycle they were in. In your log, jot down whether the answer to their question was already on the Web site.

- Using Google do a Web search for `link:www.yourdomainname.com` to measure the number of people who are linking to your Web site. You can also check your Web stats to see whether anyone has clicked through the link to find your site (check in the "referrer" summary for this information).

Measuring success isn't just about the raw numbers you can collect. Sooner or later you'll need to actually talk to people about their experience with your Web site. You may put up a survey and ask visitors what types of content they would like to see enhanced on your site and what they find easy, or confusing, about your site. Create goals where the unit of measurement involves talking to your customer. If you already have a site but don't want the hassle of programming a survey, try SurveyMonkey (`www.surveymonkey.com`). It is easy to use and free for a limited number of questions and responses.

You must consider all of the possible outcomes before you look for answers. Decide ahead of time how you will deal with *both* satisfactory and unsatisfactory results. You do not need to implement massive change—in fact, it is much easier to implement small changes and measure the effectiveness of the new change made. If you change too many things at once, you won't know which bit was effective and which bit was not.

Attainable Goals

Your Web site probably won't be able to solve world hunger. But that doesn't mean you can't successfully raise funds for a local charity. Be reasonable when you create your site goals. Tasks that seem impossible are hard to start and even more difficult to finish. This doesn't mean you can't reach for the moon! If you do have very ambitious goals, break them into smaller milestones that are plausible and attainable. Think of complementary goals that will help you achieve each of your larger goals. The following are some examples.

- **Lofty goal.** Be the number-one Web site for Cajun food recipes.
- **SMART goal.** Be the top-ranked Web site in the Google search engine for the keyword combination *Cajun food recipe* during the month of September.
- **Complementary goal.** Get five new relevant incoming links to your Web site every week. Links may include interviews, syndicated recipes, and blog comments.
- **Complementary goal.** Conduct one media appearance every month. Media appearances may include podcast or Internet interviews as well as traditional print, TV, and radio interviews if they're relevant to your site.

Relevant Goals

If you have a hard time staying focused, this part of the SMART goals may be difficult for you. When you create new goals, make sure they align with the driving mission or vision for your business. Relevant goals may include the following characteristics.

- If you are profit-driven, a relevant goal would be to increase the amount of money customers spend at your Web site.
- If you are participation-driven, a relevant goal would be to increase member contributions. An ancillary outcome of this may include more ad revenue if the person creates new pages that hold more ads.

Do you have community members who are excellent mentors and can help you convert low-level contributors into active contributors? Think about all aspects of your site to create goals that are relevant to your core vision.

Timed Goals

Create a sense of urgency for yourself. Create plausible deadlines and work toward them. Break your tasks into realistic subtasks that you know you can achieve within a given time period. Everyone I know works best when given a deadline. Many of the people I know work harder as the deadline approaches. If this describes you (I know it describes me), give yourself a lot of small goals with tight timelines instead of having only huge tasks drag on for ages.

Sadly, there is no magic formula to calculate how long it takes to build a Drupal Web site. Once your Web server is configured, you can install Drupal in less than ten minutes, but that's just one step. What if you want to create a very large content portal? In this case, installing Drupal is just the beginning.

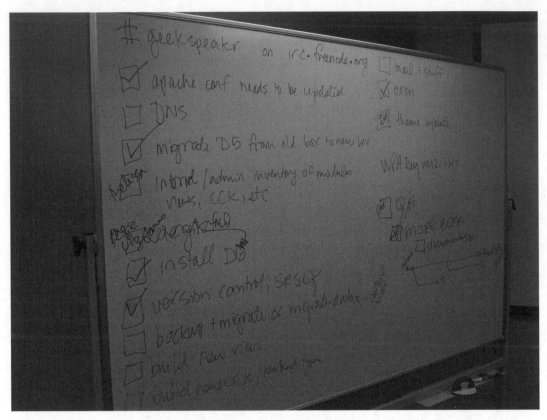

FIGURE 5.1 Planning board for the GeekSpeakr site migration

To create a time estimate for your project, you need to know every single step that is required. Figure 5.1 shows the planning board we used to migrate the GeekSpeakr Web site (www.geekspeakr.com) from one Web server to another. A dozen people were working on the migration, and we managed to finish the core tasks within an evening. Twelve people each working three hours that evening would be nearly a week of full-time work for one person! The expertise of everyone in the room meant that many of the tasks took less time than they might have otherwise.

Do you know what tasks need to be completed for your Web site? List every single thing you can think of. If you were going to create a Web site that features your products, your task list might include the following.

• Write descriptions of all products.
• Take photographs of all products.

- Buy a domain name.
- Find Web hosting.
- Install Drupal and relevant contributed modules.
- Create a content type that includes the product photo, short description, long description, and price.
- Add the product descriptions to the Web site.
- Create a product listing page that includes the title and a short description.
- Alter the product listing to include single image for the product. (This is listed separately because dealing with images is not the same as dealing with text.)
- Create a design for the Web site.
- Convert the design to a Drupal theme.
- Write text for the About page and other nonproduct pages.
- Add the text for extra pages to the Web site, and configure the menu items.
- Enable and configure the Contact module. Add contact details and hours of operation for your business.
- Test the site, and look for design and content errors and omissions.

Depending on how many products you have and how complicated their descriptions are, each of these tasks may take you two to three hours to complete. There are 13 tasks, so a rough time estimate to build this site is 39 hours. If you've never worked with Drupal before and you are hoping to accomplish each task on your own, you should double this time estimate. If you are more experienced with Drupal, you will be able to halve the time estimate.

Create an action plan calendar from the list of tasks that you created by completing the following steps.

1. Group related tasks. For example, finding Web hosting doesn't really have anything to do with taking photos of the products you will be selling on your Web site.

2. As best as you can tell, put each of the groups of steps you listed earlier into the order they need to be completed in. For example, you cannot accept PayPal payments before you've set up a PayPal account; however, you can hire a photographer to take photos of your products while you write the text for your About page.

3. Many of the steps, or groups of steps, can happen simultaneously. Decide which you would prefer to work on first and which you'd prefer to work on second. This order may be related to when you have time and when you'll have money if you need to use outside contractors for parts of your Web site.

4. Sort your list of tasks into approximate weeks and months starting from today. Assume that every task you can identify will take one unit of time. Depending on how full your schedule is, this might be a week or a month. It doesn't need to be perfect, but it should give you an idea of when you might hit your major milestones.

5. Put your milestones onto a calendar. Stick to the deadlines that you've set for yourself.

> **Keep Track of Time**
> Keep a log book at your desk, or a spreadsheet if you're digitally inclined, and take notes on how long tasks take you to complete. If you like paper-based time tracking and playing games to stay motivated, check out the free Printable CEO templates available from www.davidseah.com. If you're interested in online time tracking, check out Freckle (www.letsfreckle.com). For a great video on why you should keep track of your time, check out Time Management for Anarchists (http://nomediakings.org/vidz/time_management_for_anarchists_the_movie.html). It's more fun than a bowl of kittens.

Your calendar will be a living document, because you may realize there were things you forgot to note and tasks that take less time than you'd originally planned. Document how long each of the steps actually took in your calendar. This will serve as your guide for the next time you need to work on a Web site. The more time you spend working on your Web site, the more accurate your time predictions will be. In general, it is safe to work in weeks or months as your unit of time (although many tasks may happen simultaneously within the same week). For example, it will take a week to register your domain name and get it hooked up to a Web hosting account. It may take a bit less time, but this is a safe unit of time for your estimate.

Your Competition

If you've completed the exercises to date, you know what your site is going to do and how you're going to measure its success. How does the competition stack up? To ensure you have a solid idea for your Web site, look at what people are already doing. Scour the Internet and find sites that have content similar to yours and also sites that have a similar engagement model, even if the content is different. For example, if you are thinking about creating a Web site for stamp collectors, you may find useful community models on Web sites for figurine collectors.

You need to know what your competition is offering to be able to make your site shine. If you are making a membership site, create accounts on your competitors' sites. Engage with the community and find out what you do, and do not, like.

Create a chart for yourself that shows what other sites offer and how your site will be different (Table 5.1). You need to be able to define your site without comparison as well. Once you know what makes you unique, emphasize only that part of your site. Avoid the temptation of saying things like, "It's like Facebook but different." Focus instead on what is exciting and engaging about what you offer.

This comparison chart may also include a pricing scheme that shows how much your product or service will cost in comparison to your competitors' services. This is not a waste of time. In fact, this chart can be used as part of your marketing information on your Web site. Some of the best services I use have clear charts that allow me to compare services. Sometimes the services a company is offering are all the services I don't actually need. It can help to see this information detailed in something other than text.

The following process will help you identify who your online competitors are and what you will need to do with your Web site to make it stand out.

TABLE 5.1 Comparing Your Site to the Competition*

	Sales History (What Did You Get Him Last Year)	Gift Cards	Monthly Newsletter with Reminders About Holidays	Discount Coupons	Local Products/ Flowers
My business	x	x	x		x
FlowersXpress		x		x	
Chocolate Bouquets		x			x
Flower Expressions	x	x			
McInney Flowercart		x	x	x	

* Features across the top, customers down the side, and check boxes in the middle as appropriate

1. Determine your competitive set. Who leads the field in your industry, and who are your competitors? Analyze their Web sites to see who you need to compete with and in what ways you can grow your site. Search broadly for this initial list. Use the same tools your customers may use (search engines, print advertising, word-of-mouth, links from popular Web sites).

2. Choose the 10 to 20 sites that are the closest match to your own business for the remainder of the steps. It may not be easy to choose only 20 (or find even 10), but try to limit yourself because the goal is to work on your own Web site, not lose yourself looking at everyone else's.

3. Create a feature set. List all the features offered on all the sites you found. Include relevant offline features. Categorize the features in terms of the following.

   a. Ones that you know you can provide now (or already provide)

   b. Features you may want to offer in the future

   c. Features you know for sure are *not* a good match for your business

4. Pick a select group of trusted customers and ask them which features they

   a. currently use,

   b. think they might use, and

   c. know they'll never use.

5. Write yourself a little summary. Your findings are fresh in your mind right now, and it is important not to have to spend too much time deciphering your notes two months down the road.

It's not always easy to find those "trusted customers" referred to in step 4 from the list. Be sure to do the other parts of the activity and tuck everything into a folder. When the right adviser (whether it's a customer or a friend) does show up, you can pull out the file and ask them to take a quick look.

Summary

This chapter has asked you to take a look at the success of your Web site. Most people want to jump right into their Web site and skip the planning stage. They become frustrated and upset when their new (very expensive) Web site doesn't seem to solve the problems that the business has. Taking the time to think carefully about what you want to do *will* save you time and money. Careful planning will allow you to budget your time and your money. It will allow you to see when you have too many features planned for your site for the amount of time you have between today and launch day.

If you've done each of the activities suggested in this chapter, you will now have done the following.

- Come up with SMART goals that you can share with your team and that define exactly what you are trying to accomplish and by what date you want to be completed.

- Written a comparison chart that shows the features offered by your business and your primary competitors. If it's relevant, this chart may also have pricing comparisons.

- Examined your existing Web site statistics and looked for popular entry and exit pages.

- Defined the functionality and attributes your site will have based on the sample sites that were offered.

With your business goals in hand, let's take a look at who you will be building your Web site for.

Chapter 6

Human-Friendly Web Sites

The success of your site depends on the success your visitors have. In this chapter, you will learn how to think like one of your Web site's visitors. Through their eyes, you will look at your project's goals and identify whether you *really* need to add all the features on your wish list. Ignore this chapter at your own peril: Site visitors tend to get restless if they feel their needs are being ignored.

Defining Your Audience

By correctly identifying the desires of your site's visitors, you can transform your Web site from a bland hypertext archive to an interactive experience that engages new customers. Whether you are interested in nurturing an online community or creating an e-commerce Web site, you need to put your guests' needs before your own.

If you are trying to sell products or services, what information will *your customers* need to order your product? Shipping rates? Pricing? Minimum orders? Currency? You need to make sure the information is easy to find so that the customer can easily order your product. And if you are running a community Web site, there are questions that also need to be answered. Are your guests coming to your Web site to find out when the next meeting is? Do they want to register for a workshop? Or are they looking for the discussion board? By knowing who your audience is, you can organize your Web site accordingly.

The more you know about your customers, the easier it will be to create a Web site that meets their needs. You should know the kinds of people who will be interested in what you're offering. Let's "flesh" them out a bit.

To focus on your most important customers, we will be creating *personae*. A persona is the archetype of your user—you may have also seen it called a *customer profile* by marketing or businesspeople. Each group of users that has a significantly different need or set of requirements should have its own persona. If you are selling a series of products, you may have a different target market for each of your products. Wherever there is overlap, try to combine users into a single persona.

For example, a garden-supplies Web site may have both retail customers who purchase individual plants and wholesale customers who order plants a season in advance. Although both customers are buying plants, their approach to the Web site will not be the same. However, a small business wanting to decorate the front of their store and a home owner decorating their front lawn may both want to find the same kind of information.

There are many different ways of preparing a persona. Firms that specialize in creating profiles will charge tens of thousands of dollars for each profile they create. The profiles are expensive because they are based on ethnographic interviews with thousands of real people. These interviews are then distilled into a one- to two-page description of an "average" person. Fortunately, you do not *really* need to hire an expert to get a sense of who your customers are—you just need to think about your experience with the kind of customer that you would like to attract more of.

Personae will help guide your decisions about Web site features, information structure, and even visual design. By designing for your "someone" whose goals and behavior are understood, you can satisfy the broader group of people represented by the archetype. Each persona you create should have the following characteristics described in their summary.

- **Primary goal.** What do they want to accomplish while visiting your Web site?
- **Attitudes about Web sites and businesses like yours.** Create a one-sentence "quote" that describes the essence of this particular type of site visitor.
- **Environment and technical profile.** Include their Internet connection speed; comfort with computers; and whether they are accessing the Internet from work, from home, on the road, or all of the above.

- **Completely fictional details to bring the persona to life.** Create a name, occupation, and income. Define their age, gender, and marital status. Include a photograph and personal details such as the number of children and any pets the person has.

Sample Personae

The following are some personae I've developed when creating Web site–building workshops. They helped me pick the topics I needed to cover and the order in which I presented the information. The names and details are completely fictitious, of course.

Bobbie Dunphy

Age: Late 50s.

Occupation: Author/poet (self-employed).

Family: Married, three children.

Technical profile: Updates her own Web site using established templates. Uses an up-to-date Mac computer.

Internet use: 10 to 15 hours/week. Mostly e-mail and researching grant applications.

Summary: Hands-on technical.

Additional details: Bobbie has taken a self-publishing workshop and has produced short "chap books" using sophisticated desktop publishing software. She writes grant applications for organizations and receives grants as an individual writer. Although Bobbie is more interested in starting projects than the daily monotony of running them, her brain is a constant flood of information that would be of interest to her community.

Quote: "I want to learn how to make and update my own pages. I don't want to rely on anyone else to accomplish my morning routine."

Pearl McGee

Age: Late 20s.

Occupation: Potter (self-employed).

Family: Single.

Technical profile: Uncomfortable with technology. Uses an old computer with out-of-date software and a dial-up Internet connection.

Internet use: 5 hours/week. Checks e-mail and occasionally visits a Web site or two.

Summary: Technophobe.

Additional details: Pearl works for mostly private clients but has also done some larger corporate projects. She is interested in reducing telephone and travel costs by working with customers online. Pearl takes her products to some trade shows but does not seem to be as focused on developing client relations as she should be—she prefers the making part of the business to the selling part of the business.

Quote: "I want to learn how to share files and pictures over the Internet. But I don't want to waste my time learning new software that won't work on my computer."

Owen Harbour

Age: Early 40s.

Occupation: Liaison officer (bureaucrat).

Family: Married, no kids.

Technical profile: Mostly uses the Internet at work (high-speed connection). Familiar with the tools installed by the office technician.

Internet use: 20+ hours/week. Constantly connected to e-mail. Whenever possible, Owen will send out a quick e-mail to avoid the interruption of the phone.

Summary: Tool user.

Additional information: Owen works as a liaison officer and frequently has to travel to any one of the businesses serviced by his regional office. On meeting days, Owen can spend as much as four to six hours in the car. Although he doesn't want to be a technical person, Owen likes understanding what his options are. The in-house technical staff is too busy keeping the office working to research new solutions. Owen is exploring the idea of creating an e-newsletter to send human-friendly versions of his media releases to all of his (interested) contacts.

Creating Your Own Personae

Based on your current knowledge of your existing clients, create one persona for each *substantially different* group or type of person who visits your Web site. You may do this task with either your current customers in mind or the customers you would like to have. Remember, a persona should not describe only one person; rather, it should be the average of several people. You may want to write a list of all your best customers and then group them according to similar characteristics. It's OK to have several different persona to work from. They should each represent a different kind of customer that is important to your business. Generic personae that match no one will be of no use to you. Instead, you need to figure out the characteristics your customers have in common.

The following are some ideas to get you started.

- Who are some real-life people that you think use your site? Choose 10 to 15 real people to start. Write down their names and a description. What characteristics do they have in common (combine these into one "person").

- What kind of technical constraints does your audience have? Do they live in the country with a dial-up Internet connection? Are they connecting from work with a high-speed connection and a firewall that lets only limited data through?

- Add fake stuff. Give your person a name, an age, and a family (and maybe even an income). You may want to clip a photograph from a magazine to really give your sample person a personality.

It may take you several days, if not several weeks, to create a persona that really matches your needs. Try to have no more than two or three personae—each should represent a kind of customer or guest with completely unique goals. Your profiles should be printed out and hung in the office. Whenever you are faced with a design decision (technical, informational, or visual), you should ask yourself, "What would Bobbie like?" or "Could Owen use this feature if I built it like this?"

You may also want to create the antipersona. You know, the people who suck away your time and never actually pay you anything? It can't hurt to remind yourself of who these people are when building your Web site. You can practice saying no to your antipersona in the privacy of your own home. It's probably cheaper than therapy too.

With your personae created, it's time to put them to the test. The following tips can be used to test the accuracy of your personae.

- Use your Web site statistics to see what browsers your actual Web site visitors are using. This will help you identify the ratio of technowhiz to technophobe. Depending on the granularity of these numbers, you may also be able to look at "visitors" and "buyers" (or community members) separately.

- Again, using your Web site statistics, look for the incoming links (the *referrers*) and compare which incoming links provide the longest visits to your site.

- If you have a physical shop, conduct a survey of your shop customers to see who visits your Web site and what they hoped to find (or did find) on your site.

If you don't have a physical shop *or* a Web site, you can put together a quick survey using SurveyMonkey. Appendix A contains a presite sample survey. It asked realistic questions that helped identify the types of people who would be using the site, their expectations, and their capabilities. A word of caution on listing features: Don't list too many "pie-in-the-sky" Web site features that may not end up being implemented. People may get disappointed and feel they weren't listened to if you decide not to implement their favorite feature.

Take any requests for new features with a grain of salt. People are often more enthusiastic about a new technology than their time permits them to be in reality. For example, your survey shows that your community *needs* an online gallery. Before building the gallery, check to see whether other community groups, with goals similar to your own, are also using gallery software. Has the gallery been kept up to date for more than six consecutive months? Do you think the software has been successfully integrated into at least half of the sites you look at? This reality check allows you to see in which areas your peers and competitors succeed *and* fail to meet their goals.

User Scenarios

The visitors to your Web site will be constantly interacting with it. A simple Web site may only offer links between pages as points for interaction, allowing visitors to view pages and navigate between them but not much else. On a community Web site, where visitors are able to interact with one another and add their own content to the Web, you will need to consider more fully how visitors and community members interact with your Web site.

Visitors to your site need to be able to discover all of the things your Web site has to offer. They need to have a clear understanding of what everything on the screen means before they can take an appropriate action (or make an appropriate click). Every screen in your Web site represents multiple decision points. Each time a visitor clicks, they have to guess what will happen next. Successful Web sites are good at giving clues about what's on the other side of a click; the resulting page will be immediately obviously right or obviously wrong, based on what the visitor was looking for. To achieve success within your Web site, visitors must be able to name the task they want to accomplish, perform the task, and then verify the task has been successfully achieved.

If you completed the activities in Chapter 5 and earlier in this chapter, you should have a list of features for your site and cast of characters who will be using your site. You can now run each of your personae through your competitors' Web sites to see whether you can accomplish your goals while pretending to be each of the personae you've created. Writing user scenarios do not need to be difficult, but they may be time-consuming.

Using these very simple steps, you will be able to create many scenarios for your Web site.

1. Update your personae from earlier in this chapter, and add a realistic Web site goal related to the important Web site features you identified in Chapter 5.

2. Using your favorite thinking tool (mind-mapping software, a text editor, sticky notes, and an empty wall), write down all the steps that your personae will need to take in order to complete the goal you identified in the previous step.

3. On sheets of paper, create each of the Web pages a user will need to pass through to accomplish each of the steps you've identified. You may want to use index cards or sticky notes for this step.

4. Complete the first three steps for each persona's goal, identifying where you have screens in common between each person and task.

5. Create a summary document that describes the individual screens necessary. In the summary document, identify the elements that need to be programmed for the functionality to work.

For example, Bobbie wants to create a blog to share her thoughts with others. She's hired you to build the Web site that she will use to put her blog entries online. She's really excited about not having to update templates by hand anymore. The following are the steps she will need to successfully complete in order to create new blog entries.

1. Bobbie goes to the front page of her Web site and clicks the "login" button.

2. She is taken to a login form where she enters her user name and password. Programmer task: Create user account for Bobbie.

3. Once logged in, Bobbie must find the button to "create content," click it, and then choose "blog entry" from the list of content types. Interface design note: This sequence must be very easy to navigate. A custom "home" page will be needed that offers a limited set of tasks for Bobbie to perform.

4. To add a new blog entry, Bobbie must add a title, blog content, and categories/tags. She must scroll to the bottom and click "save" to successfully post her blog entry to the front page of the site.

5. Once the blog post has been successfully saved, Bobbie should be given a clear notification that the blog entry has been successfully saved. Options should be presented to either visit the new blog entry on the home or log out.

This scenario is very simple, but it lists each of the tasks that you will be able to use to "test" your Web site and guess how effective it will be at helping you reach the business goals you identified in Chapter 5. Your user scenarios can also become the foundation for your site's documentation.

Technical Profiles and Minimum System Requirements

In the personae you developed earlier in this chapter, you included a brief technical profile. It is important to understand the technical capabilities of your Web site visitors. There is no sense installing a streaming Webcam of your garden if you know that every person visiting your site is in cottage country and is limited to an old computer with a dial-up modem.

Be realistic. Tools should enhance the visitor's experience, not distract or detract from it. Overbuilding a site also runs the risk of losing customers who find your site slow, frustrating to use, or simply inaccessible for whatever reason. As E. F. Schumacher said, "Small is beautiful." He also said some very clever things about appropriate technology and not giving gas-powered tractors to people living in the middle of the African desert.

Summarizing the technical requirements before starting to build your project can help prevent feature creep. For example, if you know you are required by law to be accessible to individuals with low vision or mobility impairments, you should probably think twice about that plan to include an interactive sheep-counting game on your Web site.

Browsers

Cross-browser compatibility is just about the bane of every Web designer's existence. Internet Explorer doesn't quite behave the same way as Firefox or Chrome. Sometimes you can get very lucky and be asked to design a Web site on a corporate intranet where every single person accessing the site is using the same type of browser. This is not very common, though. When taking into account which browsers you will optimize your site for, remember that the site does not need to look identical across all browsers. It needs to look intentional, and it needs to be functional. Minor variations of a pixel here or a rounded corner there are not going to determine the success of your project. Do have a list of browsers that you are committed to achieving beauty for, and do be accessible to all devices regardless of their age. Just remember, being accessible doesn't mean visually identical.

If you already have a Web site, go ahead and take a look at the statistics for it. Can you see a trend in the types of browsers that visit your site? Within my own Web sites, the profile of browsers varies considerably. Within my own portfolio of Web sites, small-business owners visiting HICK Tech tend to use Internet Explorer, but site visitors to emmajane.net, which has a lot more about open source software, tend to use Firefox or Chrome.

Even if your site is not getting a lot of mobile devices accessing your site, having a mobile version can make all the difference for someone who is traveling and really needs access to information contained on your site. This is especially true for hotels, restaurants, and travel-related Web sites.

Internet Connectivity

In addition to the accessibility of information on your site to mobile devices, you will also need to consider the total size of download for your Web site. As more and more people are accessing the Web from metered mobile devices, the size of your Web site has once again become relevant. Unlike the days of the dial-up, it's not necessarily about speed so much as it is the concern of cost. Although visitors may not tie your site directly to an increase in their data charges, they will be savvy enough to recognize which sites should be avoided while on the road. And if this isn't enough of an incentive, search engines are now using page download to rank sites. If you want your site to rank well in search engines, you need to make it load faster than your competitor's site.

There are also niche markets for whom the land of dial-up is very much a reality. This could be travel-related sites and also rural industries such as farming, agriculture, and exotic sports such as horse racing, polo, and mountaineering. To be fair, I'm not entirely sure that anyone else was checking their e-mail from Arthur's Pass this summer; however, nerds do like to stay connected.

Accommodating Everyone

When planning how visitors will interact with your site, you need to think about the tools your Web site visitors are using to capture and consume the content on your Web site. Will you need a printer-friendly version of your pages, a high- and low-bandwidth template, a mobile version of your site, or a private members-only area for your site? If your Web site is updated regularly and you are providing an RSS feed for your content, you will also need to consider the attributes for this feed. Will you publish the whole story or merely a content summary?

Your Web site should never prevent people from accessing public content. Consideration should be given to people who will use adaptive technology to access your site. In most cases, it makes good business sense to accommodate everyone, but in some cases you are also required by law to provide your content in an accessible manner. You will find more information on creating accessible Web sites in Chapter 17.

Summary

To make your site achieve your goals, you will need to realize it's not about you. In this chapter, you learned how to do the following.

- Identify your primary visitors
- Create scenarios that will enable you to efficiently deploy a successful Web site

No matter what kind of Web site you are creating, this chapter has given you the tools to ensure your project is a user-centered design. As you proceed through the rest of this book, remember to refer to the task lists you created in this chapter. In the next chapter, you will add the next layer into your plan: information design.

Chapter 7

Information Architecture

When I'm dining out, I'm frequently overwhelmed by the choices on a menu. Especially when traveling, I really want to try everything that is in season and locally grown. Like many others, I'll stare blankly at a menu before giving up and having one of my default menu selections of fish and chips or lamb. While staring at a menu, recently a friend of mine gave a name to this overwhelmed feeling: *option paralysis*. Having a name for the term didn't make choosing what to have for supper any easier, but I did like being able to label my affliction.

In this chapter, you will learn how to help prevent option paralysis on your Web site. You will learn about the importance of tying site and user goals to menu options as well as techniques to effectively categorize and label information on your Web site.

Information Architecture

Information architecture gives you the guiding principles necessary to organize your Web site's content in a way that will make sense to your visitors. It will help you determine what order the pages should go in by examining the methods a visitor will use when looking for information on your site. Although many of the processes in this chapter are easy in principle, they can consume much of your time as you struggle over whether to put "tiger" under "giant cats" or "felines." To make the right decision, refer to the goals and personae you defined in earlier chapters as you work your way through this chapter.

You must consider four components when designing the information structure for your Web site.

- **Organization.** When people think of information architecture, they typically think of this component. Much of this chapter focuses on different ways to organize your content.

- **Labeling.** These are the titles you put onto groups of information. Labels will appear in your menus and as the headings for categories of grouped information. Labels should be clear and use natural language wherever possible. Avoid short forms and company-specific or project-specific jargon. This may include the text used on breadcrumb navigation.

- **Navigation.** How do your visitors get from the front page to the page they're looking for? This is the navigation system. It defines the location of and functionality of your menu system and subsection navigation structure. This may include breadcrumb navigation.

- **Search.** When all else fails, Web site visitors will search. (Many users will arrive on your site as a result of a search too.) A number of Drupal modules can enhance the on-site search experience for your visitors.

You will have a high degree of control over organization and labeling information architecture components when working with Drupal, which you will learn more about in chapters 12 and 13. You will need to use natural language, appropriate labels, and organization to ensure you have findable content. Labeling will require a heavy dose of common sense on your part. Organization systems are discussed in depth throughout the remainder of this chapter.

Defining Content Types

When building Web sites with Drupal, you are not limited to simple Web pages. You can create as many different *kinds* of content as you need. Your Web site might have the following types of content: Article, Basic page, and Event. Each of these types of content would have its own form with custom fields that content authors would use to create and edit new content (Figure 7.1). Separating discrete bits of content into fields means you have more control over how that information is used. For example, by storing a person's birthday separately, you can create a birthday calendar.

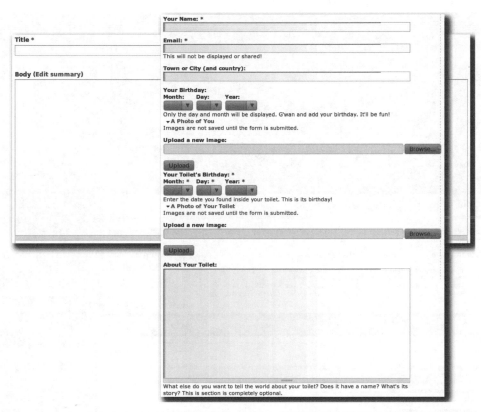

FIGURE 7.1 The form used to create a new instance of the content types Basic page (bottom) and Toilet (inset)

Although it is tempting to think of content types as "types of Web pages," resist this temptation. When you create a new unit of content (for example, a new Basic page), Drupal uses the term *node* to refer to that content. A single Web page that is displayed in a Web browser may contain several nodes along with other page components (see Figure 7.2).

Origins of the Word *Node*

The dictionary defines a *node* as the point on a plant stem from which leaves or lateral branches grow. Computer scientists define *node* as an abstract unit that contains either data or a link to more nodes—a single item that is connected to a network. If you think of a tree, the leaves on a tree are like the units of content stored in your database, and the sections in your Web site are like the branches on a tree.

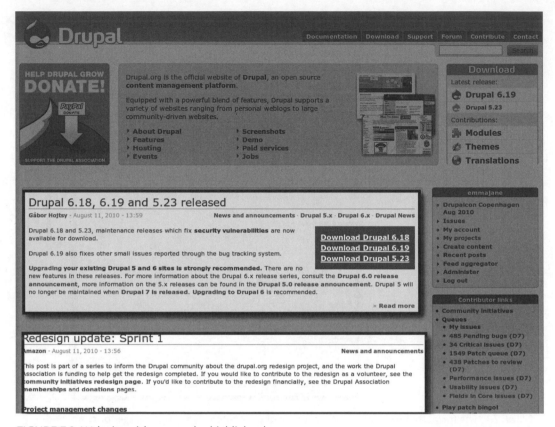

FIGURE 7.2 Web site with two nodes highlighted

Before building your new Drupal Web site, you must carefully examine the content that will be entered into the Web site. Look closely for similarities in the structure of your content to find all necessary fields for each of your content types. Perhaps your content can be contained within a simple Basic page content type, which allows you to enter only the title and a "body" of information. With this content type, however, you will be limited to sorting information based on the date the story was created or last updated and its title. For example, if you are storing a library of books you have read in your Drupal Web site, you may also want to list the books according to the name of the author, the year of the book's publication, the date when you read the book, and perhaps your quality rating for the book. Unfortunately, the content type Basic page, without modification, does not permit sorting books based on these fields. As such, it would not be a suitable content type to store information about the books you have read.

To create suitable content types on your site, you must first describe your content. Start with a list for each different kind of content displayed within your Web site. Ask yourself the following kinds of questions to determine the attributes of your content types.

- Does this content have a corresponding image?
- Are there categories for this content (and do the categories have icons)?
- Is the author's name displayed with the content?
- Should the creation date or last-updated date be displayed?
- Is this a date-based event that will be displayed in a calendar?
- Are there video and audio files associated with this content?
- Can people leave their comments on this content?

For every type of content that you need to display on your Web site, create a little diagram of how it will look on the page and what form fields you will need to build this page. Don't worry if you don't know exactly how the form will look yet. (It's easy, I promise.)

Extra Content

In addition to the content that is specific to your Web site, there are also several pieces of content your Web site should include. This content is (more or less) standard across the Web. Your visitors will expect to be able to find the following information. Depending on your business, these pages may be more or less relevant to what you are doing.

General Information

These types of content cover a range of topics that most Web sites will need to address.

- **Contact.** How to get in touch. This page should also give geographical context. What country are you in? Many of us like to deal with local companies to cut down on freight and increase neighborly behavior.
- **Feedback.** This page typically helps people get in touch directly with the IT team for the Web site to report a problem. You may want to incorporate this into your contact page if you are a relatively small company.
- **What's new.** This may include media releases or other persistent news stories. A "What's new" page will typically be updated less frequently than a blog and be a bit more formal. If you have a blog, you may not need a "What's new" section (and vice versa).

- **Blog.** Typically this is an informal series of short articles or snippets of information about the latest happenings related to the Web site.

- **About this site/company.** This is information and context about who you are, what the site is about, and why you are an authority on the information contained on the Web site.

- **First-time visitors.** If your site is information dense but there are a few "getting started" pages that people should start with, go ahead and let them know what they should read first.

- **Help and FAQ.** I'll admit it, I hate FAQs, and I rarely remember to click the Help button. Wherever possible, provide this information in context instead of isolated in its own area. But if you must, lots of Web sites do have this type of extra content. Go ahead and add it to your site if it makes sense to do so.

Search-Related Pages

These types of content tend to be menu items or navigation pages. In most cases, you will need to configure Drupal to generate them automatically. There is more information about the items described here in Chapter 16.

- **Link to the home.** Everything in life deserves a "do over" button. This is your visitor's opportunity to start at the beginning. In addition to a Home link, many Web sites will also link the company's logo back to the home page.

- **Site map.** This helps search engines and human visitors navigate your site. This page will organize content according to topic or section.

- **Index.** Unlike the site map, the index lists all content alphabetically. There is more about alphabetical organization in the "Organizing Lists of Content" section later in this chapter.

- **Quick links.** This is a list of links to pages that are very commonly requested but are not appropriate to have as top-level menu items for browsers.

- **Search.** This is a search box or a link to a search form.

Legal Pages

The next set is all the legal stuff. *Yawn.* Although you may be tempted to combine several of these pages into a single page, your audience may be looking for key labels and miss a grouped page. Do whatever is most appropriate for your audience.

- **Disclaimer.** Is there anything you need to get off your chest about your company's affiliations or to absolve yourself of responsibility? This is the page you should do it.

- **Privacy policy.** If you're collecting personal information, you'll need to have a privacy policy to let people know what you do with their information. You are allowed to update this document if things change, but do ensure you let people know *before* they sign up that you may change this policy and that you share the responsibility with your visitor to keep them up to date on any changes that make take place.

- **Terms and conditions.** Include information that your visitors expect about the service you are providing and under what conditions you make your information and services available to your visitors.

- **Cancellation and returns policy.** This is relevant if you are allowing individuals to purchase tickets or physical goods.

> **Not All Lawyers Are Boring**
> Don't for a second think that all lawyers are boring. Some of my favorite people are lawyers. Please take a moment to check out Megan Langley Grainger (@meglg) and Jon Penney (@jon_penney) on Twitter.

Organizing Content

Content can be organized in a lot of ways. In this section, we look at how Web site visitors can navigate through content. By understanding how you want to arrange lists of content on your site, you will be better equipped to choose the most appropriate tools to build these lists.

The rest of this section describes common ways to sort content into lists of content. Each of these examples has a different implementation pattern in Drupal. Read through these examples and make a few notes on which ones you think best match the content for your Web site. It is possible that you will implement more than one of these options.

Content Audit

A content audit is a process whereby you list every single thing you may want to use on your Web site. These bits of content become your "assets," which must be stored and organized for visitors to find. You will use the results of this content audit in sub-sequent steps to build your navigation system and menu labels. You will also use the results as a checklist to know which content you already have and which you still need to develop.

I typically do content audits directly on cue cards (aka recipe cards or index cards... you may even want to use sticky notes), which I can reuse for the card-sorting exercise that is described later in this chapter. Cue cards allow me to write more information. Small sticky notes, on the other hand, can use a file folder as their wall for organization and can be easily photocopied to share with others. There is no requirement to use paper for this step; I'm incredibly tactile, and I like being able to move around bits of physical things. If you want to do this outline digitally instead, go for it! Try to avoid deleting things, though. There will be plenty of time for that later.

To perform a content audit for your own Web site, you must complete the following steps.

1. Brainstorm a list of all content you want to include on your site. Consider categories of information such as "services my business offers," "how visitors can get in touch with me," "when the next meeting for our group is," and "how people join my group."

2. Mark content according to whether this is content you already have or content that you will need to create. Write down the file name where this content resides if it is available digitally. You may want to color code based on "content that I have," "content that I need," and "content that is written but still needs images."

3. Review your business goals (Chapter 5) and make sure no content is missing from your list.

4. Review your personae (Chapter 6) and make sure everything your best customers want to know is captured in your list.

The next step will be to sort the information you have identified in your content audit.

Organization Structures

Before you can begin your sort, let's take a look at some of the different ways that content can be sorted.

Chronological Organization

Most Web site visitors are highly familiar with the chronological form of content organization, because it is commonly seen in blogs and calendars. In a blog, the units of content (blog entries) are sorted from most recent to oldest. Visitors to the Web site must navigate through the history of the Web site to find each unit of content. When using the Blog module, Drupal displays new entries on the front page of the Web site by default (see Figure 7.3).

A variation on this sort of chronological organization is a display calendar. This format is most appropriate when listing upcoming events (Figure 7.4). It may also be appropriate to show an archive of stories if the information is date-specific (for example, a Web site that reports on community events). Think about how people will access and use the list of content. Consider how many events will be added as well. In some instances, it will be appropriate to use a full display calendar as well as a quick summary organized as a bullet list of the next 10 events.

FIGURE 7.3 A blog is a series of short entries sorted by reverse chronological order.

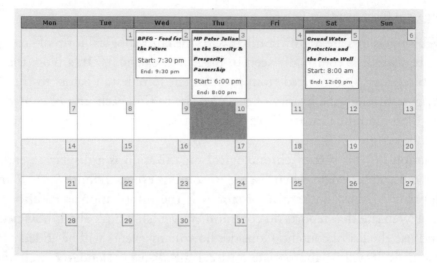

FIGURE 7.4 Upcoming events displayed as a calendar

Linear Organization

Novels have a beginning, a middle, and an end. Authors create stories and assume they will be experienced in a linear way. Similarly, your Web site may have sections that ought to be read from start to finish, just like a book. For example, linear organization is appropriate for instructions and documentation, where you build on the knowledge that was obtained in a previous section or where there is a logical progression of ideas from start to finish (Figure 7.5).

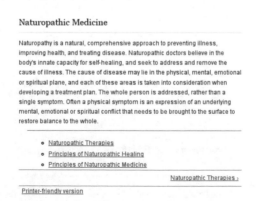

FIGURE 7.5 A section of content with built-in navigation. Pages within the group are listed below the introductory paragraph.

Topical Organization

If your content is sorted hierarchically into sections and subsections, visitors to your site will be able to browse each of the different categories to find information that is of interest to them (Figure 7.6).

Within Drupal, you may choose to implement a controlled vocabulary with pre-determined categories, or you can opt to use "free tagging" and allow categories to be entered when the content is created. Both approaches have merits. A controlled vocabulary generates a rigorous system that is predictable for both content editors and Web site visitors (as is shown in Figure 7.6). Free tagging, by comparison, is often more appropriate for community-generated content where thousands of users may enter slightly different types of content into your Web site.

Alphabetical organization works best when users know the exact name of the thing they are looking for. This is especially true with very long lists of content. The word *the* is perhaps the biggest enemy to alphabetical organization. Although your Web site visitors may know exactly what they are looking for, *the* can end up putting the content in an unexpected spot in machine-sorted lists of content. If possible, try to limit alphabetical lists of content to a single display page. In other words, avoid paginated lists of alphabetical content. This approach will allow users to more easily scan the full list of options to find what they are looking for.

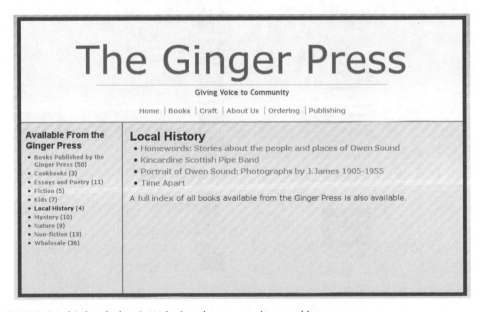

FIGURE 7.6 On this book shop's Web site, the content is sorted by category.

Popularity-Based Organization

Many social networking sites feature popularity-based content organization for their front pages. Figure 7.7 shows crochet patterns sorted according to their ratings and also the number of times they've been viewed. A FAQ, or set of help pages, may also be ordered according to how often the content is requested.

Task-Based Organization

From the very beginning of your Drupal installation, you will be working with task-based organization. Your Web site might include tasks such as adding new content, moderating comments, searching or filtering the content, and viewing recently updated content. Figure 7.8 shows the task-based menu that Drupal provides to help organize these actions. You may also have a set of tasks that are available to different roles within your team of authenticated users.

Task-based organization is appropriate for the presentation and navigation of action-oriented pages as opposed to content-oriented pages. You will need to decide

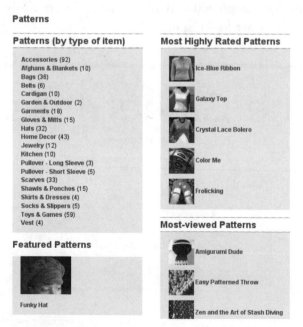

FIGURE 7.7 Crochet patterns sorted according to popularity

FIGURE 7.8 Task-based links are grouped into the administrative toolbar, the shortcuts menu, and the user menu (shown top to bottom).

how related tasks are grouped and how they are ordered within that group. You will also need to decide how to integrate the tasks into the page. In some cases, tasks may be available from a menu option (for example, Create Content); in other cases, tasks may be presented as tabs on a page (for example, Edit This Page). The administration area of Drupal allows you to build scenarios of related tasks. For example, the user menu and the shortcut links, as shown in Figure 7.8, group task-based navigation in easy-to-access navigation areas across the top of your site. You can add to these menus and create your own utility links, as well. Administrative shortcuts are covered in Chapter 3, and customizing menus is covered in Chapter 11.

Defining Structure for Your Content

Once you have captured a list of all the content that may go onto your site, you can start organizing your content. Review the list of organizational structures described previously in this section and the goals of your site and your visitors that you identified in earlier chapters. Pretend you are one of the personae you developed. How would the information be easiest to navigate for each of your personae?

Using the following steps, organize the items you collected in your content audit into groups of content. This activity is known as *card sorting*.

1. Group each of your cards by topic.
2. Assign each group of cards a label. It is easiest to create a "label" card that appears at the top of your group of cards. You may want to color code this card to make labels easy to spot.
3. Within each group, organize your cards from general information (top tier) to specific information (lower tier in the navigation structure).

These groups of content will become the basis for each of the sections of your Web site. Think of a label for the topic that will fit easily onto a Web site menu. Shorter labels are typically easier to fit into a Web site design; however, don't make them so short that they no longer make sense. Subtopics are often placed in an area of the Web site that can accommodate longer menu labels.

If you use sticky notes, you can do this activity on an empty wall in your office. If you use small sticky notes, you can use a manila folder to store all of your cards. Either way, having a backup never hurts. You can take a photograph with a digital camera of the wall or a photocopy of the folder to capture the information. This snapshot can be shared with others or tucked away for future reference.

> **Card Sorting Isn't Just for Web Sites**
> I've been a card sorter since the early 1990s when I first used the technique to organize arguments for essays. I was thrilled to find out how popular it is in information architecture as well. The technique is visual and tactile and much less prone to distraction than using a computer.

Conveying Content Structure

As your content structure starts to take shape, you will need to formalize the structure into a document that can be shared with others. It is especially handy if you can share this document with other people over the Internet. Having everyone working in the same office has become a bit of a luxury that doesn't extend to companies that have hired Web development firms or that have distributed teams that work all over the planet.

It can be easy to convert your organized content audit to a linear document that captures all the content you will include on your site. Linear planning documents may include sequential headings that assign a number to each piece of content in the site hierarchy. Legal documents are often written with this detailed linear heading assignment. They typically follow the numbering scheme of *Number.lower case letter.roman numeral* (for example, 2.c.iii). If you are working from paper, assign each sticky note or cue card a number as follows.

- All top-level topics covering first-tier (general) questions are assigned a numeral (for example, 1 to 10).

- All tier-two content that is a subsection of a tier-one page is assigned the tier-one topic number as well as a lowercase letter (for example, 1.a, 1.b, 1.c, 2.a, 3.a).

- All third-tier content that answers specific questions for site visitors should also be assigned a roman numeral (for example, 1.a.iii).

If your content has more than three levels, you will need to extend this numbering system to suit your needs.

Once you have assigned your numbers, you will never again need to worry about losing the order of your cards. These numbers can also be easily transferred to your digital planning document and allow you to easily see whether you've missed any cards.

A visual display of information is often the most useful for people to see how a site fits together. The information may have a formal structure (flow charts) or represent a natural flow of ideas (mind mapping).

Use Mind Mapping

Mind maps allow you to dump your thoughts onto a page in a quasi-organized manner without having to worry about truly sorting information. Mind maps allow you to easily show relationships between content. To get past the inertia of a blank page, I used FreeMind, an open source mind-mapping tool, to dump my ideas onto a page. Figure 7.9 shows the mind map for this chapter.

Mind-mapping software can also be used to organize simple Web sites. Generally, mind-mapping software should be limited to organizing Web sites that have 20 to 30 pages in no more than 3 to 5 primary topics.

Flow Charts

Flow charts are more formal versions of mind maps where symbols representing content are attached to each other using connectors. They are used to map everything from electrical circuit diagrams to complex Web sites. They may be describing a very simple five-page Web site (Figure 7.10), or they may be very complex—representing hundreds of pages. No matter how complex the diagram, the goal is always the same: to describe how, and by what labels, content will be connected.

Using the content audit from the previous section, create a linear flow of your content by completing these steps.

1. Assign a topic label to each group of cards.
2. In your favorite digital drawing program (such as Photoshop, Dia, Illustrator, and so on), create a box for each group of cards with its label.
3. Draw connections between the boxes to show the hierarchy of the topic labels.

FIGURE 7.9 The mind map for this chapter. Sections are not organized, but the relationships between ideas are marked.

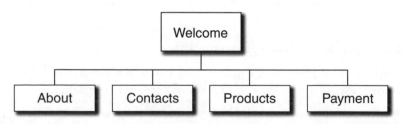

FIGURE 7.10 Minimal Web sites can still benefit from having all pages represented in a flow chart.

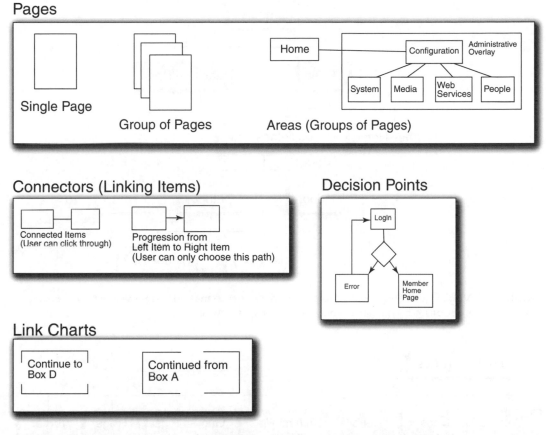

FIGURE 7.11 A minimum number of shapes are required to represent a complex Web site.

You may have seen complicated flow charts that also act as decision trees. Generally, there are only a few shapes needed for a Web site. Figure 7.11 shows the six basic shapes useful for most Web sites: page, stack of similar pages, continuation of the chart on another page, areas (grouped pages), connectors, and decision points.

A complete vocabulary of shapes for flow charts is available at www.jjg.net/ia/ visvocab/.

Flow charts will show you whether your content will be accessible via a navigation system. For example, visitors who are new to the topic you are presenting may be overcome by option paralysis if you have too many choices on the landing page. Beginners need a navigation system that is narrow and deep (Figure 7.12); advanced visitors who are capable of dealing with complex topics will have an easier time dealing with a broad selection of menu choices that lead to a relatively shallow set of pages (Figure 7.13).

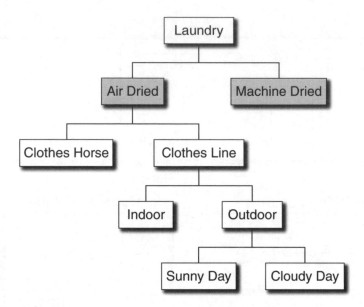

FIGURE 7.12 Visitors who are new to a topic will find it easier to make decisions where they choose between fewer options. This is a narrow but deep content structure.

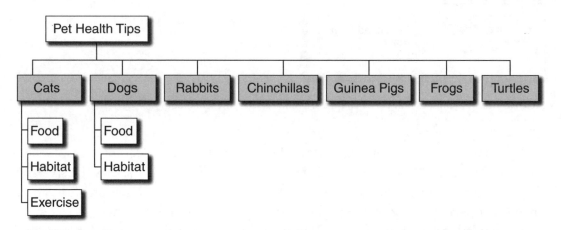

FIGURE 7.13 Visitors who are experienced with a topic will be better equipped to deal with many choices presented to them at once. This is a broad but shallow content structure.

Your flow chart will also be the basis of your navigation system and your menu labels. Each level of navigation potentially represents a menu. George Miller's famous "7 plus or minus 2" rule can be used to help choose the number of items that a person can keep in short-term memory. Menus that are fewer than ten items are definitely easier to style (visually). It may be unfair to assume that our visitors will need to memorize menu labels for a navigation system to be effective. Rather than using only an arbitrary number for your menu items, consider what your site visitors already know about the topics you cover on your Web site. Beginners will be more effective at navigating menus with fewer items because they must memorize more relationships and hold that information in short-term memory; however, a Web site geared to visitors with a high degree of prior knowledge will be able to navigate longer menus with greater ease than their novice counterparts.

Testing the Organizational Structure

Ask your visitors for feedback on how you've organized your site. Although it may make perfect sense to you, it's possible you've created a teaching aid (a shortcut for yourself) rather than a learning tool (a shortcut for your visitor). There is no need to blow the budget (time or money) on this testing. Usability expert Jakob Nielsen has reported that a sampling as small as 5 people for usability testing and 15 people for card sorting will reveal significant errors.

The card sorting test is the same as the activity you completed earlier in this chapter. If possible, find participants who closely resemble the personae you developed in Chapter 6. Shuffle the cards you have created for your own content audit, and give them to the participants to sort into relevant, labeled categories. Check their organization structures and labels against your own. If they're the same, great! If they're not, it's possible you're using industry jargon to describe your products and services. Consider adding more text to your site so that the key words your visitors need are included.

Summary

Throughout this chapter, you learned how to help your visitors overcome option paralysis to make the right decisions about how to find content on your Web site. If you completed each of the activities described in this chapter, you will have done the following.

- Defined the types of content that will be displayed on your Web site
- Performed a content audit and identified which material is already written and what material still needs to be assembled

- Organized your content audit into one of several organization strategies that was appropriate for the goals defined in Chapter 5 and the personae defined in Chapter 6
- Created a flow chart representing all the content that will be available on your site and that lists the menu labels you will use in your navigation system
- Performed user testing on your content structure

In the next chapter, you will create the beginnings of a beautiful Web site.

Chapter 8

Design for Drupal

Drupal has a bad reputation of being hard to create designs for. It's true: There are a lot of working parts that go into a Drupal theme. But that means you get *more* control over how a Drupal site will look. By taking the time to plan your design with Drupal in mind, you will be able to easily snap together the site of your dreams. In this chapter, you will learn about the most powerful concepts needed for Drupal layout: regions, wireframes, and grid-based layout. There are also some tips for those who don't consider themselves designers at all.

Planning Your Page Layout

Armed with your detailed description of each content type and the structure for your lists of content, you are ready to start filling in the gaps of your Web site's page template. Around the outer edges of the content, you will need to fill in navigation areas, logos, and maybe even spaces for ads. Common interface components are listed in this section, though your own site may have additional requirements that go beyond this list.

Page Elements

When you are designing a Web site template, you must decide where the content, navigation, and logo will go. If every Web site were this simple, life would be so much easier. But most Web sites these days have a lot more to them than this. When designing your Drupal site, you will need to be able to place all your page elements into a template so that you know how to build your site. Without planning how the elements fit together, you will end up with an unruly site that feels cluttered and complicated.

Gather up a list of all the page elements ("things") that will appear on your site. Divide them according to page type, if it's appropriate. The following is an example of the types of pages your site may have.

- **Home page.** Sign-up for newsletter (call to action), featured product of the month, recent blog posts (establish company personality), money-back guarantee (reassurance text).
- **Product page.** Featured image, alternate images, price, description, dimensions, shipping information, "click to buy" button, link to return policy, links to related products.
- **Staff profile.** Photo, name, contact information, short bio, areas of expertise.
- **All pages.** Logo, Main menu navigation, sidebar subnavigation, search box, copyright notice.

Many of today's Web sites also include advertising. Whether you are soliciting ads from specific companies or using an ad service that places advertisements on your Web site automatically, you may need to consider at some point how you will display ads. Perhaps you will end up designating different areas on your page for different levels, and different kinds, of advertising. For example, you might make a distinction between text-based ads and graphical ads. Even if you do not plan to rely on advertising as a source of revenue, you may need to recognize sponsors. For example, your content may highlight large events with corporate sponsors, or your organization may need to acknowledge that it has received funding from a specific agency for one of its projects. Consider each of these interface components as you design your Web site templates.

A little planning now will help your Web site start out on the right foot and also allow it to grow with elegance as you add features over time. To your list of page elements, add anything you are planning to add in the future, even if you know you're not going to build it straightaway. The goal is to set aside the space (or know how you need to change the space) to accommodate your future self.

Regions

Drupal uses *regions* to place elements onto a Web page. These regions hold *blocks*. The blocks can be made up of almost anything, such as the content for any given page (a *node*), navigation menus, a search box, or recent comments on a blog. Blocks are provided by *modules* that are created by programmers. Although Drupal programmers have thought of *almost* everything you might want to build into your Drupal site, make sure you know that what you need is available before incorporating it into your design.

Regions can be as narrow as a column or as wide as a banner. Size constraints are created by the theme. So if you're building your own theme, you are limited only to what HTML and CSS has as constraints. In other words, regions are rectangles of whatever height, and width your little heart desires. This makes me exceptionally happy because I like drawing rectangles.

In a Drupal site, the largest region is typically reserved for content, whereas other, smaller regions contain other page elements such as navigation.

Some of the more extensible premade Drupal designs have as many as 12 different regions! This sort of organization gives a lot more flexibility than merely choosing between a two- or three-column layout. Figure 8.1 displays the Fusion base theme

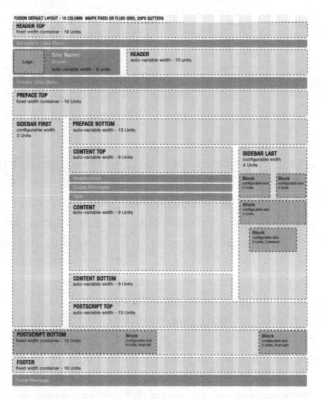

FIGURE 8.1 The Fusion base theme comes with 12 regions that you can stylize.

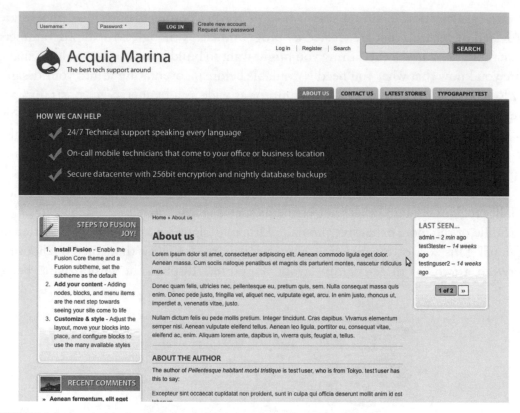

FIGURE 8.2 Acquia Marina is a completed theme that uses Fusion as its base.

onto which you can add your graphic embellishments—by default there are 12 available regions in this theme. Figure 8.2 shows a sample theme that uses the Fusion base.

There are no hard-and-fast rules about where each page element needs to be placed on your site, but there are a few conventions that might help you make decisions about where stuff goes. For left-to-right languages (such as English), Web site visitors tend to scan content starting at the top-left corner of a Web page—working their way out from that corner by scanning from left to right in bars. This makes an *F* shape. To capture attention, important content should be placed at the top left of the page. This top-left region is sometimes referred to as *the golden triangle* (Figure 8.3).

Web site visitors expect content to be placed in the regions outlined in Figure 8.4. You don't *need* to use these regions for your Web site, but it isn't bad to use conventions.

Key locations include content in the middle, navigation along the top or side, help and e-commerce checkout links in the top right, and company information along the bottom.

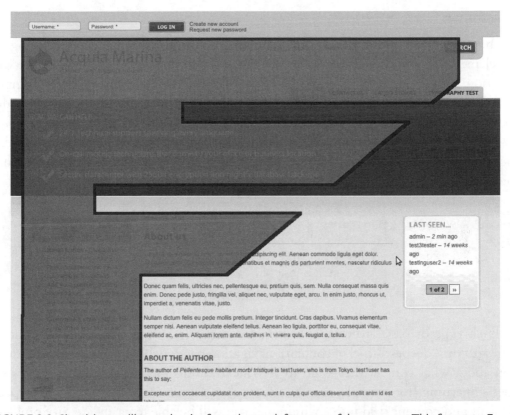

FIGURE 8.3 Site visitors will scan the site from the top-left corner of the page out. This forms an *F* shape that is referred to as the golden triangle.

Home Link	Advertisements		Search	Shopping Cart	Help
Navigation					
Navigation	Content			External Links	
				Help	
Search					
Navigation				Advertisements	
External Links		About Us			

FIGURE 8.4 Visitors expect content to appear in specific regions on each Web page.

Wireframes

At this stage you need to sketch out what your Web site will look like, including all the elements that will be displayed on the page. Wireframes establish how the site will function before starting the visual design process. They are comprised of "components" (navigation bar, content, logo, page title) placed in a basic shape that provides an outline of how each Web page will be formed. You may use graphical tools to create your wireframes, or you may draw them by hand. Effective wireframes do not resemble the final Web site. In fact, the more sketchy they look, the less people will worry about the visual design of the site.

> **Always Make Wireframes**
> I wish technology were so advanced that I could make this section blinking pink. Wireframes are super important. They are used during the initial site build to ensure that each page element is inserted correctly into your site. Think of them as a visual checklist.

Each type of page layout should have its own wireframe. This includes content pages (to the "deepest" level of content), navigation pages (where the user makes a decision about what content they want to view next), and function pages where the user does something (for example, search forms, submission forms). By placing every page element and content field into a wireframe, you will be able to easily identify problem areas where things have gotten too squished.

> **Make Space**
> Be sure to add more than enough regions into your template. You may not need them all now, but you will probably need them as your site grows. For example, will there be a time when you might want three columns of information in your footer instead of just one?

Figure 8.5 shows the wireframe for the design you will build in Chapter 15 (Figure 8.6).

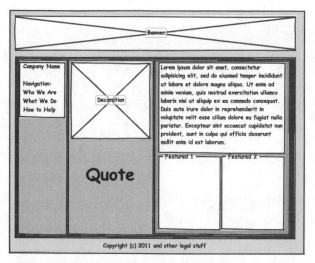

FIGURE 8.5 Wireframe for the home page of the theme Domicile

FIGURE 8.6 Completed design for the theme Domicile (design by Betty Biesenthal of www.design-house.ca)

> **Find the Right Tool for You**
>
> Lots of tools can be used to easily create wireframes. Some of my favorite free tools include Pencil (www.evolus.vn/Pencil/), Gimp (www.gimp.org/), Inkscape (www.inkscape.org/), and Skencil (www.skencil.org/). I also like Balsamiq Mockups (www.balsamiq.com/products/mockups), an inexpensive and very easy-to-use wireframe tool. A free version is also available for use online or as a desktop application. You don't have to use this software to make your wireframes. In fact, you don't even need to use a computer—you can go lo-fi with pen and paper!

Looking at your wireframe, you should also be able to answer the following questions.

- Where am I in the site?
- How do I get back to the main page to start over?
- What's available on this site?
- Where can I get help?
- I've been to a page before that I want to find again; where is it now?
- I know what I want; can I search for it?

You may need to create several wireframes if you have multiple content types that differ significantly. For pages that are several clicks away from the home page, remember to include all the relevant levels of navigation in your wireframes. These rough sketches will be your wireframes that follow you into the next phase of development: visual design.

Next, we'll refine your rough wireframes into a grid-based layout. As you become more experienced with Drupal, you may find yourself skipping the rough sketch stage and using a grid to sketch your layout ideas. Sometimes I skip the rough sketches, and sometimes I skip the refined grid sketches, but I never skip the wireframing process.

Grid-Based Layout

Humans have been using grids to shape the structure of how information is displayed on a page for almost as long as we've had the page to display it on. The grid of choice for print page layout has changed over the centuries with the height of its use in the 1980s. With the adoption of desktop computing, there has been a decline in the use of grids as graphic designers rebel and amateur designers use their personal inspiration instead of formal training to create layouts. Fortunately, we are starting to see a trend back toward the use of grids on the Web.

Using a grid as the base for your design does put an artificial constraint on how your page is laid out. Like a swimmer doing laps in a pool, the artificial (and perhaps arbitrary) lane markers allow you to focus on making each page element part fit into the whole page design. Grids allow you to be a little bit lazy and give you a grid to snap your page elements together. By using a grid, you also allow a whole community of designers and developers to help you with cross-browser compatibility. By using their CSS rules, you can, with a pretty comfortable degree of certainty, know that your design is going to *just work* if you have used a grid and corresponding CSS grid framework. But perhaps most importantly, working with grid systems makes building Drupal themes really easy.

By their very nature grids are rigid. But that doesn't mean all grids are built the same way. The grid system described here is the 960 Grid System. You can download the related resources from `http://960.gs/` for both a fixed-width design and a fluid design. The technical part of how to use a grid system is discussed later in this chapter. In this section, you will learn how to take advantage of your newfound structure.

Figure 8.7 shows the three shapes you need to be aware of in a grid: columns, gutters, and margins. Columns can exist only if there is space between them to show you the boundaries where one column ends and the next column starts. The space

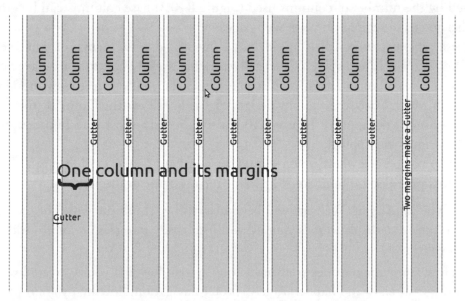

FIGURE 8.7 A grid is comprised of three shapes: columns, gutters, and margins.

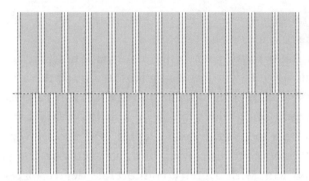

FIGURE 8.8 Choosing between a 12- (top) or 16-column (bottom) grid does not affect the total width of the page.

between each of the columns is referred to as the *gutter*. Around the entire design is an additional, calculated space that separates the edge of the content from the edge of the container (browser window). This outer space, referred to as the *margin*, is half the width of the gutter in the 960 Grid System. This is because the margin exists both on the left and right sides of the column. When two margins butt against one another, they create a doubly wide space—the gutter.

The first step in using the 960 Grid System is to choose whether you want your page divided into 12 columns or 16 columns. The total width of the page will not be affected by the number of columns used (Figure 8.8). These columns can be grouped together to create regions on your Web page.

These regions can be filled by sidebars, content, advertisements, or whatever else your Web site needs to display. I almost always start with 12 columns if I have no constraints. It gives a bolder layout with stronger lines for your eye to follow. It's also less space with which I can screw up my design. Figure 8.9 shows the Domicile theme with the 12-column grid applied. Figure 8.10 and Figure 8.11 show a second design with the 12-column grid applied.

To help you decide whether you should start with a 12- or 16-column grid, look for constraints provided by your site. The following are some examples.

- If you know your Web site will have advertising, check the width of the ads you need to display. Does your ad width fit easily into the 12- or 16-grid layout?
- How many menus does your navigation system have? If you've created wireframes already and happen to have footer navigation, how many columns did you need to display each of the relevant menus?

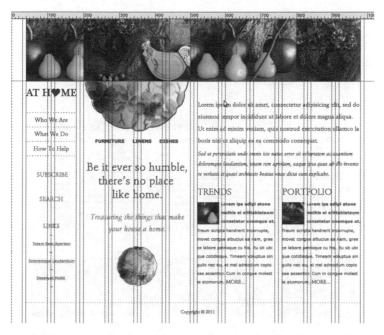

FIGURE 8.9 Domicile theme with the dotted lines representing the 12 columns and gutters from the 960 Grid System

FIGURE 8.10 Home page of the HICK Tech Web site

FIGURE 8.11 Home page of the HICK Tech Web site with the 960 Grid System 12-column grid applied

- Do you have a specific number of products you want to highlight on your home page? Does this number divide evenly into either 12 or 16?

- Will your site feature large content areas for photographs, maps, videos, or some other rich media asset? When you shave off the rest of the space for navigation, are you left with an appropriate number of columns?

This is not an exhaustive list of constraints. Your site may have some other constraint that makes the decision obvious. If there is no obvious choice, start with 12 columns. You can always change your mind later.

Your wireframe may show you that you need a two-column Web site; however, what it won't show you is how wide the two columns should be. Should the left column be 200 pixels wide? How do you even know? This is where the refinement step comes in. Use your constraints listed previously to set your column widths. If you don't have any constraints, look at the content you want to put into the sidebar to see whether it has a "shape." For example, if you have only short menu titles, you can make your navigation column narrower than if you have really long menu titles.

The most comprehensive list of grid-based tutorials and Web sites I've ever seen is available from www.noupe.com/design/ultimate-guide-to-grid-based-web-design.html. If this page disappears, look for it in Archive.org's Way Back Machine.

Go ahead now and refine your rough wireframes into a grid-based layout. It will make building your Drupal site a lot easier if you do this work now. Once you have all your page elements into your grid, you should be able to see where there is room for visual embellishments. If your grid is too full, you may need to shuffle your template so that you have room to make your pages beautiful instead of just jammed with content.

Embellishments

When I wrote that heading, every single graphic designer drew in a sharp breath—offended that I called their visual design an "embellishment." Visual design is a *lot* more than a toss-away flourish. In addition to setting the tone of a Web site, visual design helps site visitors answer the question, "What should I do next?" It is well beyond the scope of this book to teach you to be an exceptional designer; however, I will be able to give the nondesigners a few tricks on how to add tasteful embellishments that enhance their Web site design.

Type and Fonts

A well-designed grid will start with a typeface and use measurements that are derived from it. It is more typical in Web design, however, to pick a grid and then plunk a font into the design somewhere down the line. Don't feel too bad if this sounds like you. But do make sure you know at least a little bit about typography.

Think back to the days of movable type and letter presses. Each letter and every space was set by hand to form a page of words. When selecting which letter to place, the printer would choose letters from a single font with shared characteristics between letters (for example, a 12-point boldface Times New Roman font). Whenever the printer wanted to change the characteristics of the type they were using, they would look within that typeface to a different font (for example, a 12-point italic font).

In the digital world, a font is a subset of a typeface that has only one characteristic. Typefaces that contain multiple options (for example, Arial and Times New Roman, which both offer regular and bold options) are actually a collection of many different fonts. Decorative *fonts* are typically comprised of only one style and one weight and are scaled digitally, making them a true font as opposed to a font within a typeface.

**This is a serif font.
The Ts have feet.**

This is a sans serif
font. The Ts do not
have feet.

*THIS IS A
DECORATIVE FONT.
IT'S JUST WILD
AND CRAZY.*

FIGURE 8.12 Sample serif, sans serif, and decorative fonts

Within the world of typefaces there are generally three different styles available to you (Figure 8.12).

- Serif fonts that have little feet and little handles on the tips of the letters (Times New Roman or Georgia)
- Sans serif fonts that do not have little feet (Arial and Helvetica)
- Decorative fonts that are . . . whatever they want to be

Sans serif fonts are usually easier to read on the screen, but in print serif fonts are usually easier to read. This is, in part, because computer screens don't project as clear of an image and the extra decorations on the serif fonts are less clear for us to read. (Yes, your Kindle probably has a serif font set as its default, because the image quality is superb.) Web designers will often pair sans serif body type with a serif heading. This distinction allows the reader to easily scan a page because they can use shape, size, and possibly color to distinguish between the main text and headings.

You don't have to choose special fonts for your Web site. This is especially true when you are working with a CSS framework because the framework designer has already selected and assigned fonts that are appropriate for most Web sites.

If you do want to use decorative fonts for your headings, you will need to use some custom code to make it work. Several options are available. Check which fonts these alternatives offer so that your design files are using a font that's really available for online use.

- The CSS3 property `@font-face` is getting better browser support and is now supported by the latest browsers. I quite like the service Kernest. It allows you to embed open source fonts into your Web site for free. This resource is available at www.kernest.com. The Google Font API is also popular. There is a Drupal module available (http://drupal.org/project/google_fonts), and the fonts can be viewed online at www.google.com/webfonts.

- Make pictures of words. This method isn't accessible to screen readers and search engines, but it does give visually predictable results. To avoid having to make every single heading for your Web site, use one of the Drupal-contributed modules that does this conversion of text to image on the fly. Several modules are available for Drupal 6. Ideally by the time this book gets into your hands, Textimage (http://drupal.org/project/textimage) and Signwriter (http://drupal.org/project/signwriter) will both have stable Drupal 7 modules available.

- Use JavaScript to perform dynamic text transformations to your desired font. The online service Typekit (www.typekit.com) has opened up a whole new fonty world for designers. For a small fee you can make your Web site appear using exactly the font you want. Pair it up with the Drupal module (http://drupal.org/project/typekit) for no-code fonts. There is a small fee for Typekit (the Drupal module is a free helper). If you need a completely free option, you may want to consider the contributed Drupal module Cufon. I personally found this module added a lot of JavaScript to the page in ways that annoyed me. Check it and see what you think, though: http://drupal.org/project/cufon.

Be careful with these powerful tools. Web sites shouldn't look like ransom notes (unless you want them to). Try to limit the number of typefaces that appear on your page to no more than two of three. Does your company have a style guide for its print material? Now would be the perfect opportunity to match it up with what you're doing online, limiting your own design work to the number of fonts (typeface variations) that are allowed in the print style guide.

Color

It would be a bit silly to include a lesson on color in this black-and-white book. But you probably already know that bright colors make for "happy" Web sites and dark colors are "moody." I probably don't need to tell you to keep your palate relatively simple, choosing no more than a few main colors and a few accents. If you do want more color theory, a quick search in your favorite search engine will get you started.

There are a lot of great online resources to help you choose appropriate colors for your Web site. My favorites include the following Web sites.

- Colr.org allows you to choose a palate from a photograph (`www.colr.org`).
- Color Scheme Designer helps you pick palates (`http://colorschemedesigner .com`).
- Colour Lovers is a community of people who love color. Go figure (`www. colourlovers.com`).

To be accessible to the largest possible audience, choose colors that stand out from the background color. In other words, pair up light and dark colors. Several online services can help you (for free) ensure your site is visible for folks who are color-blind. These include the Colorblind Web Page Filter (`http://colorfilter.wickline .org/`) and Vischeck (`www.vischeck.com/vischeck/vischeckURL.php`).

Imagery

Whether your site is using the cute Twitter bird (or the fail whale) or stunning photography, you will need to consider images in the context of the whole palette (unless you're using a minimalist look that uses no images at all). Some people choose their images first and then pick colors to complement their imagery; others start with a corporate branding guide with exactly the shade of red and go looking for images to match. No matter what order you use to choose your design elements, you will need to take the time to ensure everything fits together.

If you are using your own illustrations, fabulous! There's little else I need to tell you at this point; however, if you're using photographs, you will need to make sure you have consent from the person you are photographing (or the location you are photographing if you are on private property) before incorporating the image into your design. A simple model photo release is available from `www.diyplanner.com/templates/ official/misc/photorelease`. If you are working with a professional photographer, ask for a copy of the signed model release forms for your records. It is especially important if you are photographing kids to get their legal guardian to sign the model release. It's really hard to delete things from the Internet (look for the Google Cache option or visit Archive.org and plunk in your favorite Web site's URL).

With those warnings in place, the following are some great online resources for design elements.

- Compfight searches Flickr for images that have been licensed for use under the Creative Commons license (`www.compfight.com`). If the site is down, check back later. They've been known to have brief outages.
- Lullacons are GPL icons created by Lullabot that you can use on your own Web site (`www.lullabot.com/articles/free_gpl_icons_lullacons_pack_1`).
- Open Clip Art has illustrations that are available under a CC-0 (public domain) license (`www.openclipart.org/`).
- From Old Books has a good collection of wood engravings and wood cuts scanned from old books (`www.fromoldbooks.org`).

A search for *public domain* or *royalty-free* images will also turn up even more free resources than this short list.

I also use iStockPhotography if I'm looking for images of people and don't want the hassle of tracking down model release forms. The images do cost a bit of money, but the fee of a few dollars per image for a Web-quality photo is typically a lot cheaper than doing paperwork to track down people and get them to sign a release form.

Applying Embellishments to a Wireframe

You will only look as professional online as your graphic design abilities. If you're unsure and your budget allows it, hire a Web design professional to create your Drupal theme. If you can't afford that, hire a graphic designer to create a banner. And if you absolutely must, jump right in and make your own design. By sticking with a relatively simple layout and only a few embellishments, you'll have no problem creating a pleasing Web site.

There are a lot of good step-by-step tutorials online to help you create a Web site layout in a graphic design program. Start with `http://designreviver.com/tutorials/35-premium-photoshop-layout-tutorials-for-web/`, and once you've worked through those, do a search for *photoshop web design tutorials* to get even more. Most of the free tutorials you find online will be generic enough that you can use whatever software you'd like to use. I personally use Gimp instead of Photoshop for all of my Web layout work. Call me economical or cheap, but I'd rather spend my money on fonts and chocolate than a graphic design program. Your mileage may vary.

Design Resources for the Graphically Challenged

If you are a developer who is intimidated by graphic design, you will find that a lot of excellent templates are readily available that can be easily adapted to suit your needs. For their part, experienced designers who are new to Drupal can use these templates to get a sense of what is possible beyond the basic themes that Drupal provides by default. Drupal.org lists a number of themes that can be downloaded and customized (`http://drupal.org/project/Themes`) to suit your project's needs. To see each of these themes on a real Web site, visit the Theme Garden (`www.themegarden.org/drupal6/`). Of course, the Web and its design inspirations are much larger resources than the limited set of information found on the main Drupal Web site.

> **⚠ Copyright**
> The designs listed in this section are not necessarily free to modify and use. Many of the templates are licensed under the Creative Commons or the General Public License (GPL) and can be used if appropriate credit is given to the original designer. Please be sure to respect the terms of the individually licensed designs.

CSS Zen Garden (`www.csszengarden.com`) is an excellent design resource. The content of each page is identical, but the page has been restyled by applying a unique Cascading Style Sheet (CSS) prepared by an expert designer. Figure 8.13 shows a summary of all designs available in this unique theme browser. CSS Zen Garden shows you exactly how easy it ought to be to apply a new theme to your Drupal site. You will be able to achieve a nearly instantaneous visual overhaul of this Web site by changing only the style sheet that is applied to the underlying HTML. If the CSS Zen Garden can perform such a dramatic transformation with only a style sheet, imagine what you will be able to do by combining this capability with Drupal's powerful theme system.

If you need more ideas, even more template sites are available on the Internet. Scan through these resources for inspiration, or use the templates as a starting point for developing your own Drupal theme. The Open Web Design (`www.openwebdesign.org`) and Open Source Web Design (`www.oswd.org`) sites provide a wide range of sample layouts. From these sites, you can download a package containing HTML, CSS, and image files. These files must then be converted into a Drupal theme; instructions on how to build a Drupal theme are included in Chapter 15. The Open Source Web Design (OSWD) site also has an excellent "See Designs in Use" section where you can see how the OSWD templates have been modified and implemented on real Web sites (`www.oswd.org/links`).

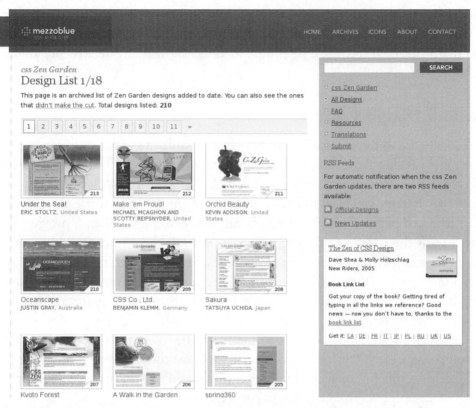

FIGURE 8.13 Each theme in the CSS Zen Garden uses the same underlying HTML markup. The visual design is overhauled by changing only the style sheet.

Photos

By changing only the photo used in a design, you can change the whole feel of a Web site. If you decide to include photos of people as part of your site, make sure you have their permission. High-quality photos with the appropriate model releases can be purchased for very little money from stock photography Web sites. If you are using your own photos of people, be sure your models sign a release form. A sample form is available from www.istockphoto.com/docs/languages/english/modelrelease.pdf.

When developing your page design and layout, you can choose to start with a premade Drupal theme, or you can have a template from your existing Web site that you are migrating to Drupal. If you are new to Drupal, the easiest approach is to start with a Drupal theme and customize it as needed. You can also choose to convert an existing

Web site template into a Drupal theme. Alternatively, you may want to create a theme from scratch. You will find useful information throughout this book on creating and customizing Drupal themes. The fundamentals of how to create a theme are covered in Chapter 15.

Test Your Design Structure

Just like we tested the information architecture of your site with a card sorting activity in the previous chapter, it's a good idea to test your design as well. Usability experts will typically use a technique called *paper prototyping* to test their designs.

For this activity you need to have a printout (a wireframe is sufficient to test menu labels) for each page of your Web site. With your printouts in hand, provide the participant with the wireframe for the first page and ask them to complete a task that is relevant to your personae. Each time they "click" a menu label, provide them with the corresponding page. Repeat these steps until the participant has successfully completed the task you gave them. Having a separate person record actions (or a video camera) will make the exercise faster; however, it is not necessary.

A sample task for a bookshop Web site might be "What are the shipping rates for this company?" Ideally the participants pick the most direct route though your navigation system to this information, but if they don't, you may have saved yourself a lot of money by catching a mistake at the paper stage.

If you want to know more about testing your designs, read *It's Not Rocket Surgery* by Steve Krug.

Summary

Planning your design and being able to name every page element is a *key skill* needed to make Drupal look like your imagination. Too many people skip this critical planning stage and jump right into site building and then get frustrated when Drupal looks like Drupal instead of their imagination. Ideally, you'll remember to come back to this chapter each time you build a Drupal site and every site you build will look exactly right because you did your planning homework.

If you've done each of the activities suggested in this chapter, you will have the following.

- Created and then refined wireframes to use a grid-based template
- Inserted all page elements into your new design templates

- Embellished your wireframes into design templates with stylish fonts, colors, and imagery

This chapter was just the beginning of your journey to designing great-looking Drupal sites. In Chapter 15 you will learn how to convert a design file into a completed Drupal theme.

Part III

Case Studies

Chapter 9

Community Site

For this site recipe you will learn how to build a micro Web site with basic pages and images. The site features the capabilities of Drupal's core modules. You will learn how to create content, create a navigation system for your Web site, and configure relevant site settings. You will also become familiar with Drupal's administrative interface.

You will learn the following key concepts as you build each feature.

- Categorizing your articles with the taxonomy system
- Creating sidebar content with blocks and placing that content into regions
- Creating menus that link to nodes and other pages within your site
- Adjusting permissions to allow site visitors to use specific parts of your Web site

Site Profile

For this site we will be rebuilding the Bruce-Grey-Owen Sound Greens Web site. This is a political party aiming to elect both a provincial and federal member of parliament. This site is a real site, although you'll notice our sample has some "fake"

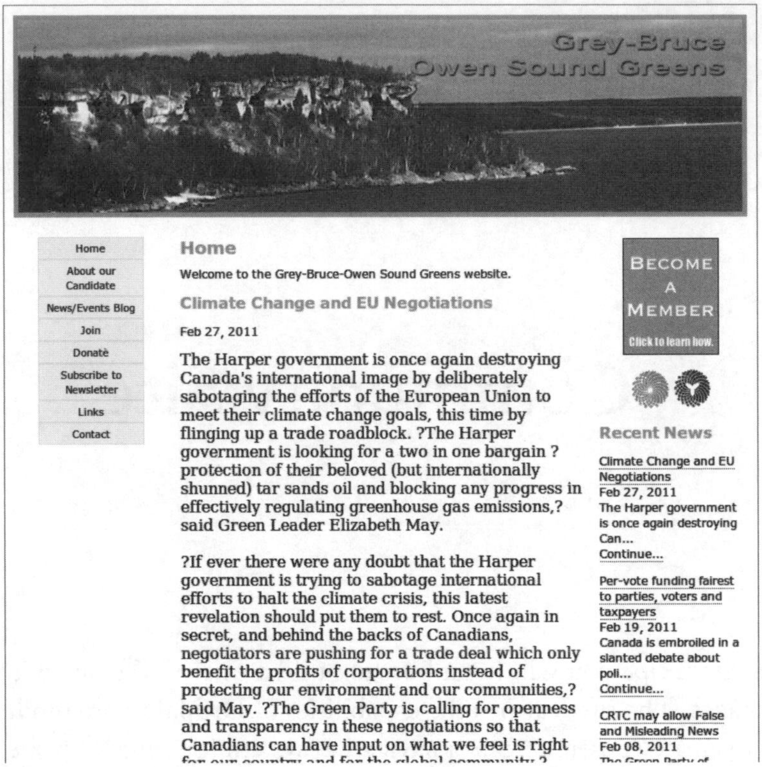

FIGURE 9.1 The Bruce-Grey-Owen Sound site before its makeover

content. The old site (Figure 9.1) uses four different technologies (including Web pages that are coded by hand, phpList to send announcements to list members, Blogger, and phpBB for internal communications).

Our revised site integrates each of the features used by the group into a single point of access. The only bit that remains external to Drupal is the announcement mailing list. Currently the group uses phpList (`www.phplist.com/`). This is a great free software application you can install directly onto your server. There's also a Drupal module that allows you to publish newsletters from your Drupal site (`http://drupal.org/project/phplist`). If you're just getting started with a community site, you have fewer than 1,000 members, and you're not very tech-savvy, I recommend using MailChimp instead (`http://mailchimp.com`). This system allows you to automatically send out e-mail newsletters every time you post a new blog entry.

The functionality that we'll be building in this site includes the following.

- RSS aggregation to pull content into the site from off-site sources
- User blogs that all executives will have permission to post to
- Members-only forum
- Hierarchical content for the site's content
- Polls

Specific theming features that we'll be adding to the site include the following.

- On-the-spot, point-and-click styling (no text editor required)
- Custom fonts
- Multiple nodes promoted to the front page

With the theme applied, the home page of the site will look like Figure 9.2.

For this site recipe, you will learn how to enhance Drupal's core modules. The basic functionality is provided by Drupal core, but to avoid a bunch of custom PHP

FIGURE 9.2 The revised home page of the Bruce-Grey-Owen Sound Web site

TABLE 9.1 Modules Used to Build the Community Web Site

Functionality	Module
Recent news. Currently uses Blogger.	Blog (available in Drupal core)
RSS aggregator to pull content automatically from the federal and provincial party Web sites.	Aggregator (core)
Private, community discussion forum (current phpBB).	Forum (core), node privacy by role (contributed)
Basic pages that can be structured according to jurisdiction (in other words, wind turbines are a power generation issue and therefore provincial; waste from the nuclear power plant, however, is a federal issue).	Book (core)
New functionality: polls.	Poll (core)
Contact form.	Contact (core)
Newsletter. Currently provided by phpList.	Hard-coding the sign-up form (full HTML into a block)

programming, we'll install some contributed modules. Through experience you will learn which modules suit your needs and how to search for modules to fill in the missing elements. We'll use the modules listed in Table 9.1 to build this site.

Currently, user logins are created by hand. In the new version, the Drupal default will be used: Anyone can create an account, but administrator approval will be required to activate the account. The link to the account creation page (`http://example.com/user/register`) is hidden on the new site; however, it could easily be linked to from the join-up information page.

The functionality of this site exists in silos. There is little to no connection between the forum and the blog, the join-up page, and the issue/about pages. Navigation will be restricted to the Main menu across the top and book menus down the side. Breadcrumb navigation will be added to the forum only.

The build for this site is a "simple" matter of installing and configuring each of the modules listed in Table 9.1. (Don't worry, there are instructions!)

Basic Configuration

The first step in building a Drupal site is to . . . install Drupal. Instructions are covered in Chapter 2. Once Drupal is installed, adjust the site information as follows.

1. Navigate to Administration > Configuration > Site information.
2. Set the Name, Slogan, and Email settings appropriate for your site.

3. Set the default front page to the path for the node you'd like to use for a welcome message. Custom paths are covered in the section called "Customizing URLs."

4. Set the Default 403 (access denied) page URL to "user." This will give members trying to access the forum a way to easily log into the site.

5. Scroll to the bottom and click "Save configuration."

Create Roles

Not everyone visiting your site should be able to do everything. This is a good thing—you don't want unauthenticated folks adding content to your site. Drupal has a very granular permission system that allows you to apply specific permissions to groups of people easily. Most community groups Web sites have three types of people visiting: members, nonmembers, and special executive members. Any visitor who does not log into the site will be treated by Drupal as an unauthenticated site visitor. This role is appropriate for nonmembers. We will, however, need to create two additional roles for Members and Executives.

To add your new roles, complete the following steps.

1. Navigate to Administration > People, go to the Permissions tab on the top right), and then go to the Roles tab on the top right.

2. Next to the button "Add role," type your new role name (such as Executive).

3. Click the button "Add role."

Repeat steps 1 to 3 for each role you want to add to the site.

Now when you create new account, you will be able to assign any of the existing (Administrator) or new (Executive, Members) roles to each account.

Enable Core Modules

Most of the modules used to extend Drupal's out-of-the-box functionality in this site are core modules. We'll enable them first.

1. Using the administrative toolbar, click the button Modules.

2. Locate each of the modules listed here and ensure its corresponding check box is enabled.

   • Aggregator

   • Blog

   • Book

- Contact
- Forum
- Poll
- Tracker
- Update manager

3. Scroll to the bottom of the page and click Save.

These modules are now enabled. We will configure them after we've downloaded and enabled the contributed modules as well.

Download and Enable Contributed Modules

Install the latest Drupal 7 version of each of the following contributed modules. In order of preference, look first for a module that's Recommended (green). If there isn't a Recommended release available, look for Other releases (yellow) and finally Development releases (pink). As of Drupal 7, there are multiple ways to install a contributed module. For now, we're going to use Drupal's administrative interface to quickly install the modules listed in Table 9.2.

TABLE 9.2 Contributed Modules to Download and Install

Functionality	Module Name	URL
Point-and-click design changes	CTools. Required by Sweaver; install first.	http://drupal.org/project/ctools
Point-and-click design changes	Sweaver.	http://drupal.org/project/sweaver
Private member forum	Access control list (ACL). Required by Forum Access; install first.	http://drupal.org/project/acl
Private member forum	Chain Menu Access API. Required by Forum Access; install first.	http://drupal.org/project/chain_menu_access
Private member forum	Forum Access.	http://drupal.org/project/forum_access
Place content into non-content regions	Nodes in Block.	http://drupal.org/project/nodesinblock
Generate "fake" content for your Web site; optional module	Devel.	http://drupal.org/project/devel

If your Web site is available from a public Web server, you can use the following steps to install contributed modules (this will work for most people).

1. Locate the latest version of the module you want to install. Make sure the version you have selected matches your version of Drupal. For example, you cannot use Drupal 6 modules with Drupal 7.

2. Copy the download link for the module you want to install. On a Windows computer, right-click the download link and select "Copy link location." On a Mac, Ctrl-click the download link and select "Copy link location." The text may differ slightly for your browser.

3. In your Drupal installation, use the administrative toolbar to navigate to the Modules page.

4. Click the link "Install new module." If the link is not available, make sure you have the module Update manager installed and enabled.

5. Paste the link you copied in step 2 into the URL field. Scroll to the bottom of the screen and click Install.

6. Enter your authentication information for the Web server. This is the same user name and password that you would use if you were connecting to your Web server with an FTP account, not your Drupal user name and password. Contact your hosting provider if you are unsure of this information.

7. Assuming there were no errors during this process, you should now be able to enable your module. Using the toolbar, navigate to Modules. Scroll through the list and find the module you just installed. Enable the check box beside the module name, scroll to the bottom of the screen, and click "Save configuration."

Your module should now be available for configuration. Repeat these steps for each module you want to install. If this method does not work with your server, refer to the instructions in Chapter 11.

Configure Modules

We will now build the site. At this point, you will be working exclusively from the administrative area. Once you've built up the site and entered some content, you will create the theme for the site and finally place content into the theme's regions using the administrative user interface.

Aggregator

This core module allows you to pull in content from public RSS feeds. Content is available as a page showing the title, publication date, and as much text as is available in the RSS feed or as a block with titles linking to the original source of the news. If your community group has a hard time keeping fresh news on the home page, pulling in content from off-site sources with the Aggregator module is a great way to cheat. You can combine several sources of news into one category or display a per-feed block.

1. Navigate to Administration > Configuration > Feed aggregator.
2. Click the link "Add category."
3. Enter a title and click Save. (Add as many categories as you'd like at this point.)
4. Click the tab List.
5. Click the link "Add feed."
6. Enter a title and the RSS feed's URL. Select the appropriate categories from the list at the bottom of the screen.
7. Click Save.
8. You must now tell Drupal to go and fetch the news stories from the Web. On the tab List, next to each feed, click the link "Update items."
9. By default, only administrators can read the news. Navigate to Administration > People > Permissions. Under the Aggregator module, enable the option "View news feeds" for all roles listed. Leave the option "Administer news feeds" set to "Administrators only."
10. Scroll to the bottom of the permissions configuration screen and click Save.

The content is now available and ready to be placed on your site. In our site, we'll be placing blocks on the front page after the theme is built. For now you are finished with the configuration of the Aggregator module.

Blog

Blog entries are much like the core content type, Articles; however, additional functionality is built into the module to permit you to read blog entries by any given content author. There is also a block created with "Recent blog posts." However, blog entries have only a title and body. They do not permit image uploads. If you'd like to add images to your blog entries, you can add the extra field by completing the following steps.

1. Navigate to Administration > Structure > Content types.
2. Next to the content type "Blog entry," click the link "Manage fields."
3. Under the label "Add new field," enter the label Image, and select Image as the field to share.
4. Scroll to the bottom of the screen and click Save.
5. It is appropriate to leave the default settings. Continue to the bottom of the screen and click "Save settings."

You will now be able to upload an image along with your blog entries, as if they were articles.

Book

Book pages are used to create static pages that have hierarchical content. The Book module automatically creates a new navigation block for each new book created. According to the Drupal help pages, this content type is well suited to "creating structured, multi-page content, such as site resource guides, manuals, and wikis. It allows you to create content that has chapters, sections, subsections, or any similarly-tiered structure." By default new entries made from this content type

- Are published but not promoted to the front page
- Accept user-contributed comments
- Are not version controlled

On public Web sites, such as the one we're creating, I like to turn off comments and turn on revision control. To make these adjustments, complete the following steps.

1. Navigate to Administration > Structure > Content types.
2. Next to the content type Book page, click the link "edit."
3. Click the tab "Publishing options." Enable the option "Create new revision."
4. Click the tab Comment setting. Change the Default comment setting for new content from "open" to "closed."
5. Scroll to the bottom of the screen and click "Save content type."

The settings for this content type have been adjusted. Next you will need to adjust the permissions for this content type.

1. Navigate to Administration > People > Permissions.
2. Scroll to the Book module. It is appropriate for content authors (these are probably only people with the role of Administrator or Executive) to have the following permissions: "Administer book outlines," "Create new books," and "Add content and child pages to books." It is appropriate for all rolls to have the permission "View printer-friendly books."
3. Scroll to the Node module, and locate options starting with Book page. It is appropriate for all content authors to have all permissions. It is not appropriate for anonymous users to have any of these permissions.
4. Scroll to the bottom of the screen and click "save permissions."

You are now ready to start adding hierarchical content to your Web site with auto-generated navigation. Are you as excited as me? I bet you are!

1. Let's start by creating a container that will hold your book pages. From the shortcut menu, click the link "Add content."
2. Click the link "Book page."
3. Enter a title and the body for your new page.
4. Scroll to the tabs at the bottom of the screen and click the tab labeled "Book outline." Change the Book setting from <none> to <create a new book>.
5. Scroll to the bottom of the screen and click Save.

You've just made your first book and its first page. To add more pages to this book click, the link "Add child page." You should be aware of several administrative options for books.

- Any content type can be added to a book. Configure which content types you would like to place into books at Administration > Content > Books > Settings.
- Once pages have been placed into a book, they can be easily reordered at Administration > Content > Books > List > edit order and titles.
- To add any single page to a book, navigate to that page and click the tab Outline. Then select the book you would like to add the page to and click "Add to book outline."
- Each book page can belong to only one book at a time.

Customizing URLs

For every page you create, you can also customize the URL. By default basic pages and articles will get a URL that starts with "node" such as `http://example.com/node/12`. This isn't very search engine friendly compared to `http://example.com/my-queen-bee-is-named-gloria`. To adjust the URL for each basic page, navigate to the page and then complete the following steps.

1. Click the tab Edit.
2. Scroll to the bottom of the editing screen and click the tab "URL path settings."
3. In the "URL alias" field, enter the URL you would like to use for this piece of content. Enter only the bit that comes after the domain name.
4. Scroll to the bottom of the screen and click Save.

Your new URL should now be activated. Note: You can also complete these steps as you are creating new nodes.

There are a few quick tips that you can implement now to improve your search engine ranking by adjusting only the URLs for each of your pages.

- Use only lowercase, such as About => `about`.
- Replace spaces with dashes, such as New Camel Yarn => `new-camel-yarn`.
- Use keywords, not all words, such as A Story About Ping The Duck => `story-ping-duck`.
- Use slashes to indicate structure, such as Bread Recipes => `recipes/bread`. (This doesn't automatically create a page at `recipes` too.)

Creating URL aliases automatically is covered in Chapter 10 profile, and search engine–friendly optimization is covered in more depth in Chapter 16.

Contact Form

The contact form is disabled by default in your new Drupal site. To start using the contact form, you will need to enable the appropriate module and set the permissions to allow people to use the contact form. First, enable the Contact module using the following steps.

1. From the administrative dashboard, navigate to Modules.
2. Scroll down to Contact and check the box.
3. Scroll to the bottom of the screen and click "Save configuration."

You can now set up the contact form. From the modules page you can click the link Configure, or you can use the administrative dashboard and navigate to Structure > Contact form. By default one category has been added to your contact form. You will need to add the recipients' e-mail addresses for this form. Click the "edit" link for the "Website feedback" category. Then configure the following settings.

- **Category.** This is displayed only if you have more than one category.
- **Recipients.** You can add one or many e-mail addresses. These can be any address you like, such as Hotmail or Gmail e-mail addresses, or even the e-mail address for a discussion mailing list.
- **Auto-reply.** Enter the text you want to send to everyone who completes this form.
- **Weight.** If you have many categories on your Web form, you can choose the order in which they appear in the drop-down menu. By default all categories are given the same ranking and are sorted alphabetically.
- **Selected.** If you have more than one category, you can choose the default with this toggle.

Your contact form is now configured. You can add as many categories as you need, such as Website feedback, Sales, and Customer support.

You must now allow people to use the contact form by adjusting the permissions for this module.

1. From the administrative dashboard, navigate to People.
2. Click the tab Permissions.
3. Scroll to the module Contact.
4. Next to the permission "Use the site-wide contact form," enable the checkboxes for "Anonymous user" and "Authenticated user."
5. Scroll to the bottom of the screen and click "Save permissions."

Now you must create a link to your contact form so that people know where to find it.

1. Using the administrative dashboard, navigate to Structure > Menus.
2. Next to the Main menu, click the link "add link."
3. Enter the following required settings.
   - **Menu link title.** Contact
   - **Path.** contact (note, this is lowercase)
4. Scroll to the bottom of the configuration screen and click Save.

5. A summary of all links in the Main menu is now visible. Adjust the order of these links by dragging and dropping them into the correct order. If you do make changes, remember to scroll to the bottom and click "Save configuration" to lock in your changes.

Finally, if you would like to add your mailing address, your phone number, or a message to the contact form, you can do so with a custom block.

1. Using the administrative dashboard, navigate to Structure > Blocks.
2. Click the link "Add block."
3. Enter a block description (used in the administrative section only) and the text you want to appear on the Contact page (this goes into the Block body).
4. Scroll to the fieldset for the region settings. For your theme, set the appropriate region name. Depending on your theme, this could be something like "Content" or "Above content."
5. Scroll to the Visibility settings. Select the tab Pages. Enable the option "Only the listed pages." In the large text area below the option you just enabled, type **contact** (no quotes, all lowercase).
6. Scroll to the bottom and click "Save block."

Your new message should now appear on the contact form. Navigate to this page to check your work.

Search

Drupal ships with a built-in search engine. It's not as sophisticated as Google, but it's not too bad. It is enabled by default, but only administrative users are allowed to use it. If you would like site visitors to use it, you must adjust the permissions. We'll use the same technique to make the search form public as we did to make the contact form usable by all visitors.

1. Use the administrative dashboard to navigate to People > Permissions.
2. Scroll down to the Search module.
3. Next to the permission "Use search," enable the check boxes for "anonymous" and "authenticated users."
4. Scroll to the bottom and click "Save permissions."

Visitors to your site will now be able to search content.

To see what site visitors are searching for, use the administrative dashboard to navigate to Reports > Top search phrases.

To configure the Search module, navigate to Configuration > Search settings. From here you can adjust the following.

- The size of the words that get indexed. By default words must be at least three characters long.
- Content ranking factors. For example, you can set content with a lot of comments to be automatically "better" than pages that have fewer comments.

In general, the default settings are appropriate for most small-business and personal Web sites; however, if your site is a little unique, you may want to play with these settings to suit your needs.

Forum

A forum topic starts a discussion thread within a forum. People can then discuss this topic by adding their comments to it. Figure 9.3 shows the structure of structure forums. Containers and forums are both taxonomy terms, topics are nodes, and comments are, surprisingly, comments.

By default new forum topics are as follows.

- Published but not promoted to the front page
- Enabled for comments
- Not version controlled. Each time a forum topic is saved, it replaces the previous contents. There is no "undo," and you cannot revert to a previously saved version of the forum topic.

Fields for this content type include only the Title and Body settings. You can extend this content type to include other fields as described in the "Blog" section.

You can enter default topics for discussion by completing the following steps.

1. Navigate to Administration > Structure > Forums.
2. By default there is only one discussion forum, "General discussion." To add a new forum, click the link "Add forum."
3. Enter a forum name and description to let people know what topics you'd like discussed under this heading. Scroll to the bottom and click Save.

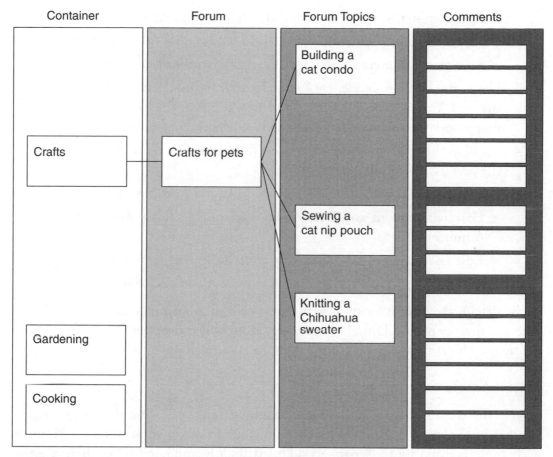

| Container | Forum | Forum Topics | Comments |

Crafts — Crafts for pets

Building a cat condo

Sewing a cat nip pouch

Knitting a Chihuahua sweater

Gardening

Cooking

FIGURE 9.3 Hierarchy of Forums: Containers, forums, forum topics, and comments

Repeat these steps for each of the new topics you'd like to add. (Hint: Start with fewer forums rather than more forums.) You can nest forums inside one another by changing the parent element while adding a new forum.

The next step is to adjust the permissions of the Forum module and the Forum content type.

1. Navigate to Administration > People > Permissions.
2. Under the Comment module, adjust the permissions as follows.
   - **Administer comments and comment settings.** Administrators only
   - **View comments.** All roles

- **Post comments.** Members, Executive, and Administrators
- **Skip comment approval.** Members, Executive, and Administrators
- **Edit own comments.** Members, Executive, and Administrators

3. Under the Forum module, ensure the forum can be administered by Administrators. You can also allow Executive to administer the forum. It would be inappropriate to enable this permission for Members or Anonymous Users.

4. Scroll to the Node module and then to the section for "Forum topic." Adjust the permissions as follows.

   - **Create new content.** Members, Executive, and Administrators
   - **Edit own content and Delete own content.** Members, Executive, and Administrators
   - **Edit any content and Delete any content.** Executive and Administrators

5. Scroll to the bottom of the configuration screen and click Save.

By default the Drupal forum is available to be read by anyone visiting the Web site. The site that we're rebuilding has a private forum where members can discuss issues before they hit the public pages of the Web site. Let's lock down access now.

Forum Access

Enable the contributed modules `chain_menu_access`, `acl`, and `forum_access` if you have not already done so. With these modules in place, you can now administer each container and forum separately. (This is slightly annoying if you have a lot of forums or containers; did you heed my warning to limit the number of forums?)

> **Rebuild Permissions**
> You may need to rebuild the permissions if you already have content. You will know if you need to do this if this warning appears: "The content access permissions need to be rebuilt." If you see this error, click the link "Rebuild permissions" in the error message and follow the on-screen instructions.

1. Navigate to Administration > Structure > Forums.
2. Next to the forum/container that you'd like to make private, click the link "Edit forum."
3. You will be presented with the configuration screen displayed in Figure 9.4.

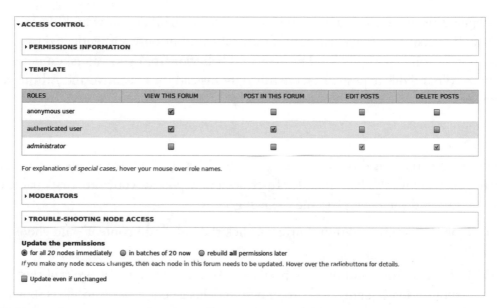

FIGURE 9.4 The Access Control settings will appear in a new fieldset for each content type.

4. Configure the access control for this content type according to your preferences. The configuration options are as follows:
   - The fieldsets "Permission information" and "Trouble-shooting Node Access" are both help files. Read them if you need.
   - The fieldset "Template" allows you to apply the access defaults from another forum/container to this one.
   - The fieldset "Moderators" allows you to create superusers that have all permissions regardless of settings. The moderates are set by name, not by role.

   To participate in a private forum, the permissions must be assigned to roles as follows.
   - View this forum
   - Post in this forum

   Trusted roles may also be allowed to do the following.
   - Edit posts
   - Delete posts
5. With the appropriate boxes selected, scroll to the bottom of the screen and click Save.

Repeat this process for each of the containers/forums that you would like to set to private. By default everyone can read forum content, but only authenticated users can post to it. If you expect any kind of malicious behavior from your users, do not allow them to edit and delete posts. Reserve this right instead for Executive and Administrators users.

Poll

If you've ever found it difficult to get a straight "yes" or "no" from your site visitors, you're going to love the Poll module. To create a new poll on your site, first enable the Poll module and then complete the following steps.

1. From the administration shortcuts, click the link "Add content" and choose Poll.

2. Enter a question and possible responses. You may change the order of the responses by dragging and dropping the fields into a new position, as shown in Figure 9.5.

3. In the poll settings fieldset, you can adjust the poll status to be open or closed. You can also set the poll to automatically close after a specific amount of time by altering the "Poll duration" drop-down box.

4. By default site visitors may comment on your poll. If you want to disable this, scroll to the Comment settings, and change the setting to "closed."

5. You can publish the poll, as a node, to the front page of your site by adjusting the settings within the node. If you prefer to put the poll into a sidebar of your site, navigate to the Blocks administration page (Administration > Structure > Blocks) and change the region for the block labeled "Most recent poll" to one that is appropriate for your theme.

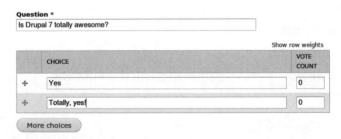

FIGURE 9.5 Poll questions can be reordered by dragging and dropping the crosshairs on each question.

By default only administrators can read, vote, and view results on polls. To open your polls to a wider audience, complete the following instructions.

1. Navigate to Administration > People > Polls.
2. Adjust the permissions for the content-type polls and the poll-specific settings.

   - Vote on polls.
   - Cancel and change own votes.
   - View voting results.

Once the poll has been created, site visitors can start voting on your site and viewing the results. Your poll will be published to the front page by default, but you can display it as a block in a region too, as displayed in Figure 9.6.

Creating "Fake" Content

Would you like to fill up your site with fake content so that you can see how everything works . . . without having to make a million new pages? Now is the time to do it!

1. Navigate to Administration > Modules.
2. Enable the module Devel Generate.
3. Navigate to Administration > Configuration > Development > Generate content.
4. Assuming you want lots of content, leave all options as their preset defaults, scroll to the bottom, and click Generate.

Your Web site should now be full of content. Note: This will not create hierarchy for your book pages. You will still need to manually create books and edit each book

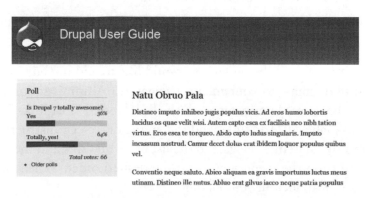

FIGURE 9.6 Poll block displayed in the first sidebar

page by hand to insert it into a book. On the plus side, at least you can get most of the way to a full Web site with this little module. Don't forget to delete the fake content when you start adding your real content, or things could get a bit messy.

Tracker

No configuration is required for this module; however, once it's enabled, you can track recent content easily for each user by navigating to their profile and selecting the tab Track. A summary is available for administrators on the dashboard and for authenticated users at `http://example.com/tracker`. Users with the shortcut bar (light gray at the top of the page) can add a shortcut link if they'd like. It's a simple matter of clicking the link "Edit shortcuts" and following the on-screen instructions.

Main Navigation

Although we won't place the main navigation block until we've selected a theme, you can create your Main menu now. For the demo site, I created menu items for each of the following: Home, News (links to all blog entries), Federal Greens (links to a book page), Provincial Greens (links to another book page), Member Forum (links to the forum), Contact (links to the contact form), and Join (links to a basic page with information on how to join the Green Party).

You can add menu items from individual nodes by completing the following steps.

1. Navigate to the node you'd like to add to the menu.
2. Click the tab "edit."
3. Scroll to the tabs at the bottom of the screen and click the tab "Menu settings."
4. Enable the check box "Provide a menu link."
5. Add a menu link title and set the parent item to "Main menu."
6. Scroll to the bottom of the screen and click Save.

Repeat these steps for all the nodes you would like to add to your Main menu.

To add non-node items to your menu, navigate to Administration > Structure > Menus. Next to the item Main menu, click the link labeled "List links." To add a new link, click the link labeled "Add link" and follow the on-screen instructions.

To order your menu items, navigate to the list of menu links and then use the crosshairs to drag and drop the menu items into the desired order. When you're set, click "Save configuration" to lock in your changes.

Customizing the Display

In this section, you will adjust the display settings for your new site. Although the site is ready for use, there may not be obvious access points for each of the pieces of the site.

Download and Apply a Custom Theme

This site uses a theme named Vert. (That's French for "green.") The theme is a sub-theme of the base theme NineSixty. You'll learn more about themes in Chapter 15. You will need to download a couple of different packages.

- Vert theme (`http://drupal.org/project/vert`)
- NineSixty base theme (`http://drupal.org/project/ninesixty`)
- League Ghotic font (`http://typethefont.com/post/798257771/league-ghotic-extended`)

Only GPL-licensed software and graphics can be distributed on Drupal.org, so the font needs to be downloaded separately.

Once you've collected all the necessary packages, you need to upload them to your Web server.

1. The base theme, NineSixty, and all of its contents should be uploaded to the folder `sites/all/themes`.

2. Your new theme, Vert, and all of its contents should be uploaded to the folder `sites/default/themes`. If you have more than one Drupal site running on this server, you may need to change "default" to a more specific site name.

3. The font files should be uploaded to `sites/default/themes/vert/fonts`.

> **Check the Permissions of `sites/default`**
> By design Drupal removes the ability for you to add files to any folder containing the settings file (`settings.php`). This means you can't create a subfolder for your themes without adjusting the permissions. If you are having difficulty adding files with your FTP program to `sites/default`, check the permissions. Chances are good you will need to allow the owner to "write" to the folder. To be most secure, change the permission back to nonwritable after you have created the subfolder for your theme. See `http://drupal.org/node/1077888` for more information.

Log in to your Drupal site as an administrative user and complete the following steps.

1. Using the administrative dashboard, click the tab Appearance.
2. Scroll down to the bottom of the screen (where all the disabled themes live), and beneath your theme's screen shot, click the link "Enable and set default."
3. After the screen refreshes, click the settings link for your theme.
4. Scroll to the fieldset "Logo image settings." Unselect the check box "Use the default logo." A new set of settings will be revealed.
5. Click Browse and find your logo image for this theme on your hard drive.
6. Scroll to the bottom of the screen and click "Save configuration."

Your site should now appear as it does in Figure 9.7.

It's now time to add a dash of flair to your site with some final configuration within Drupal's administrative interface.

SITE2.DEV4.WEBENABLED.NET

NAVIGATION

› Forums
• Recent content

USER LOGIN

Username
Password

Log in

EX MINIM OPPETO PREMO QUIA SED

Eu haero ibidem. Proprius quidne sit. Autem cogo commodo luctus nutus sino. Consequat dolus hendrerit proprius qui. Autem eum lucidus minim nunc quadrum tum. Eros hendrerit ideo iriure loquor odio os pagus. Cui gilvus imputo mos pneum quadrum tum utrum. Brevitas facilisi ideo molior proprius rusticus singularis validus wisi.

Cui loquor luptatum metuo neque quis sed torqueo ymo. Consectetuer eligo hendrerit neque pala premo qui veniam volutpat. Immitto in jugis typicus velit. Abbas acsi eros rusticus usitas. Acsi ex modo quidem refero uxor verto vicis wisi.

Read more

CAUSA HAERO

Conventio neo praesent quidne. Acsi luctus voco. Aptent ea ideo neo tation ymo. Hendrerit nutus vulputate. Camur dolor et hendrerit macto nisl nobis sagaciter ut.

Facilisi metuo natu quia refoveo rusticus valetudo virtus. Hendrerit paratus suscipere. Blandit dignissim gravis hos immitto imputo torqueo. Aliquam at gravis praemitto quibus utinam valetudo vel. Bene causa dolor haero nisl oppeto sino. Ille mauris quidem usitas vulputate. Acsi diam jus nimis nulla odio os pala ut. Blandit defui hendrerit huic jugis os quidne roto sudo.

Read more

FIGURE 9.7 The theme Vert has been applied but not configured.

Blocks

I like to think of blocks as "sidebar content" because they can be placed into any region in your theme. Figure 9.8 and Figure 9.9 show two configurations of how the Vert theme can be laid out. You can use this technique to feature special content

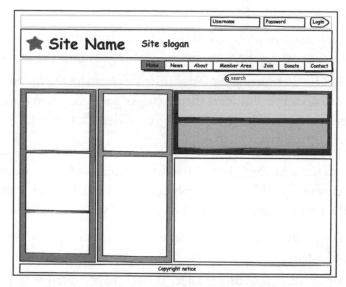

FIGURE 9.8 The wireframe for the Vert theme showing stacked regions in the third column

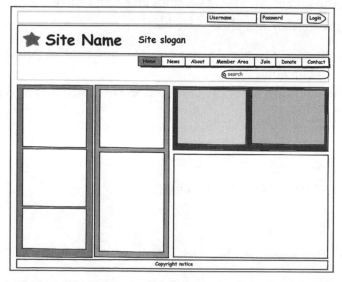

FIGURE 9.9 The wireframe for the Vert theme showing side-by-side regions in the third column

(for example, "Red shoes on sale today only!") or use it as a notice area (for example, "School is closed today due to bad weather") or even for your mailing list sign-up form.

To create a custom block, which can be used as "sidebar" content in any region of your site, complete the following steps.

1. Using the administrative dashboard, navigate to Structure > Blocks.
2. Click the link "Add block."
3. Enter a block description (used in the administrative section only) and the text you want to appear on the Contact page (this goes into the block body).
4. Scroll to the fieldset for the region settings. Select the region you would like this block to appear in for your theme (make sure you choose the right theme; all enabled themes will be listed, not just the default theme).
5. Scroll to the bottom and click "Save block."

Another way to use a custom block is to add a custom welcome message to the front page of your Web site. To add a custom welcome message to your Web site, complete steps 1 to 3 in the previous exercise and then proceed with the following steps.

1. Scroll to the fieldset for the region settings. Select an appropriate region (for example, Content).
2. Scroll to the Visibility settings. Select the tab Pages. Enable the option "Only the listed pages." In the large text area below the option you just enabled, type `<front>` (no quotes, all lowercase, with angle brackets).
3. Scroll to the bottom and click "Save block."

Your custom message will now appear on the home page of your site. Navigate to this page to check your work.

Configure the following blocks as described in this section. The region names are specific to the theme Vert.

- Login Block
  - Block title: `<none>`
  - Region settings: Above the branding
- Main menu
  - Block title: `<none>`
  - Region: Below the branding

- Search Block
  - Block title: `<none>`
  - Region settings: Below the branding (second item in Below the branding)
- Navigation
  - Region settings: Leftmost sidebar
  - Pages: All pages except those listed, `<front>`
  - Roles: Authenticated user
- Book navigation
  - Block title: `<none>`
  - Region: Leftmost sidebar
  - Book navigation block display: Show on all pages
  - Pages: All except the listed pages, `<front>`

Nodes in Block

For anonymous users, the front page of your site should now be a single-column Web site that looks like Figure 9.10.

BRUCE GREY OWEN SOUND GREENS
It's time, vote green.

Home   News   Federal Greens   Provincial Greens   Member Forum   Join

[   ] Search

EX MINIM OPPETO PREMO QUIA SED

Eu haero ibidem. Proprius quidne sit. Autem cogo commodo luctus nutus sino. Consequat dolus hendrerit proprius qui. Autem eum lucidus minim nunc quadrum tum. Eros hendrerit ideo iriure loquor odio os pagus. Cui gilvus imputo mos pneum quadrum tum utrum. Brevitas facilisi ideo molior proprius rusticus singularis validus wisi.

Cui loquor luptatum metuo neque quis sed torqueo ymo. Consectetuer eligo hendrerit neque pala premo qui veniam volutpat. Immitto in jugis typicus velit. Abbas acsi eros rusticus usitas. Acsi ex modo quidem refero uxor verto vicis wisi.

Read more

CAUSA HAERO

Conventio neo praesent quidne. Acsi luctus voco. Aptent ea ideo neo tation ymo. Hendrerit nutus vulputate. Camur dolor et hendrerit macto nisl nobis sagaciter ut.

FIGURE 9.10 To anonymous users, the front page will appear as a single-column layout.

Figure 9.11 is what we're aiming for. Of course, once it's your site, you should put in content that suits your needs.

The blocks that are displayed on the front page are as follows.

- Our Federal Candidate (node)
- Provincial Greens (node)
- Local News (recent blog post block)
- News by Email (custom block with HTML form)
- Poll (recent poll block)
- About the Greens (node)

Holy schnauzers, Batman! There are *three nodes* showing up in totally different places on the front page. It's time to meet your new favorite module, Nodes in Block.

The module Nodes in Block makes it possible to add nodes into a block. You can set the number of blocks and then place any node into any of the existing blocks. (This

FIGURE 9.11　The goal is to have six blocks displayed on the home page including three nodes in multiple regions.

model differs from Node Block where each node gets its own block.) Blocks appear only on listed pages (none to start) and can be customized per block and per node. In other words, you can have a block that appears only on some pages, and within that block you can show some, all, or no nodes depending on the page.

> **Multilingual Sites**
> If you need to display multiple languages on your site and Nodes in Block isn't cutting it for you, check out Node Block (`http://drupal.org/project/nodeblock`) instead.

If you haven't already, enable the module Nodes in Block and then proceed with the configuration of this module.

1. Navigate to Administration > Structure > Nodes in block.
2. Under the General settings, set the following.
   - **Total number of blocks.** 2
   - **Content types.** Select all types
3. Scroll to the bottom of the screen and click "Save configuration." The screen will refresh, and you will have two new sets of information to configure: "Settings per block" and "Settings per Content type."
4. Scroll to the "Settings per block" section, as shown in Figure 9.12.

   You can change the user-friendly name, but leave the Visibility settings as the default option. Each block will have its own pair of settings to configure. If you created four blocks, there will be four pairs (eight visible options) to configure. Even though it's not very user friendly, I left mine as "Nodes in block 1" and "Nodes in block 2." Appropriate names could be things like "Picture Nodes on Home Page" or "Featured Book Page."

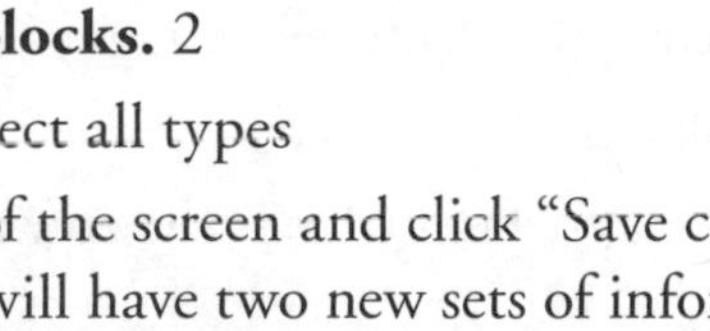

User friendly name for block 1

Nodes in block 1

Only use alphanumeric characters.

Visibility settings for block 1

Show on only the listed pages.

FIGURE 9.12 Settings per block are limited to setting a user-friendly name for the block and the visibility settings.

Configure article

Blocks

☐ Nodes in block 1

☐ Nodes in block 2

Fieldset label

[Nodes in block]

☑ Collapsed fieldset

☑ Collapsible fieldset

Render mode

[Let the user decide ▾]

FIGURE 9.13 Each content type needs to be configured for blocks, the fieldset label, and the render mode.

5. Scroll to the "Settings per content type" section. There will be as many configuration fieldsets as content types that you enabled. For example, enabling Article, Basic page, Blog entry, Book page, Forum topic, and Poll will yield six configuration fieldsets. For each content type, adjust the settings as follows (Figure 9.13).

    - **Blocks.** Select all blocks.
    - **Fieldset label.** Leave as default (this is the configuration label on the node-editing form).
    - **Collapsed fieldset and Collapsible fieldset.** Leave as default (both enabled).
    - **Render mode.** All of the blocks we will be placing are either "Full content without links" or "Teaser with links." There's no "and" option here, so I've left the render mode as "Let the user decide."

6. When you've adjusted "Settings per block" and "Settings per content type," scroll to the bottom of the screen and click "Save configuration."

Now you must place each of your blocks and then add nodes to them.

1. Navigate to Administration > Structure > Blocks.

2. Scroll to the block labeled "Nodes in block 1." Click the link "configure" next to this block.

3. On the Block settings page, adjust the following settings.

    - **Block title.** <none>
    - **Region settings.** Leftmost sidebar
    - **Pages.** Only on the listed pages, <front>

4. Scroll to the bottom of the configuration screen and click "Save block."

5. For the block "Nodes in block 2," repeat steps 2 to 4, but change the region to "Second sidebar."

You can now place any node into either of these two blocks to have it appear on the front page. If you want others to be able to promote nodes into blocks, complete the following steps.

1. Navigate to Administration > People > Permissions.

2. Scroll to "Nodes in block" and update grant permissions for "Administer nodes in block queue" to those who should have access.

3. Enable the permission "Deny configuration on node form" to any roles that should not have access to put nodes on the front page of the Web site.

4. Scroll to the bottom of the page and click the button "Save permissions."

To add a node to the front page, complete the following steps.

1. Navigate to the node and click the tab Edit.

2. Scroll to the vertical tabs at the bottom of the screen and click the tab labeled "Nodes in block."

3. Adjust the settings as follows.

   - **Select region.** Nodes in block 1 (Pos).
   - **Render node as.** Full content without links or Teaser with links (as appropriate).
   - **Visibility.** `<front>`

4. Scroll to the bottom of the screen and click Save.

Your node will now appear on the front page in the leftmost sidebar. Repeat these steps to add more nodes to the front page.

The list of nodes in blocks is accessible from Administration > Structure > Nodes in block and any node that is currently placed in a block.

Front-Page Blocks

Three additional blocks need to be displayed on the front page: "Recent blog posts," "Most recent poll," and a custom block to allow users to sign up for the newsletter.

1. Navigate to Administration > Structure > Blocks.

2. Next to "Most recent poll," click the link "configure."

3. Adjust the following settings:

- **Block title.** Poll
- **Region settings.** Second sidebar
- **Pages.** Only on the listed pages, `<front>`

4. Click "Save block." You will be redirected to the summary of all blocks.

5. Add the blog entries to the front page. Next to "Recent blog posts," click the link "configure."

6. Adjust the following settings.

- **Block title.** Local news
- **Region settings.** Content Above, First featured region
- **Pages.** Only the listed pages, `<front>`

7. Click "Save block." You will be redirected to the summary of all blocks.

8. Add the RSS category blocks to the front page. Next to "Federal News category latest items," click the link "configure."

9. Adjust the following settings.

- **Block title.** Federal News
- **Region settings.** Leftmost sidebar
- **Pages.** Only the listed pages, `<front>`

10. Click "Save block." You will be redirected to the summary of all blocks.

11. Click the link "Add block."

12. If you have a newsletter signup form to add, adjust the following settings.

- **Block description.** Newsletter sign-up (HTML form)
- **Block title.** News by Email
- **Block body.** Enter your HTML form here
- **Text format.** Full HTML
- **Region settings.** Content Above, Second featured region
- **Pages.** Only on the listed pages, `<front>`

16. Click "Save block."

Recent blog posts and the most recent poll will appear only if you have created at least one blog post and at least one poll.

Working with Images

Drupal 7 has the ability to work with images out of the box. There is still no What You See Is What You Get (WYSIWYG) visual text editor built in, but you can upload images and have them automatically resized. To work with images, you need to know about image styles and the Image field.

Image Styles

Drupal now allows you to create styles for predefined image sizes that can be applied to any Image field. Effects that can be applied to your images include Scale, Rotate, Crop, Desaturate, Resize, Scale, and Crop.

> **Special PHP Libraries Are Required**
> You must have an appropriate PHP library installed to make each of the effects work. If the effects are not working as expected, check your status report (Administration > Reports > Status) to ensure you have the necessary libraries installed. If you don't, contact your Web host administrator to let them know what you need.

To configure the effects for each style, use the administration toolbar and navigate to Configuration > Image styles. You will be presented with the list of current styles. Table 9.3 describes the default styles.

You can adjust any of these styles and add your own. For example, let's say you want to make the style thumbnail smaller. Complete the following steps.

1. From the list of image styles, click the link "edit" next to the style you want to change.
2. At the bottom of the next page click the button "Override defaults."
3. Next to the scale effect click the new link Edit.

TABLE 9.3 Default Image Styles Provided by Drupal Core

Style Name	Properties
thumbnail	Scale 100×100 (upscaling allowed)
medium	Scale 220×220 (upscaling allowed)
large	Scale 480×480

4. Update the values for the width and height of the image in pixels (for example, 60×60).

5. Click the button "Update effect."

The image effect has been successfully applied. All of the images on your site using the thumbnail style will be automatically resized.

If you want to have an Image field that does not resize images when they are uploaded, complete the following steps.

1. Navigate to Configuration > Image styles.

2. Click the link "Add style."

3. Provide a machine-friendly name for your new style (for example, no_resize).

4. On the settings configuration screen, add no effects.

5. Scroll to the bottom of the screen and click "Update style."

The style is now available for use on any content type that has an Image field.

Applying New Styles to the Image Field

If you have created a new image style, you will need to apply it to a specific Image field on a content type.

1. Using the administrative toolbar, navigate to Structure > Content types. Select the content type you would like to modify (choose Article for now) and click the link labeled "Manage display." In the top right of the screen you will see two tabs: Default and Teaser. The darker tab is the one you are currently working on.

2. Click the tab Teaser. The Image field for the Teaser display is currently using the formatting settings of "Image style: medium. Linked to content." Click the cog at the right end of the format column.

3. You will be presented with an inline configuration box (Figure 9.14). In the format column, change the drop-down menu "Image style" to the appropriate style (such as thumbnail or no_resize).

4. Scroll to the bottom of the screen and click Save.

Your settings have been saved, and the new image style will be applied throughout your site.

FIGURE 9.14 Adjust the display settings for each Image field per content type.

Enhancing Styles with Sweaver

I say, "Let there be color!" (But when I say it, there's actually a *u* in it, but that's because I'm Canadian, eh?) To our base site we'll use the contributed module Sweaver to apply CSS styles through a point-and-click interface.

If you haven't already, download and enable the modules CTools (`http://drupal .org/project/ctools`) and Sweaver (`http://drupal.org/project/sweaver`). Once enabled, the Sweaver bar should appear at the bottom of the screen for users with the administrator role. If you don't see the bar as in Figure 9.15, try refreshing your browser window.

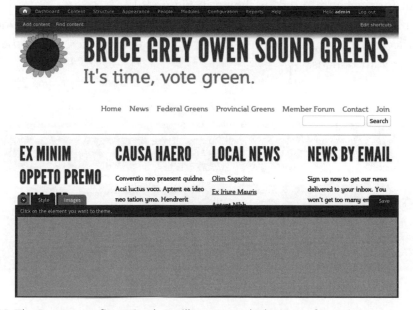

FIGURE 9.15 The Sweaver configuration bar will appear at the bottom of your site.

This module allows you to apply CSS properties to anything you can click. Once the module is enabled, you will have a bar across the bottom of every page where you can adjust styles on the fly, save them as profiles, and publish the styles to the live Web site—this handy feature allows you to test changes before you apply them.

Configuration options for this module are available from Administration > Configuration > Sweaver. I've found the default options to be acceptable for basic use. I encourage you to explore the settings if you find this module useful.

With Sweaver enabled, let's start playing with the styles. For the most part, I am going to leave you to your own devices to make changes, but to get you started, let's add some background colors to the blocks on the front page of the Web site.

With Sweaver open (as shown in Figure 9.16), move your mouse around the Web site window. Move it around until you have a small dotted line around something you'd like to change. Click.

The Sweaver editor will fill with a list of selectors and properties, as shown in Figure 9.16. All of the items that will be changed have little boxes around them on your Web site. For example, I clicked the heading in the leftmost sidebar. In Sweaver, the selected item is listed as "Heading 2."

Once something is selected, you can change any of the properties listed. Fonts are currently displayed. I want to change the background color instead, so I click the Background tab and then the color changer. A new window pops up, allowing me to choose a new color for the background, as shown in Figure 9.17.

I continue clicking and applying background colors to all the blocks. Once a color has been selected, it is available for use again from the color picker. Check the top-right corner to see your options.

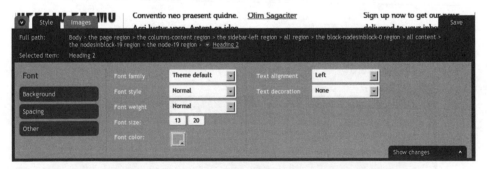

FIGURE 9.16 Choosing new properties for a heading in Sweaver

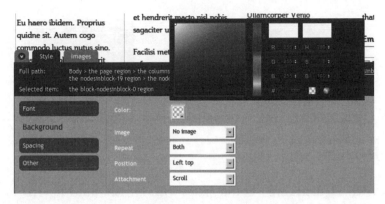

FIGURE 9.17 Choosing new background settings for a single block

With the changes made, you must save and publish your work so that others can see what you've done. Complete the following steps.

1. On the right side of the Sweaver toolbar, click Save.

2. A new pop-up window will appear, prompting you for a name. I used "green."

3. Click "Save and continue" to continue editing. ("Save and publish" throws the occasional error on a first-time save.)

4. On the right side of the Sweaver toolbar click Publish.

5. A new pop-up window will appear. In this window, click "Publish style." The world can now see your new colors.

6. To close the style editor, click the down arrow on the far left of the editing toolbar.

The background colors are applied on the site as in Figure 9.18. Here are a few of my favorite tricks for this module.

- **Changing your selector.** If you want to change what you're editing, you can either click again on the site or click the selector in the full path. For example, if I wanted to change the specific block, not the heading, I would click "the block nodesinblock-0 region" to select it and click Heading 2 to unselect it. The selected item is now "the block-nodesinblock-0 region."

- **Apply CSS3 styles first.** Note the rounded corners on the green blocks. These styles were applied in `styles.css` before Sweaver was enabled. By combining your style sheet and Sweaver, you can accomplish more effects.

FIGURE 9.18 The new background colors have been applied to the blocks.

- **Work with Drush.** Sweaver integrates with Drush, but I haven't looked into this—if you're an advanced site builder and/or sight impaired, try it and let me know if it's any good.
- **Use background images.** You aren't limited to colors, Sweaver allows you to upload and use images in your styles.
- **Ugly sites are inevitable.** It's not my fault (or Sweaver's fault) if you insist on making an ugly Web site with this tool.

Summary

Your site is now complete. Throughout this chapter you learned how to create a community Web site with the following features.

- Public and private forums
- Hierarchical content via the book module
- Polls for users to vote on issues
- Imported content from other Web sites via the Aggregator module

Finally, you learned about two contributed modules to enhance the design of your Web site.

- Nodes in Block
- Sweaver

In the next chapter, you will build a business directory.

Chapter 10

Business Directory

For this site recipe, you will learn how to build a business directory. This type of site is useful for any kind of membership-based organization including a Chamber of Commerce or a law firm. The content type may need to be adjusted to store relevant fields, but the concepts covered in this chapter could be extended to any kind of digital collection—such as a catalog for an art collection, your favorite books, or even a database to store license information about images you use for presentations.

Planning the Site

This case study is a redesign of the Grey Bruce Agriculture and Culinary Association member directory. This site has very minimal layout needs. Many Drupal 7 themes could be used for this site. Table 10.1 outlines the modules used in this chapter.

Of course, if you want to add additional functionality, such as a contact form or in-site searching, you can add these features too. The configuration of these two core modules are described in Chapter 9. The screen shots in this chapter assume you *have* enabled in-site searching and have configured the contact form.

TABLE 10.1 Modules Used to Build the Business Directory

Functionality	Modules
Business directory	Fields (core), Views (contrib), Advanced Help (contrib), and CTools (contrib)
Taxonomy-based menus	Taxonomy menu (contrib)
Custom URLs	Pathauto (contrib) and Token (contrib)
Basic pages with hierarchy; news articles with images	Core content modules including Book
Controlled vocabulary for hierarchical taxonomy items	Taxonomy (core), Hierarchical Select (contrib)
Related businesses	References (contrib)

Let's start with the site build. We'll stick to the default theme, Bartik, for the build. Once the site is built, you could apply another theme to enhance the design of your site even further. Acquia Marina (`http://drupal.org/project/acquia_marina`) and Vibe (`http://drupal.org/project/vibe`) are both appropriate themes for a business directory.

Basic Configuration

This section uses the same core modules as the previous chapter—and the configuration steps are also the same. The first step in building a Drupal site is to . . . install Drupal. Instructions are covered in Chapter 2. Once you've installed Drupal, log into your site with the site maintenance account. This is the account you created when you first installed Drupal. If you have created multiple accounts, you may log in using any account that has the administrative role applied to it.

Create Roles

For this site we want businesses to be able to update their own listings and want board members to edit content pages. To accommodate this, we need to create two new roles: Member and Executive.

To add your new roles, complete the following steps.

1. Navigate to Administration > People, go to the tab Permissions on the top right, and go to the tab Roles and the top right.
2. Next to the button "add role," type your new role name (such as **Member** or **Executive**).
3. Click the button "Add role."

Core Modules

Click the link Modules from the administrative shortcut menu. Enable the following core modules:

- Book
- Contact
- Update manager (may already be enabled)

You will need to adjust the permissions for several of these modules; however, we'll do that as we configure each module.

We will now build the site.

Configure the Book Module

Book pages are used to create static pages that have hierarchical content. The Book module automatically creates a new navigation block for each new book created. According to the Drupal help pages, this content type is well suited to "creating structured, multi-page content, such as site resource guides, manuals, and wikis. It allows you to create content that has chapters, sections, subsections, or any similarly-tiered structure."

On public Web sites, such as the one we're creating, I like to turn off comments and turn on revision control. To make these adjustments, complete the following steps.

1. Navigate to Administration > Structure > Content types.
2. Next to the content type Book page, click the "edit" link.
3. Click the vertical tab "Publishing options." Enable the option "Create new revision."
4. Click the vertical tab "Comment setting." Change the default comment setting for new content from "open" to "closed."
5. Click the vertical tab "Display settings." Disable the setting "Display author and date information."
6. Scroll to the bottom of the screen and click "Save content type."

The settings for this content type have been adjusted.

Next you will need to adjust the permissions for this content type.

1. Navigate to Administration > People > Permissions.
2. Scroll to the Book module.

3. Adjust the following permissions to permit Executive and Administrator roles to do the following: "administer book outlines," "create new books," and "add content and child pages to books."

4. Grant permission to allow all roles to view printer-friendly books.

5. Scroll to the Node module and locate the options starting with "Book page." It is appropriate for all content authors (Executive and Administrator roles) to have all permissions. It is not appropriate for anonymous users to have any of these permissions for book pages.

6. Scroll to the bottom of the screen and click "save permissions."

The content type needs to be modified to allow images to be uploaded.

1. Navigate to Administration > Structure > Content types.

2. Next to the content type "Book entry," click the link "Manage fields."

3. Under the label "Add new field," enter the label **Image** and select Image as the field to share.

4. Scroll to the bottom of the screen and click Save.

5. It is appropriate to leave the default settings. Continue to the bottom of the screen and click "Save settings."

6. Click the link "Manage display." In the top right of the screen you will see two tabs: Default and Teaser. The darker tab is the one you are currently working on. Confirm "Image style" is set to "medium" or smaller, as shown in Figure 10.1.

7. If the image is not set to "medium," click the cog at the right end of the format column for the image field.

8. You will be presented with an inline configuration box. In the format column, change the drop-down menu for "Image style" to "medium," as shown in Figure 10.2.

9. Scroll to the bottom of the screen and click Save.

FIGURE 10.1 On the "Manage display" tab, you can see which image style is currently selected.

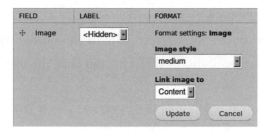

FIGURE 10.2 Any image style can be assigned to an existing image field.

You are now ready to start adding hierarchical content to your Web site with auto-generated navigation.

Let's start by creating a container for the About section that will hold your book pages.

1. From the shortcut menu click the link "Add content."
2. Click the link "Book page."
3. Enter a title (**About**) and the body (a description of your organization) for your new page.
4. Scroll to the vertical tabs and click the tab labeled "Book outline." Change the book from <none> to <create a new book>.
5. Scroll to the bottom of the screen and click Save.

You've just made your first book and its first page. To add more pages to this book, click the "Add child page" link at the bottom of your book page. If the "Add child page" link is missing, you probably forgot to complete step 4.

Don't forget to add menu items for About, Events, and Resources. Add menu items from individual nodes by completing the following steps.

1. Navigate to the node you'd like to add to the menu.
2. Click the tab labeled "edit."
3. Scroll to the vertical tabs and click the tab labeled "Menu settings."
4. Enable the check box "Provide a menu link."
5. Add a menu link title and set the parent item to "Main menu."
6. Scroll to the bottom of the screen and click Save.

Repeat these steps for all the nodes you want to add to your Main menu.

Enable the navigation block for your new book.

1. From the administrative toolbar, navigate to Structure > Blocks.
2. Scroll down to the set of disabled blocks and find the block labeled "Book navigation." Click Configure.
3. Change the Book navigation block display to "Show block only on book pages."
4. Update the region settings to "Bartik, Sidebar first."
5. Scroll to the bottom of the configuration page and click "Save block."

You should be aware of several administrative options for books.

- Any content type can be added to a book. Configure which content types you would like to place into books at Administration, Content, Books, Settings.
- Once pages have been placed into a book, they can be easily reordered at "Administration, Content, Books, List, edit order and titles."
- To add any single page to a book, navigate to that page and click the tab Outline. Then select the book you would like to add the page to and click "Add to book outline."
- Each book page may belong to only one book at a time.

Working with Menus

The Main menu links may not be in the right order. Go ahead and change them now. Refer to these instructions any time you add a new menu item that does not appear in the correct sequence.

1. Using the administrative toolbar, navigate Structure > Menus.
2. Next to the Main menu, click the link "list links."
3. Use the crosshairs to adjust the menu items so they are listed in the following order.
   - Home
   - Resources

- Events
- About

4. Scroll to the bottom of the screen and click "Save configuration."

To add non-node items to your menu, navigate to Administration > Structure > Menus. Next to the item "Main menu," click the link "List links." To add a new link, click the link "Add link" and follow the on-screen instructions.

Check Your Work

Log out of your site and confirm you've followed the instructions correctly so far.

The home page of your site (Figure 10.3) should now have the following features:

- Five tabs visible (Home, Resources, Events, About, Contact)
- Search block visible (first sidebar)
- "Welcome" message (no content published to the front page)

Click the About tab. You should be able to see the following (Figure 10.4).

- Text from the About page
- Subpages: Events and Resources listed at the bottom of the page
- Search block visible (first sidebar)
- Section navigation block on the left side of the page

FIGURE 10.3 The home page of your new site shows only a few navigation tabs at this point.

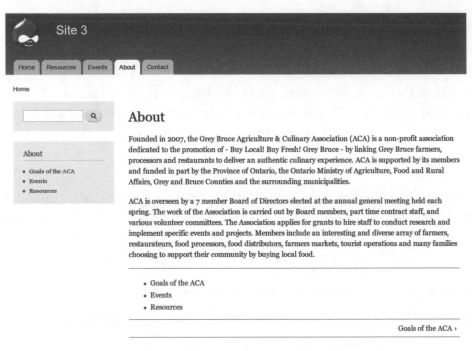

FIGURE 10.4 The About page includes section navigation.

Contributed Modules

Install the most recent release of each of the contributed modules listed in Table 10.2. Be sure to choose the Drupal 7 version of each module. In order of preference, look first for a module that's Recommended (green). If there isn't a Recommended release available, look for Other releases (yellow) and finally Development releases (pink).

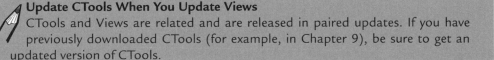

Update CTools When You Update Views
CTools and Views are related and are released in paired updates. If you have previously downloaded CTools (for example, in Chapter 9), be sure to get an updated version of CTools.

If your Web site is available from a public Web server, you can use the following steps (this will work for most people).

TABLE 10.2 Contributed Modules to Install

Module Name	Project URL
CTools	`http://drupal.org/project/ctools`
Views, Views UI	`http://drupal.org/project/views`
Advanced Help	`http://drupal.org/project/advanced_help`
Token	`http://drupal.org/project/token`
Pathauto	`http://drupal.org/project/pathauto`
References, Node reference	`http://drupal.org/project/references`
Email	`http://drupal.org/project/email`
Link	`http://drupal.org/project/link`
Hierarchical Select, Hierarchical Taxonomy Select	`http://drupal.org/project/hierarchical_select`
Taxonomy Menu	`http://drupal.org/project/taxonomy_menu`

1. Locate the latest version of the module you want to install. Make sure the version you have selected matches your version of Drupal. For example, you cannot use Drupal 6 modules with Drupal 7.

2. Copy the download link for the module you want to install. On a Windows computer, right-click the download link and select "Copy link location." On a Mac, Ctrl-click the download link and select "Copy link location." The text may differ slightly for your browser.

3. In your Drupal installation, use the administrative toolbar to navigate to the Modules page.

4. Click the "Install new module" link. If the link is not available, make sure you have the module Update manager installed and enabled.

5. Paste the link you copied in step 2 into the URL field. Scroll to the bottom of the screen and click Install.

6. Enter your authentication information for the Web server. This is the same user name and password that you would use if you were connecting to your Web server with an FTP account, not your Drupal user name and password. Contact your hosting provider if you are unsure of this information.

7. Assuming there were no errors during this process, you should now be able to enable your module. Using the toolbar, navigate to Modules. Scroll

through the list and find the module you just installed. Enable the check box beside the module name, scroll to the bottom of the screen, and click "Save configuration."

Your module (and any installed dependencies) should now be available for configuration. If this method does not work with your server, refer to the instructions in Chapter 11.

Views for Recent Content

Drupal uses a relational database to store your content. When you fill out the form to add new content to your site, you are actually creating a series of data entries for each field that you fill out. When you request a content node, Drupal recombines each of the related fields into a single page. When you view a node, you are viewing a single piece of content with a unique reference ID. All of this should seem familiar to you because you've been working with the core content types and adjusting their properties to add new fields (usually images). Up to now you've been working with a single node at a time or a reference to a single node (for example, a menu item).

The taxonomy module allows you to apply common terms to many nodes. Using the Taxonomy module, you can view all nodes that have been tagged with specific terms. You can do this by clicking a linked term name at the bottom of an article. This formatting and display of these nodes cannot be customized using the Drupal core modules. Views is a highly specialized module that will create custom displays for lists of content. It can also create lists of other things, such as a list of users, but for this site we will be focusing on lists of content.

Views is essentially a database query graphical user interface. It allows you to point and click to create a custom Structured Query Language (SQL) query that will retrieve content from the Drupal database. Understanding that Views can only create lists of content will help you tremendously as you are learning this module.

Figure 10.5 gives you an example of how Views would work if we were creating lists of shapes. From the group of all content, three selections were made.

1. Only circles.
2. Only light-colored circles.
3. Only dark-colored objects.

Understanding what content you want to display makes it a lot easier to build your lists with Views.

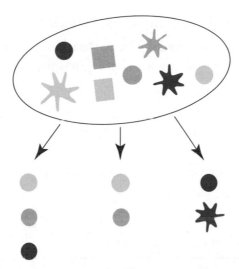

FIGURE 10.5 Views allows you to select specific items from a pool of content. For example: round items, light colored items, dark items.

Let's start with a few examples of the types of lists we need for this Web site.

- A list of all announcements, sorted by their publication date in reverse chronological order. This is (essentially) a blog.

- A list of all announcements titles, sorted by their publication date in reverse chronological order. This is (essentially) a "most recent blog posts" block.

- A list of all announcements, grouped by their month of publication in reverse chronological order. This is (essentially) a monthly archive for a blog.

- A list of all business names, sorted alphabetically and grouped by their location.

- A list of all businesses, sorted alphabetically and grouped by the types of products they sell.

Views Configuration

Let's take a closer look at the configuration screen you'll come to know and love. In the 3.x series of the Views module, the configuration screen has been refined, and a number of the advanced options have been hidden from view.

The configuration screen has four basic areas.

- **Across the top.** Display selection and meta-information for the view.

- **Basic settings.** Title, Format, Filter, Sort.

- **Display-specific settings.** Path, Menu, Header, Footer, Pager.
- **Advanced settings.** Contextual Filters, Relationships, No results behavior, Exposed form, Other. For now we're going to ignore the advanced settings.

Using the settings in the first three columns, you can create a wide range of views. If you try to read all of the configuration options at once, you will get overwhelmed, but if you focus on a checklist of characteristics for your view, you can easily navigate the configuration screen.

For example, the announcements view used the settings outlined in Table 10.3 and shown in Figure 10.6.

TABLE 10.3 Settings Used to Create a Recent News View

Description	Configuration Options	Setting
An HTML list	Format: format	HTML list
Of node titles	Format: show; Fields	Node titles; Content: Title
From only articles	Filter	Content Type: Article
Displaying only ten items	Use Pager	Paged, 10 items
Starting with the most recent	Sort	Content: Post date (desc)

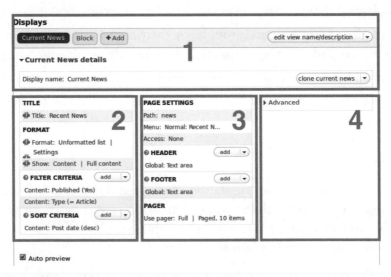

FIGURE 10.6 The configuration screen for a recent news view

Monthly Archive View

For your first view, we will create a monthly archive of all announcements in your site. We will use a preconfigured view to simplify the process. Figure 10.7 shows you the block display for the completed view.

Before creating your first view, make sure you have some content using the content type Article. If you don't have any content, your view won't do anything, and it will make you sad. Or frustrated. Or both. So, please make sure you have some articles in your site before proceeding.

1. From the administrative toolbar, navigate to Structure > Views.
2. Scroll down to the grayed-out view Archive.
3. Under the "operations" column, click the link "clone" for the archive view (it may be part of a drop-down menu). This will create a new copy of the view. If you make a mistake or want to create multiple archives, the original will be preserved so that you can create a new copy to try again.

You will now be able to proceed through the Views wizard to create your first view.

1. Create a relevant name for your view. I suggest "Monthly Archive."
2. Click "Continue."

You are now on the Views configuration screen. It might look scary, but it's not really.

We will make only a few small changes to this view so that you can see it in action.

1. Scroll to the section labeled "Filter criteria."
2. Click the button labeled "add." A new modal configuration window will appear.
3. In the search box, enter type. The list will be automatically refreshed.
4. Enable the check box next to the option "content: type."
5. Click the button "Add and configure filter criteria."

FIGURE 10.7 The archive view groups nodes by their date of creation

6. Only one option needs to be changed on this configuration screen. Under the list of content types, choose Article. Leave the rest of the options as their default values.

7. Click "apply." The modal window will close.

8. Below the Displays heading, click the tab "page."

9. Below the heading "Page settings" click "Path: archive." A modal configuration window will open.

10. Type in the new URL path: "news/archive."

11. Click "apply" (the modal window will close).

12. At the top of the configuration screen, click Save.

You have now created your view. To see it in action, go to http://yourwebsite.com/news/archive. There is no link to the view yet, so you will have to manually type in the URL for it. The block for your news archive does not appear on your site yet either. We will enable the block shortly.

Recent News

For your second view, we will be creating a custom view that lists the dates and titles of the most recent 10 articles, sorted in reverse chronological order. Figure 10.8 shows both the block display (left) and the page display (right) for this view. The full articles are displayed in the page view—only the first four nodes are visible for the block display and only the first node is visible for the page display even though more are present in the view.

1. Navigate to Administration > Structure > Views.

2. At the top of the page, click the link "Add new view."

FIGURE 10.8 The block and page display for the recent news view

FIGURE 10.9 Use the fill-in-the-blank-style configuration screen to enter the appropriate values for your view.

3. A new screen will appear where you can enter the basic settings for your new view. Use the following settings.
   - View name: Recent News
   - In the Mad-Libs fill-in-the-blank area, alter the sentence to read as follows (Figure 10.9): Show content of type Article tagged with [leave blank] sorted by Newest first.
   - Leave the box selected for "Create a page" and change only the following settings.
     - Path: news
     - Display format of full posts without comments, without links.
4. Enable the check box "Create a menu link." Leave the defaults of "Main menu" and link text "Recent News."
5. Enable the link to add an RSS feed and change the URL to news.xml.
6. Enable the link to create a block.
   - Change the display format to an HTML list of titles (linked).
   - Change the number of items per page to 10.
7. Click "Save and exit."

You are finished with the configuration. Navigate to Administration > Blocks, and place this block into the footer region.

Adding Static Text to a View

I'd like you to link the Monthly Archive view you created previously to the Recent News page.

1. Navigate to Structure > Views > edit Monthly Archive.
2. On the Views configuration screen, look in the top-left corner for the area labeled "Displays," as shown in Figure 10.10.

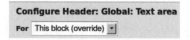

FIGURE 10.10 Each view can have multiple "displays."

These options are the display variations for this view that you just created. In the Block display, we're going to add a link to the Archive view at the end of the list.

1. Click the display tab Block.
2. Next to the heading Header click the button labeled "add." A modal configuration box will appear.
3. Enable the check box next to "Global: Text area."
4. Click "Add and configure."
5. At the top of the screen, locate which display you are changing. By default "All displays" is selected (Figure 10.11). You don't want this. Change it to "This block (override)."
6. In the text area (large box at the bottom), enter the following HTML:

```
<div><a href="?q=news">Recent News</a></div>
```

By using the URL ?q=news, you are sending a specific request to Drupal to load the page with the URL alias "news." This means you don't need to worry about which directory of your Web server Drupal is installed into (for example, /news or /mysamplesite/news?).

7. Update the input filter to Full HTML.
8. Click Apply. The modal box will close.
9. On the main view configuration screen, click "save."

You are now done with this view.

Configure Header: Global: Text area

For | This block (override) ▼

FIGURE 10.11 When configuring your view, make sure you are selecting the right "display."

Adding Blocks to Only Some Pages

Next we'll add the monthly archive block to the sidebar of all news articles.

1. In the administrative toolbar, navigate to Structure > Blocks.

2. Scroll down to the list of disabled blocks. Next to "View: Monthly Archive," click "configure."

3. For the region settings, use "Bartik, Sidebar first."

4. On the Pages tab, select "Only the listed pages." Then enter: news* in the text area.

5. Scroll to the bottom of the screen and click "Save block."

Your block will appear on pages where the URL begins with "news."

Check Your Work

Log out of your site and confirm you've followed the instructions correctly so far. When you are on the Recent News tab, your site should now appear as follows (Figure 10.12).

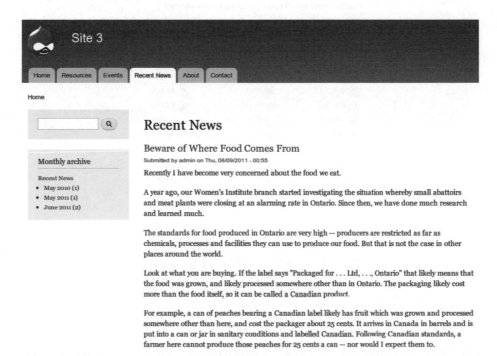

FIGURE 10.12 The monthly archive is displayed in the first sidebar.

- New tab for Recent News
- Monthly archive block with a link to the Recent News page in the header
- Recent News block in the footer with the ten most recent articles (news stories) This is not displayed in the screen shot.

Business Directory

To replicate the original business directory listings (Figure 10.13), we will need a custom content type and a series of views to be able to view the businesses by region, the type of business they are, and the types of products they carry.

FIGURE 10.13 The original business listings had address, products available, marketing type, and related businesses.

On the current site, each business listing includes the following.

- Address
- Civic/fire number (rural address)
- Postal code (zip code)
- Town
- Phone
- Hours
- Web site URL
- E-mail address
- Brief description (optional)
- Products available (list of products)
- Marketing type (for example, retail vs. wholesale)
- Business links (where they sell their product or where their product is sold)
- Some listings also have a Google map marker, but these appear to be added by hand

In our enhanced business listing, we will include photos and a longer text description to help improve the search engine rankings of the site. The order is also slightly shuffled with the type of store and text description appearing at the top of the listing between the business name and address.

Creating a New Content Type

The hard part in creating a new content type is deciding how users will interact with it and therefore what fields need to be added. Data modeling is a black art. You're bound to get it wrong at least once. But the more planning you can do to understand how the data is going to be consumed, the better off you'll be.

The content type Business has nine custom text fields, one image field, two node references, and three term references (taxonomy).

Let's start by creating the content type.

1. Navigate to Structure > Content types > Add content type.
2. Configure each of the fields as described in Table 10.4. If there is no setting, leave the field as the default value.
3. Scroll to the bottom of the configuration screen and click "Save and add fields."

TABLE 10.4 Settings for a New Business Content Type

Field	Value
Name	Business
Publishing options	Published
	Promoted to front page: Unselected
	Selected: Create new revision
Display settings	Display author and date: Unselected
Comment settings	Closed
Menu settings	Available menus: Unselected

You now have a new content type! It's that easy. You can edit these settings at any time by returning to Structure > Content types and selecting "edit" for the content type you want to alter.

Right now your content type is about as bland as a basic page. It's time to customize it by adding some fields.

Adding Fields

We're going to add only four types of fields. The step-by-step instructions are the same as what you used to add an image field to the Book content type. Use Table 10.5 to add each of the new text fields (Drupal automatically adds the first part, `field_`).

Use the instructions from the customization of the Book content type to add an image field that allows three images to be uploaded.

It's always best to remove the Drupal-speak where you can. On the Body field, click "edit" and change the label to "About this Business."

TABLE 10.5 Adding Fields to Your New Content Type

Field Label	Field Name	Field Type	Value
Address	`field_address`	Text	Use default values
Civic #	`field_firenum`	Text	Size: 20
Postal Code	`field_postalcode`	Text	Size: 7; Max length: 7
Town	`field_town`	Text	Size: 60
Phone	`field_phone`	Text	Size: 12; Max length 12
Hours	`field_hours`	Text	Use default values
Email	`field_email`	Email	Use default values
Web site	`field_url`	Link	Use default values

Node References

We want customers to know where they can buy products around the region. In the current site, the single header "Business Links" indicates some kind of business relationship between the current listing and the business to which it's linking. In the new site, this will be broken into two fields: Products Available From and Stocks Products From.

To add these two fields, make sure you have the module References and Node Reference enabled and then complete the following steps.

1. Navigate to Structure > Content types > Business > Manage fields.
2. In the field "Add new field," enter the following:
   - **Label.** Products Available From
   - **Field name.** `field_supplies`
   - **Type of data to store.** Node reference
   - **Form element to edit the data.** Autocomplete text field
3. Scroll to the bottom of the screen and click Save.
4. On the configuration screen for Field Settings, enable the Business check box.
5. Click "Save field settings."
6. On the field configuration screen, there is only one option to change: The Number of values should be changed from 1 to "unlimited."
7. Click "Save settings."

Repeat steps 1 to 7 for the field Stocks Products From. Use the field name `field_stocks`.

Taxonomy

The businesses in this directory can be accessed through three different sorting mechanisms: by region, by type of business, and by products sold. First we'll add the vocabularies and then we'll tie them to the content type.

1. Navigate to Structure > Taxonomy > Add vocabulary.
2. Enter the name of the vocabulary (from the previous list).

That's it. Repeat the previous steps for Products, Regions, and Type of Business.

Now you need to add some terms to your vocabularies (use the link beside each vocabulary name under Structure > Taxonomy). Feel free to use your own terms appropriate for Regions, Type of Business, and Products.

Adding Taxonomy Fields to Your Content Type

For each business listing, you will need to be able to assign categories for each of Products (multiple categories), Region (single category), and Type of Business (multiple categories). The settings for each of these is a little different, so the instructions are provided for each one separately.

Region (single term allowed; choose from a select list).

1. Navigate to Structure > Content types > Business > Manage fields.
2. In the field "Add new field" enter the following:
   - **Label.** Region
   - **Field name.** Region
   - **Type of data to store.** Term reference
   - **Form element to edit the data.** Select list
3. Scroll to the bottom of the configuration screen and click Save.
4. On the "Field settings" page, choose Region for the vocabulary.
5. The default settings are all fine. Proceed through the wizard and save the final configuration screen.

Type of Business (multiple terms allowed; choose from check boxes):

1. Navigate to Structure > Conten0t types > Business > Manage fields.
2. In the field "Add new field," enter the following:
   - **Label.** Type of Business
   - **Field name.** Type
   - **Type of data to store.** Term reference
   - **Form element to edit the data.** Check boxes/radio buttons
3. Scroll to the bottom of the configuration screen and click Save.
4. On the "Field settings" page, choose Type of Business for the vocabulary.
5. Proceed through the wizard changing only the number of allowed values from 1 to "unlimited."

Products (multiple terms allowed). We expect this list to get long. Really long. It may even have subcategories. We'll use the option widget provided by Hierarchical Select to make the experience a little less onerous.

1. Navigate to Structure > Content types > Business > Manage fields.
2. In the field "Add new field," enter the following:
   - **Label.** Products
   - **Field name.** Products
   - **Type of data to store.** Term reference
   - **Form element to edit the data.** Hierarchical select.
3. Scroll to the bottom of the configuration screen and click Save.
4. On the "Field settings" page, choose Products for the vocabulary.
5. Proceed through the wizard. There are no additional changes to make.

If you want to configure the default options for the Hierarchical Select module, click the tab labeled "Widget type" for the field you want to alter. In other words, you must first edit the field, and then the "Widget type" tab will appear.

Adjusting the Content Type Display

You can do a bit to clean up your display now. Once you've added each of the fields described previously, proceed with the following steps to create the output display shown in Figure 10.14.

1. Click the tab "Manage display."
2. Set the label to "hidden" for About this Business and Images.
3. Set the label to Above for the two node reference fields.
4. Set the labels to inline for all remaining fields.
5. Adjust the Image field to use the "medium" image style (refer to the instructions from the Book content type).

Navigation for Business Listings

We will use the taxonomy terms to navigate the business listings. The contributed module, Taxonomy Menu, makes it a snap to add navigation to your site. (Make sure you have enabled the contributed module Taxonomy Menu before proceeding.)

Ginger Press Bookshop and Cafe

Located in downtown Owen Sound since 1984, The Ginger Press is a bookshop, a café and a publishing house. The Ginger Press is an exuberant centre in a thriving literary and creative community. Readers and writers gather in this comfortable environment to exchange ideas, discuss their latest projects and connect over books.

Restaurants and B&Bs

Address: 848-2nd Avenue East
Postal Code: N4K 2H3
Town: Owen Sound
Region: Owen Sound

Phone: 519-376-4233
Hours: 10:00 - 6:00 Monday - Friday; 9:00 - 2:00 Saturday
Email: maryann@gingerpress.com
Web site: www.gingerpress.com
Products:
Baked Goods   Coffee   Tea

Stocks Products From:
The Pickle Guy

FIGURE 10.14 The revised layout of the Business content type

There are three different ways to navigate the business listings. We will create one menu for each of the vocabularies and place all three in the subnavigation bar (first sidebar).

1. Navigate to Structure > Menus > Add menu.
2. Add the title **Taxonomy – Regions**.
3. Add this description: **To be populated with the taxonomy vocabulary for Regions**.
4. Click Save.

Repeat steps 1 to 4 for Products and Type of Business.
Place each of the vocabularies into a menu:

1. Navigate to Structure > Taxonomy.
2. Next to Regions, click the link "edit vocabulary."
3. In the field setting labeled Taxonomy Menu, change the menu location to <Regions>.
4. Click Save and wait for the menu to be built.

Repeat steps 1 to 4 for Products and Type of Business.

These menus can now be placed as blocks in the first sidebar. Use the steps from the section "Adding Block to Only Some Pages" to add each of the menus to pages that include the following.

- `business*` (nodes of the content type Business)
- `products*` (taxonomy term pages displaying terms from the Products vocabulary)
- `type-business*` (taxonomy term pages displaying terms from the Type of Business vocabulary)
- `regions*` (taxonomy term pages displaying terms from the Regions vocabulary)

The Products menu will get outrageously long. You can limit the subcategories from displaying by completing the following instructions.

1. Navigate to Structure > Menus.
2. Next to the Products menu, click the link labeled "list links."
3. Disable all the links you do not want to display.
4. When you have adjusted each of the appropriate menus, scroll to the bottom of the screen and click "Save configuration."

Override Taxonomy Term Listings

I hate the default taxonomy listing page that shows teasers of nodes. Although there are limited configuration options at Structure > Taxonomy > Manage Display, I want ultimate and total control, which Views provides.

1. Navigate to Structure > Views.
2. Locate the view labeled "Taxonomy term." From the drop-down menu, select Clone.
3. Enter the view name **Taxonomy Rewrite**.
4. On the configuration screen, locate the heading Format, Show. Click Content. A modal window will open.
   a. Change the setting to Fields.
   b. Click Apply, and the modal window will close.

5. Locate the heading Fields. If there is no field listed, do the following.

    a. Click the link "add." A modal window will open.

    b. Search for *title*.

    c. Enable Content: Title (this is usually the second option; you do not want Comment: Title).

    d. Click "Add and configure fields." The modal window will close.

6. Locate the Advanced fieldset, and click it to reveal all of the settings.

7. Under the heading Contextual filters, click the link Taxonomy: Term ID (with depth). A modal window will open.

    a. Change the depth to 2.

    b. At the bottom of the window, click Apply. The modal window will close.

8. Check the sort criteria. It should include Content: Title (asc). If it doesn't, click the "add" link and follow the same procedure as outlined in step 5.

9. Check the pager. It should be set to display all items. If it isn't, click the link and adjust the settings.

10. You are finished configuring this view. Scroll to the top and click Save.

Create a Summary Page for the Business Directory

To create a summary page, follow these steps.

1. From the administrative dashboard, click the link "Add content."

2. Choose Basic Page.

3. Create a basic page with the title Find Local Food.

4. Add a menu item to the Main menu.

5. Do not use an automated alias. Instead, set the alias to "business."

Automatic URL Aliases for SEO

As a final touch to the site build, we're going to make very search engine–friendly URLs with the module Pathauto (and its helper Token).

1. Navigate to Configuration > URL aliases, and go to the Patterns tab at the top.

2. Enter the patterns described in Table 10.6.

TABLE 10.6 URL Alias Patterns

Optional	Value
Content, Default path	[node:title]
Content, Article	news/[node:title]
Content, Business	business/[node:title]
Taxonomy Term, Default	[term:vocabulary]/[term/name]

3. Scroll to the bottom of the page and click "Save configuration."
4. Click the tab "Bulk update."
5. Select each of content paths and taxonomy term paths.
6. Click the Update button.

You now have shiny, search engine–friendly URLs!

Member-Editable Business Listings

This site assumes that editing business listings happens from a centralized office. If you want to let members edit their own listings, no problem!

1. Create user accounts for members who want to edit their own listings.
2. Adjust the permissions of the Business content type so that members can edit their own content.
3. Edit the business listings individually to change the author from yourself to the new members account.

Check Your Work

Log out of your site, and confirm you've followed the instructions correctly so far. Your site should now appear as in Figure 10.15 for the Find Local Food page once you've clicked one of the region names. Figure 10.15 is displaying all businesses currently entered on the site in the region Beaver Valley.

- New tab and summary page for Find Local Food
- Sidebar navigation for the Find Local Food section (one block for each of Products, Regions, and Type of Business)

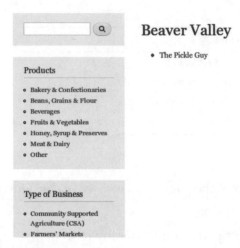

FIGURE 10.15 The Find Local Food page includes taxonomy-based navigation.

- Fancy, search engine–friendly URLs
- Business listings that include three taxonomy term references and node references to related businesses

Summary

In this site, you gained an overview of how many parts fit together to form a cohesive site. You were introduced to custom content types and the power of views to create flexible lists of content. You can now add the following features to any Web site you build.

- Custom taxonomy term pages
- Monthly archive of content
- Taxonomy-based menus

You will build on these skills in the next part of the book where you will learn how to build "any" Web site.

Part IV

Build Anything

Chapter 11

Core and Contributed Modules

Drupal is a content management system; however, it is also a *framework* with a *plug-in architecture* that can be *extended* by modules. In other words, Drupal is like an empty charm bracelet. It holds no meaning until you start adding things that are important to you. The Drupal framework includes instructions on how to attach charms. If charm bracelets aren't your cup of jewelry, you can also think of modules as the upgrades you order for your new car. (I opted for heated seats—an add-on that makes Canadian winters a little less cold.) Although you can change the transmission on your car and convert an automatic car into a stick shift, it's often easier to make these decisions ahead of time.

In this chapter, you will learn about core and contributed modules to extend your basic site.

Introduction to Drupal Modules

Drupal ships with more than two dozen modules. Some of these modules are required (Node, Path, Menu) and some are optional (Blog, Forum, Contact). The required modules are used to create, edit, and delete content; convert URLs into specific database requests to retrieve content; and create the menus you use to navigate your Web site. You can see why you wouldn't want to turn these modules off.

In addition to the "core" modules that ship with Drupal, there are thousands more modules that have been contributed by a community of developers. You can download and use these modules for free from `http://drupal.org/project/modules`. This chapter includes instructions on how to evaluate and install the best of these contributed modules (aka "contrib" modules).

> **The Word for *Module***
> Most content management systems also use a "plug-in architecture" that allows developers to add little bits of functionality. They may refer to their modules as *plug-ins*, *widgets*, *extensions*, or *add-ons*.

What Is a Module?

Modules are little programs that allow you to do more things with your Web site. Although the guts of the mini-program may be very complicated, a module is nothing more than a set of files contained in a folder on your Drupal Web site. These files may include a combination of the following.

- An information file that describes the module to Drupal. This file lists the version, files within the module directory, configuration screen shots, and a short description of the module. This file is required.

- Installation instructions for Drupal that create the necessary database tables for the module. This file is required.

- PHP scripts that hook into Drupal and allow you to perform specific tasks. These files are always present, although they're not technically required.

- Template files responsible for the output of the module. These template files can be altered by your theme. These files are optional.

- CSS files, JavaScript files, and images. These files are optional.

As a Drupal administrator, you should never need to look into a module folder. Drupal handles the installation of modules via its Web-based administrative interface.

Core Modules

When you first downloaded and installed Drupal, you were working with its set of "core" files. These files have been defined by the development community as being necessary to build a Web site using Drupal. Included is a set of 40 modules. Not all modules are enabled by default. To see which modules are enabled in your installation of Drupal, use the administrative toolbar to navigate to the Modules page. Figure 11.1 shows the top portion of the core modules. Modules may be either enabled or disabled. Those modules that are enabled can be disabled only if they are not required by another module. If a module is required, it is impossible to disable it without first disabling the dependent modules.

Modules are listed alphabetically. When grouped by functionality, the core modules are as follows.

- **Content and content authoring.** Blog, Book, Comment, Contact, Field UI, Forum, PHP Filter, Poll, Taxonomy
- **Development.** Testing
- **Media.** File, Image
- **People.** Profile
- **Regional and language.** Content translation, Locale
- **Search and metadata.** Path, RDF, Search
- **System.** Database logging, Statistics, Syslog, Tracker, Update manager

ENABLED	NAME	VERSION	DESCRIPTION	OPERATIONS		
☐	Aggregator	7.0-dev	Aggregates syndicated content (RSS, RDF, and Atom feeds).			
☑	Block	7.0-dev	Controls the visual building blocks a page is constructed with. Blocks are boxes of content rendered into an area, or region, of a web page. Required by: Dashboard (enabled)	Help	Permissions	Configure
☐	Blog	7.0-dev	Enables multi-user blogs.			
☐	Book	7.0-dev	Allows users to create and organize related content in an outline.			
☑	Color	7.0-dev	Allows administrators to change the color scheme of compatible themes.	Help		
☑	Comment	7.0-dev	Allows users to comment on and discuss published content. Required by: Forum (enabled), Tracker (disabled)	Help	Permissions	Configure
☐	Contact	7.0-dev	Enables the use of both personal and site-wide contact forms.			
☐	Content translation	7.0-dev	Allows content to be translated into different languages. Requires: Locale (disabled)			
☑	Contextual links	7.0-dev	Provides contextual links to perform actions related to elements on a page.	Help	Permissions	
☑	Dashboard	7.0-dev	Provides a dashboard page in the administrative interface for organizing administrative tasks and tracking information within your site. Requires: Block (enabled)	Help	Permissions	Configure

FIGURE 11.1 Core modules for Drupal 7. Modules are one of disabled or enabled.

- **User interface.** Block, Color, Contextual links, Dashboard, Help, Menu, Overlay, Shortcut, Toolbar
- **Web services.** Aggregator, OpenID
- **Workflow.** Trigger

You can read the description for each of these modules before enabling it. Where available, each module also has a link to its Help page, Permissions page, and Configuration page.

In addition to these modules, the following are required by Drupal and cannot be disabled.

- **Field.** Adds fields to entities such as nodes and users
- **Filter.** Filters content in preparation for display
- **Node.** Allows content to be submitted to the site and displayed on pages
- **System.** Handles general site configuration for administrators
- **User.** Manages the user registration and login system

Later in this chapter, you will learn how to enable and use a number of these core modules to enhance your own Web site.

Contributed Modules

In addition to the 40 core Drupal modules, there are *thousands* of contributed modules. Whether you are looking to add a shopping cart to your site, a newsletter, or a light box for an image gallery, Drupal has a module for it. Available modules are listed at `http://drupal.org/project/modules`. These modules have been created by professional and amateur Web developers. Each module is available under the same license as Drupal itself—the GNU Public License. By using this license, the author of the module has given you the legal authority to download, change, and include the modules in your own project. You must in turn share your code with your client under the same license.

Many of the popular Drupal contributed modules are artifacts of completed projects. For example, Views and Panels were created by Earl Miles while working at Sony Music Entertainment; the NodeEmbed and Akami modules were both created by the WhiteHouse.gov team. Developers have chosen to contribute their work to the pool of "contrib" modules because they understand the value of shared code. By releasing their work into the open, others will help find tiny errors that may be present in the code. The users may even suggest improvements and submit their own code back to the project. Whole subcommunities exist around some of the most popular modules. They have discussions using online chat software and the Drupal discussion board and sometimes even have their own Web sites for specific contributed modules.

> **Drupal Developers Are (Often) Volunteers**
> Most developers participate in the Drupal community on a voluntary basis. Being polite and helpful is always essential in the Drupal community.

The quality of the contributed modules ranges from "meh" to "OMG! Awesome!" The community carefully evaluates all code that is added to Drupal core. For example, the Content Construction Kit was first created in 2006. It allows administrators to add any custom field to any content type. Over the years it developed into an essential part of Drupal and was finally added to core in Drupal 7, where it is now referred to as the Field module. For some developers, whose job relies on how their module works, it is too great of a risk to have the community responsible for part of their job—they choose to continue development of their code as a contributed module. It is, however, very exciting when a contributed module is considered important enough to be adopted into the core of Drupal. This means more stability for site builders and those who build complementary modules on top of the base functionality of Drupal core.

Finding Modules

With several thousand modules to choose from on Drupal.org, it can be a little over-whelming to find the right one for your needs. Throughout this book, you will receive recommendations on which modules are appropriate for specific types of Web sites. This section outlines the strategies you will need to find modules that are not covered in this book.

There are a number of different strategies to choosing the module that's right for you.

- **Read a lot.** Follow the Drupal Planet news feed (`http://drupal.org/planet`) and read the case studies on Drupal.org. Read blogs, magazine articles, the Drupal.org discussion forum, and books to see what other people are using.
- **Scan the list of available modules.** Drupal.org lists modules by category. Categories are sorted by the number of modules available and range from utility (more than 900 modules) to path management (less than 20 modules).

This is the most time-consuming way of familiarizing yourself with each of the modules.

- **Search the Web for the phrase *top drupal modules*.** A number of Drupal community members have put together their personal "best of" list. Just because a module was listed as a top module does not mean you should immediately install it. Remember to install only modules you actually need. Some of these lists are also for previous versions of Drupal. For example, many list CCK; however, as of Drupal 7, this module has been incorporated into Drupal core.

- **Monitor the new modules feed.** Most won't be worth your time; however, you can stay up to date with what's being released into the pool of contributed modules by following this RSS feed: `http://drupal.org/taxonomy/term/14/0/feed`.

Once you've found a module you want to use, you need to make sure there is a version that is appropriate for your site. Drupal modules must match the core version you are running. For example, if you were running a Drupal 7 Web site and you wanted to install the module Views, it would be appropriate to download and install version 7.x-3.0-beta3, but it would not be appropriate to download and install version 6.x-2.12. There are significant database changes between each version of Drupal—the modules are not backward compatible. In other words, a module for Drupal 6 will not work with Drupal 7.

Within each major release there may be both a Recommend version and a Development version of the module. Choosing the Recommended version is almost always... recommended; however, sometimes there is a bug that directly affects you, and the fix is available only in the Development version. For small-scale Web sites, try the Recommended version first. Modules occasionally undergo a massive rewrite within a specific version of Drupal core. In this case, there may be an Other release available. Read the notes carefully when an Other release is available to ensure there are no compatibility issues with modules you have already installed on your Web site.

> **Create an Account on Drupal.org**
> All development activity is centralized on the Drupal.org Web site. To participate in the community, you will need an account on the Web site. Membership is free and allows you to post questions in the Support forum and in the individual issue queues for each of the projects hosted on Drupal.org's infrastructure. To create an account, complete the form at `http://drupal.org/user/register`.

Nine times out of ten installing a module will work exactly the way you think it should, and you'll be off to the metaphorical races. However, every now and then something bad happens. If you get an error message when you try to install your contributed module, go back to the module's project page and search for the text of the error message. A small search area is provided on each project page. You may have specific on-screen error messages you need to resolve, or you may simply find things don't work the way you thought they ought to work. If you find a solution is available in the Development version of the module, it may be appropriate to upgrade the module. If you are unsure, leave a comment in the issue queue describing how your problem is unique from what is described.

Evaluating Contributed Modules

Choosing the right set of modules for your Web site is essential. Throughout this book you will receive recommendations on which modules are appropriate for specific types of Web sites. This section outlines the strategies you will need to evaluate modules that are not covered in this book.

All modules available for Drupal are listed at `http://drupal.org/project/modules`. Figure 11.2 shows the list of all available Drupal modules. With over 8000 modules, you'll want to take advantage of the advanced search options on this page. Each module summary includes the title, the date the module was last updated, and a short description of the module.

These summaries will help you evaluate the module. Your initial evaluation should include the following check points.

- **Is there a stable version available?** Each time a new version of a module is available, the developer will decide whether this is the Recommended version (highlighted with a green background) of the module or a Development version of the module (highlighted with a pink background).

- **When was the code last released? Is there active development on this module?** Code is always being improved upon. Changes may include security fixes, new functionality, or bug repairs. Check the Date column next to the revision number. Any release that has not had at least one update in the last six months may not be suitably maintained, and there may not be an active community to answer your questions if you need help. It may also mean there are unfixed security vulnerabilities in the code.

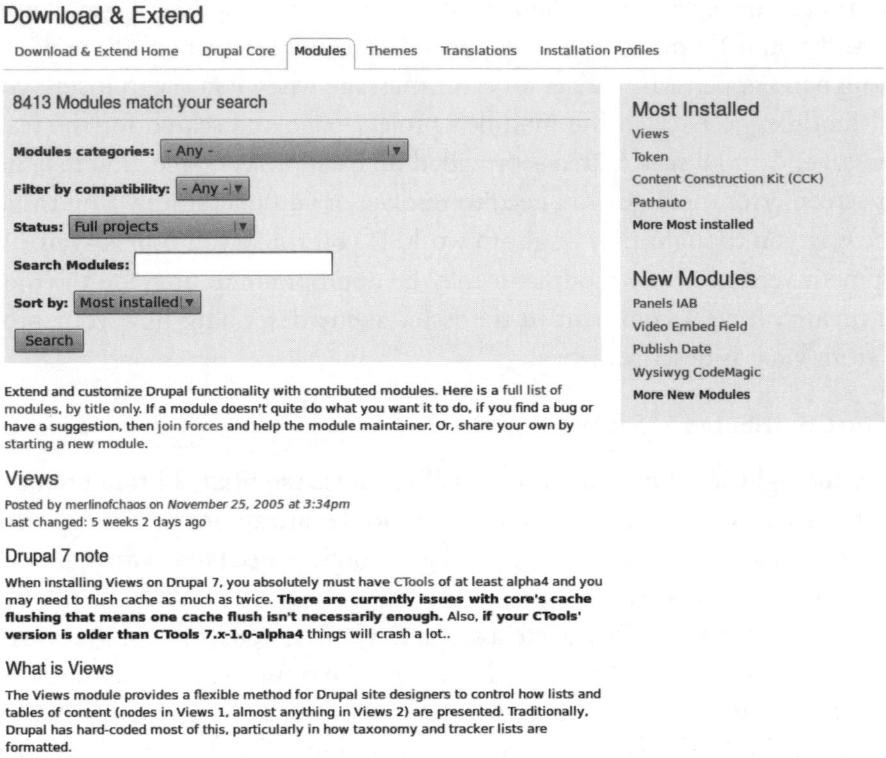

Download & Extend

Download & Extend Home   Drupal Core   **Modules**   Themes   Translations   Installation Profiles

---

8413 Modules match your search

Modules categories: - Any -   ▼

Filter by compatibility: - Any - ▼

Status: Full projects   ▼

Search Modules: [   ]

Sort by: Most installed ▼

[Search]

Extend and customize Drupal functionality with contributed modules. Here is a full list of modules, by title only. If a module doesn't quite do what you want it to do, if you find a bug or have a suggestion, then join forces and help the module maintainer. Or, share your own by starting a new module.

Views

Posted by merlinofchaos on *November 25, 2005 at 3:34pm*
Last changed: 5 weeks 2 days ago

Drupal 7 note

When installing Views on Drupal 7, you absolutely must have CTools of at least alpha4 and you may need to flush cache as much as twice. **There are currently issues with core's cache flushing that means one cache flush isn't necessarily enough. Also, if your CTools' version is older than CTools 7.x-1.0-alpha4** things will crash a lot..

What is Views

The Views module provides a flexible method for Drupal site designers to control how lists and tables of content (nodes in Views 1, almost anything in Views 2) are presented. Traditionally, Drupal has hard-coded most of this, particularly in how taxonomy and tracker lists are formatted.

Most Installed

Views

Token

Content Construction Kit (CCK)

Pathauto

More Most installed

New Modules

Panels IAB

Video Embed Field

Publish Date

Wysiwyg CodeMagic

More New Modules

FIGURE 11.2 The project modules page, `http://drupal.org/project/modules`, allows you to locate relevant Drupal modules.

- **Are there any known show-stopping issues?** Every project on Drupal has an issue queue where people can post bugs and feature requests about each module. Every project page has a link to its respective issue queue. Click through and scan the queue to see whether there are any issues that will cause you grief.

- **Whose code is it?** As a novice to the community, you won't recognize a lot of names, but the more time you spend evaluating modules, the more names you will recognize. On the summary there is a link to the primary developer's profile page. For example, the Pathauto module (`http://drupal.org/project/pathauto`) is led by Greggles. His profile (`http://drupal.org/user/36762`) indicates he's made more than 1,000 code contributions to more than 30 projects. He contributes documentation, is a member of the Drupal security team, and has been attending Drupal conferences for several years. Based on these contributions and experiences, we expect his code to be very high quality.

If the summary for the module you are interested in using passes the first three check points, you may dig a little deeper in your evaluation. Click the module title and proceed to its main project page. Figure 11.3 shows the project page for the Pathauto module (`http://drupal.org/project/pathauto`).

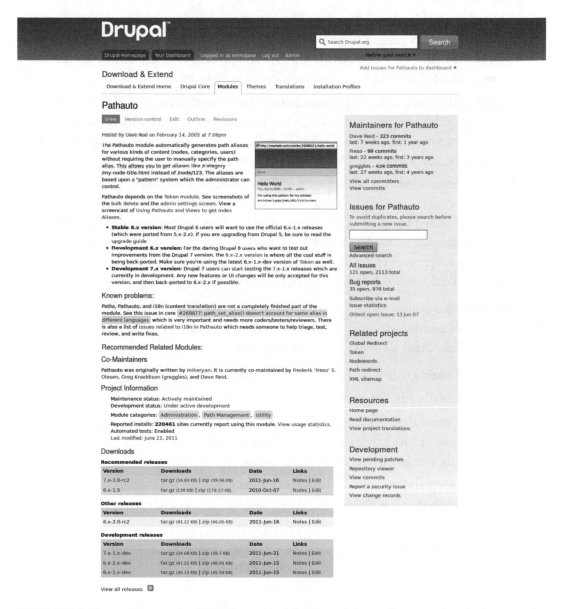

FIGURE 11.3 The project page for the Pathauto module lists active contributors and recent issues and gives a full description of the project including links to related modules and additional documentation.

On this next pass, look for the following elements.

- **Is there a link for documentation?** Check at the bottom of the page. Click through and read through the pages that are there. Does it make sense? Does it address your concerns?

- **Does the project have another home page?** This may lead to a page on the Drupal Groups subsite or an off-site Web site. If there is a project home page, follow the link and see whether there is an active and responsive community that will be able to answer any questions you may have.

- **Does this module have compatibility issues with other modules?** Some dependencies are listed on Pathauto module page; however, there are no specific versions mentioned. Installing the latest of each of the dependencies should be sufficient. This is not always the case. Read carefully.

- **Does the module do what you need it to do?** At every step of the evaluation process look carefully for things that may prevent you from accomplishing what you need to do. Even if the module has been recommended by another person, be sure to read as much as you can before committing to the module. There are often several different ways of solving a problem, and the solution that worked for another site may not be perfect for yours.

Time now for round three of your evaluation: the Drupal Modules review site (http://drupalmodules.com). Figure 11.4 shows the review page for Pathauto. There are four areas to read as part of your review.

- **Overall ratings.** Located in the top-left corner of the page.
- **Total downloads.** Located under the list of downloads.
- **Related modules.** Located to the right of the overview. Sometimes the module you've chosen isn't quite right. Check other modules listed here to see whether something else is a better fit to your needs.
- **Reviews.** At the bottom of the page is a list of all reviews written for this module. Read them all with a grain of salt and look for overall trends of content or discontent.

Equipped with your module selections, the next step is to install the modules you need to build your site.

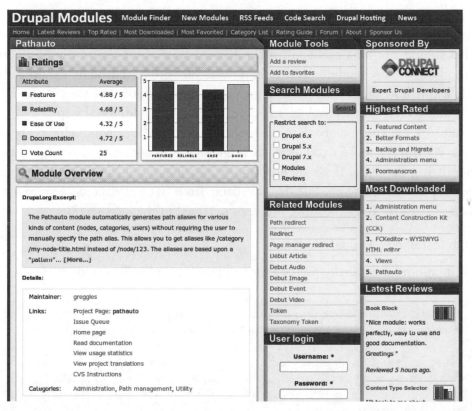

FIGURE 11.4 The Drupal Modules review page for the Pathauto module. Numeric ratings are given at the top of the review; qualitative reviews are listed at the bottom (below the visible portion of this screen shot).

Installing Modules

The hardest part of installing a Drupal module is choosing which module to install. Once you've made that decision, the installation will be easy. (Some modules get a little tricky again if the configuration requires a lot of steps.)

Be Cautious: Create Backups

Wherever possible, you should not install a contributed module on a live Web site—always test it in a development environment first. If you do not have a development environment, create a backup of your Web site before installing a new module.

Sometimes changes are made that cannot be reversed and will permanently alter the way your site functions.

This should not be a problem for the Recommended version of popular contributed modules or core modules; however, it never hurts to be a little bit cautious. If you already know how often your hosting provider creates backups of your Web site, you may be able to rely on this backup and continue without additional steps.

To create a backup, look back to the tools you used in the previous chapter to install Drupal. Within the tool set you used, there should be an option to also create a backup of an existing database. If no such option exists, make the first module you install the Backup and Migrate module. It is available from `http://drupal.org/project/backup_migrate`. Install it using the steps outlined in the next section.

Steps to Installing a Drupal Module

Installing modules is usually pretty easy and requires only a few steps.

> **Find Out More About Your Module**
> If you are working with a new-to-you module, it is generally a good idea to download the module from Drupal.org and look for a file named `README.txt` or `INSTALL.txt`. This file often contains information about what additional steps may be required to install or configure the module, help text on how to use the module once it is set up, and any additional information that is specific to this version of the module.

If your Web site is available from a public Web server, you can use the following steps (this will work for most people).

1. Locate the latest version of the module you want to install. Make sure the version you have selected matches your version of Drupal. For example, you cannot use Drupal 6 modules with Drupal 7.

2. Copy the download link for the module you want to install. On a Windows computer, right-click the download link and select "Copy link location." On a Mac, Ctrl-click the download link and select "Copy link location." The text may differ slightly for your browser. Since we are using Drupal itself to install the module, you should be able to use either the `.tar.gz` or `.zip` format. If you were downloading the module to your computer, you would need to select a compression format you could open—most operating systems are able to open a `.zip` archive without having to install additional software.

3. In your Drupal installation, use the toolbar to navigate to the Modules page.

4. Click the link "Install new module." You will be directed to a page where you can specify the download link for the module you want to install, or you can upload the module from your computer.

5. Paste the link you copied in step 2 into the URL field. Scroll to the bottom of the screen and click Install.

6. Enter your authentication information for the Web server. This is the same user name and password that you would use if you were connecting to your Web server with an FTP account. Contact your hosting provider if you are unsure of this information.

7. Assuming there were no errors during this process, you should now be able to enable your module. Using the toolbar, navigate to Modules. Scroll through the list and find the module you just installed. Click the check box beside the module name. Scroll to the bottom of the screen and click "Save configuration."

8. Your module (and any installed dependencies) should now be available for configuration. Next to each module you will see up to three links: Help, Permissions, and Configure. Click the link Configure to complete the process of installing your module. If you do not see a configuration link, there may still be configuration options for your module. In the administrative toolbar, click the link Configuration and look for your module. In very rare cases you will sometimes need to clear Drupal's cache before the module configuration screen appears. This option is under Configuration > Performance.

Install Profiles

In addition to each of the individual modules, Drupal offers prepackaged install profiles. These install profiles can be downloaded from `http://drupal.org/project/ installation+profiles`. When this book was written, there were only three install profiles available for Drupal 7. This number will increase as Drupal 7 matures and more contributed modules are upgraded. This book assumes you'll be working with Drupal core and downloading all the relevant modules for your specific use case; however, install profiles are pretty cool, and as Drupal increases in complexity, I hope the community turns more to these preconfigured versions of Drupal to help ease the installation process and overall deployment learning curve.

The install profiles, also known as *distributions*, hosted on Drupal.org include the latest version of Drupal, specific contributed modules, and a configuration wizard. Install profiles that I've either used, or had recommended to me, include the following.

- **Acquia Drupal** (`http://acquia.com/downloads`) comes with a lot of the common modules preinstalled and preconfigured.

- **Innovation News** (`http://drupal.org/project/innovationnewsprofile`) allows you to easily create a newspaper Web site. Along the same lines is Open-Publish (`http://drupal.org/project/openpublish`).

- **Demonstration Site** (`http://drupal.org/project/demo_profile`) allows you to re-create the same site over and over again. It is great for testing and sharing configuration files with your co-workers. The Patterns install profile from Gravitek may also be interesting (`http://drupal.org/project/patterns_profile`).

- **UberDrupal** (`http://drupal.org/project/uberdrupal`) is an install profile for the popular e-commerce module Ubercart.

- **Fusion Drupal** (`http://drupal.org/project/fusion_distro`) is a great install profile for site builders and designers using the Fusion starter theme by Top Notch Themes. No more running around to get their 30 or so recommended modules. They do all the tedious assembly so that you can get on with building your site.

Some additional install profiles of note are not hosted on Drupal.org because they "hack core" files in Drupal itself. My favorites include the following.

- **OpenAtrium** is an intranet in a box. It comes with five core features: a blog, a wiki, a to-do list, a shoutbox, and the most un-Drupal theme you've ever seen. You can download OpenAtrium from `http://openatrium.com`.

- **Pressflow** is a distribution of Drupal with integrated performance, scalability, availability, and testing enhancements. Chances are good that if you're reading this book, you don't need Pressflow. Still, it's good to know that when you get bigger, the chefs at Four Kitchens are ready to serve a big supper. You can download Pressflow at `http://pressflow.org`.

These install profiles may, or may not, have been updated to Drupal 7 by the time this book gets into your hands. There may be new install profiles available too.

Summary

Most sites use a combination of core and contributed modules. In this chapter, you learned how to download, install, and configure several of these modules. You also learned how to evaluate which modules are most appropriate for your needs.

With the building blocks installed and configured, we now move on to an in-depth look at creating the framework to hold your content.

Chapter 12

Working with Content Types

O rder. Family. Genus. Species. Biologists know all about the importance of finding similarities between organisms. When you're building Web sites, you need to look for patterns too. These patterns are used to create content types that accurately capture all the information you need to store and display to your site visitors. Creating custom content types allows you to get really fine-grained control of the display of your content too.

Throughout this chapter, you will learn what makes up the individual units of content in Drupal and how to customize them to suit your needs. By the end of this chapter, you will have created your first custom content type with eight unique types of fields. And you won't have to touch any code to do it! It's time to unleash your inner entomologist and get ready to spot the differences between each type of content you need to store and prepare the container it'll be stored in.

Content Patterns

When surfing the Web today, it may seem like there is no limit to the different kinds of content you run into; however, by looking for patterns among Web sites, we can find there are actually a limited number of content patterns, each with a few variations. With its custom fields, you can apply any of the content patterns covered in this chapter to content types for your own Web site. In Chapter 7 you examined your content to see what fields you would need to include on the data entry forms to be able to display this content on your site. In this section, we'll examine other types of data too. As you read about each of the content patterns, look back to your own requirements to see whether you can refine your content types even further.

Basic Content

This content type is the basic building block of any Drupal Web site. It typically includes both a title and some kind of "body" content. Embedded in that content may be images. Examples of basic content include static pages that rarely change, such as content about the company, a returns policy, shipping information, and legal pages (terms of service or a privacy policy).

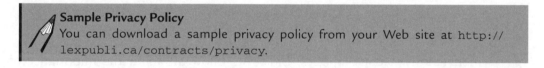

Sample Privacy Policy
You can download a sample privacy policy from your Web site at `http://lexpubli.ca/contracts/privacy`.

This content type is available in Drupal core through the "Basic page" content type. By default this content type is published, does not permit comments, and has only two fields (Title and Body). Another type of basic content is the content that is sorted hierarchically. In Drupal core, the Book module provides Book pages that can be easily sorted into a specific structure. You will learn more about sorting content in Chapter 13.

Time-Stamped Content

Whereas basic content is virtually timeless, a date-sensitive page extends the time-stamped content to add time as context. Examples of this content pattern can be seen as blog entries, newsletters, media releases, or any other type of newsworthy item that was described in the past. An article can have date-sensitive pages sorted by date—usually reverse chronologically and usually featuring date-based descriptions that have already past. This is different from an event content pattern where the event is yet to come.

This content type is available in Drupal core via Article, which is turned on by default. There is also a multiuser blog that provides the content type "Blog entry," which has almost the same characteristics as Article but without the image field. These two content types are, by default, promoted to the front page and have comments enabled.

Time-stamped content can also be syndicated from other sites. Drupal core provides the module Aggregator to allow you to manage how news feeds from outside sources are displayed on your Web site.

Future Events

Your Web site may need to feature descriptions of events that are happening in the future. With the future events content type, you can let people know what's happening in the future instead of the past. Events can be displayed in a calendar format or as a list of upcoming events.

This content type is not available in Drupal core. You can create this content type by adding one or more date fields to represent the start and end dates and times for your event. You can also add fields for the meeting location, attendees, cost, and registration information. You will need to decide for your specific needs whether events should be promoted to the front page or should have comments enabled.

Callouts

This special content type isn't really a content type at all—you may see it as a famous quote on the side of a page, a tip that's been highlighted, or some other snippet of something that appears off to the side of the main content. The easiest way to place these little nuggets is often to avoid Drupal content (the *nodes*) and instead create a custom block that can be placed into any region of your Web site. Creating custom blocks is covered later in this chapter. As a content pattern, a callout is extremely limited. It contains a blob of text, possibly formatted with HTML, and sometimes a title. Callouts are distinguished from basic content by their location (typically offset from the main content), size (typically shorter than the main content), and availability (*blocks* are available only within the context of a theme, unlike a content *node*, which is available from a URL no matter what the theme).

Resources

Resources are the catchall for any content type that includes non-HTML attachments, such as file uploads, off-site Web site links, videos, images, MP3s, and so on. These resources may be curated into collections such as vacation pictures or a portfolio of work samples, or they may exist stand-alone as individual site assets used for anything from a banner image to an instructional video.

> **More Fields Makes for More Consistent Content**
> The more fields you add, the easier it will be for people to maintain uniformity between content pages. You can leave a big empty box and hope people will enter everything correctly, or you can create highly customized content types that give a form field for every piece of data you want content authors to enter.

Figure 12.1 shows a great example of a highly customized resource. The GM Tree Watch Web site (`www.gmtreewatch.org`) catalogs where genetically modified trees have been planted around the world.

Related Items

Some content is best expressed when it is described in relation to another piece of content. For example, an author may have written many books, a singer may have sung

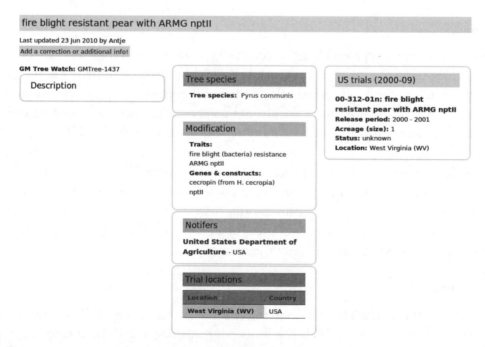

FIGURE 12.1 Sample tree report showing a highly customized content type

many songs, and a workshop may be offered multiple times a year. In these cases, it makes sense to separate the elements that don't change and put them into their own space. From any node on your site you can *reference* other nodes. If you want to use this functionality on your site, you will need to download and install the module References (http://drupal.org/project/references). This functionality was part of CCK but has not been migrated into Drupal core for Drupal 7.

> **Fields in Core Is Not the Same as CCK**
> If you are very familiar with how CCK worked in Drupal 6, you should familiarize yourself with the changes that have been made, because this key module has been rolled into Drupal 7. You can read more at http://drupal.org/project/cck.

Directory of People

A directory of people can be customized as much as any other type of content on your site. The list for each person can include their name, office hours, a photo, and a bio. Related content, such as the classes an instructor teaches, can be listed on the bio page by using references.

The most important feature of this pattern is the author of the content—either the individual is responsible for updating their own profile (each person must have their own unique e-mail address) or the profile is maintained by another person (such as a department Webmaster). If the individual is responsible for updating their own profile, you should add fields to the user profile; if the profile is maintained by a Webmaster, it usually makes more sense to use nodes, not user profiles, to maintain your people directory.

> **Find Out Who's Responsible for Updating the Content**
> Unfortunately, there are a lot of different ways you can tackle this content pattern in Drupal. I say *un*fortunately because if you pick the wrong one, it is impossible to alter content you've added to the site to use the new model without some programming knowledge—or a lot of copying and pasting.

If you choose to add fields to a user profile (instead of using individual nodes), navigate to Administer > Configuration > People > Account settings > Manage profiles. From here you will be able to add fields using the same steps as you will learn for content types later in this chapter.

Data Collection

Finally, we get to the ability to collect data from visitors and registered Web site users. Although collecting data is an action, not a content type, I include it here because there are several different ways to collect data in Drupal and, depending on how you want to use the data, several right answers on how to create a data collection form appropriate to your needs.

- **Comments.** To solicit feedback on any of your Web site nodes, you can simply enable the comment settings. This can be configured per content type and adjusted per node. For example, if you had a custom content type for Company Picnic Proposals that you wanted your employees to provide feedback on, you could simply turn on the comments to solicit feedback.

- **Poll.** Drupal has a built-in content type that allows visitors to vote on questions you create for them. Instructions on how to create polls are covered later in this chapter.

- **Contact form.** Instead of publishing your e-mail address on your Web site, why not solicit comments from people via Drupal's built-in contact form? The Contact module allows you to set up multiple categories of recipients, each of which can have multiple destination e-mails. This module was discussed in Chapter 9.

- **Custom content form.** Any content type can be used to solicit data from anonymous or authenticated site users. For example, you might want to have an application form on your Web site that potential employees use to submit their resume and contact information. Use the instructions later in this chapter to create a custom content type and then adjust the permissions so that only appropriately authenticated users can see the content submitted.

- **Extracted data.** If you want to be able to easily extract collected content from your Drupal site, you should look at the module Webform (`http://drupal.org/project/webform`). When you use this module, each node collects submissions via a Web form. These submissions can be downloaded to your computer and opened in a spreadsheet.

Custom

Sometimes these content types are extended in very specific ways with additional code. Recipes are an example of this, available from the Recipe module (`http://drupal.org/project/recipe`). This content type features everything you'd need to make an online recipe book—title, description, ingredients, and instructions on how to make each recipe. Although you could do that with a custom content type and relevant fields, the Recipe module includes many features that are specific to this content type. For example, a built-in calculator will help you convert a recipe from two servings to four, and you can export recipes in formats that are compatible with desktop applications.

Default Content Types

Drupal core ships with two content types enabled (Article and Basic page) and another four disabled but available for use (Blog entry, Book page, Forum topic, and Poll). In addition to these six content types, you can add content to your site through user-based comments and blocks. Each time you create a new instance of a content type, you are creating a node. Let's take a look at nodes generally and then more specifically at each of Drupal's core content types.

Properties of a Node

Every node in Drupal has a core set of properties. Each content type will include these basic properties and—in most cases—additional fields. These properties can be turned off or on and set to be displayed or hidden. Figure 12.2 shows a sample wireframe displaying common node properties.

- **Title.** This must be entered to create a new node. It is always displayed.
- **Body.** This is the main text for your node—technically an optional field.
- **Summary or Teaser.** This is optional. By default the first 600 characters are used as the summary text. You can adjust the number of characters used per content type. You can also change the text of the summary within the editing screen for each node.
- **Author and date information ("submitted by *author name* on *date*").** This is an optional display setting. It is turned on by default but can be disabled.
- **Node links ("read more" and related categories).** This cannot be altered from the user interface. It requires a custom PHP script to alter the display.
- **Date created and last updated.** These are not displayed. It can be used by other modules, such as Views, to create a chronological list of content.
- **Workflow.** Default toggles can be set to on/off for published, promoted to front, sticky at top of lists, and whether a new version of the content is created

each time the node is edited (like an "undo" button). By default content is published, promoted to the front page, not sticky at the top of lists, and no new revisions are created.

- **Comments.** By default comments are enabled on all content types. If you don't have spam-filtering software enabled and you don't want to solicit comments on your site, you may want to disable the Comment module instead of disabling comments per content type.

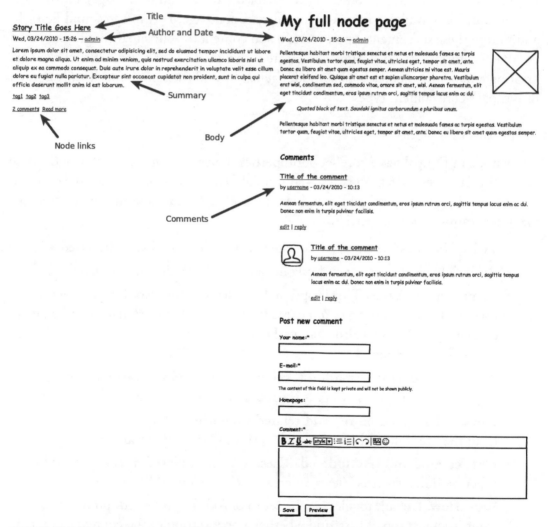

FIGURE 12.2 The sample summary (left) shows title, summary, author and date information, and node links. The sample node (right) shows title, body, author, and date information and comments.

Article

Articles are used for content that follows the time-stamped content pattern discussed earlier. By default new articles are as follows.

- Published to the front page
- Enabled for comments
- Not version controlled (in other words, revisions are not created and saved)

Fields for this content type include the following.

- Title
- Body
- Image
- Tags

The content type Article is enabled by default by Drupal.

Basic Page

Basic pages are used to create static pages that follow the basic content pattern. By default new entries made from this content type are as follows.

- Published but not promoted to the front page
- Not enabled for comments
- Not version controlled (that is, revisions are not created and saved)

Fields for this content type include only the following.

- Title
- Body

This is enabled by default when installing Drupal.

Blog Entry

Blog entries are much like the core content type Article; however, additional functionality is built into the module to permit multiuser blogs. By default new blog entries are as follows.

- Published and promoted to the front page
- Enabled for comments
- Not version controlled (that is, revisions are not created and saved)

Fields for this content type include only the following.

- Title
- Body

To enable this content type, you must enable the core module Blog. You can easily extend this content type to include an image field and tags.

Book Page

Book pages are used to create static pages that follow the basic content pattern *and* that have hierarchical content. The Book module automatically creates a new navigation block for each new book created. According to the Drupal help pages, this content type is well suited to "creating structured, multi-page content, such as site resource guides, manuals, and wikis. It allows you to create content that has chapters, sections, subsections, or any similarly-tiered structure." By default new entries made from this content type are as follows.

- Are published but not promoted to the front page
- Accept user-contributed comments
- Are not version controlled (that is, revisions are not created and saved)

Fields for this content type include only the following fields.

- Title
- Body

To enable this content type, you must enable the core module Book. You can easily extend the content type to include additional fields once it has been enabled.

Forum Topic

A forum topic starts a discussion thread within a forum. People can then discuss this topic by adding their comments to it. Forums consist of at least three levels of structure: *comments* that respond to *topics* that are sorted into *forums* (and optionally, these forums can be sorted into *containers*). Containers and forums are both *taxonomy terms,* topics are *nodes*, and comments are *comments*. (Sometimes we like to surprise people with our naming scheme.) By default new forum topics are as follows.

- Published but not promoted to the front page
- Enabled for comments
- Not version controlled (that is, revisions are not created and saved)

Fields for this content type include only the following.

- Title
- Body

To enable this content type, you must enable the module Forum. Forum topics are sometimes extended to include the ability to upload a relevant file or image for discussion. To customize the forums and containers available on your site, navigate to Administration > Structure > Forums.

Polls

If you've ever found it difficult to get a straight "yes" or "no" from your site visitors, you're going to love the Poll module. To create a new poll on your site, first enable the Poll module and then complete the following steps.

1. From the administration shortcut, click the link "Add content" and choose Poll.
2. Enter a question and possible responses (Figure 12.3). You can change the order of the responses by dragging and dropping the fields into a new position.
3. In the poll settings fieldset, you can adjust the poll status to be open or closed. You can also set the poll to automatically close after a specific amount of time by altering the drop-down box "Poll duration."

FIGURE 12.3 Enter your question and answers for the poll.

4. By default site visitors can comment on your poll. If you want to disable this, scroll to the Comment settings, and change the setting to "closed."

5. You can publish the poll, as a node, to the front page of your site by adjusting the settings within the node. If you prefer to put the poll into a sidebar of your site (Figure 12.4), navigate to the Blocks administration page (Administration > Structure > Blocks) and change the region for the block labeled "Most recent poll" to one that is appropriate for your theme.

6. By default only administrators can read, vote, and view results on polls. To open your polls to a wider audience, navigate to Administer > People > Polls. Adjust the permissions for the content type polls and the poll-specific settings: "Vote on polls," "Cancel and change own votes," and "View voting results."

Once the poll has been created, site visitors can start voting on your site and viewing the results (Figure 12.5).

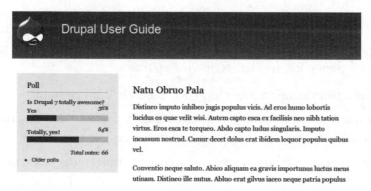

FIGURE 12.4 Your poll will be published to the front page by default, but you can display it as a block in a region too.

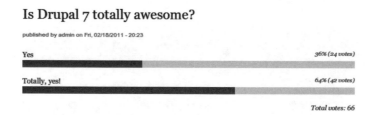

FIGURE 12.5 The results from the new poll

Blocks

You can make custom content appear in *any region* on your Web site using blocks. I like to think of blocks as "sidebar content." You can use blocks to feature special content (for example "Red shoes on sale today only!") or use it as a notice area (for example, "School is closed today due to bad weather") or place any custom HTML into the sidebar of your site (for example, your mailing list sign-up form).

To create a custom block that can be placed into any region of your Web site, complete the following steps.

1. Using the administrative dashboard, navigate to Structure > Blocks.
2. Click the link "Add block."
3. Enter a block description (used in the administrative section only) and the text that you want to appear on the contact page (this goes into the block body).
4. Scroll to the fieldset for the region settings. Select the region you want this block to appear in for your theme (make sure you choose the right theme; all enabled themes will be listed, not just the default theme).
5. Scroll to the bottom and click "Save block."

    One way to use a custom block is to add your mailing address, your phone number, or a message to your site's contact form. (You will need to enable your site's contact form for this to work. Instructions are in Chapter 9.) Complete the previous steps 1 to 3 and then proceed with the following steps.
6. Scroll to the fieldset for the region settings. Select the region you would like this block to appear in for your theme (make sure you choose the right theme; all enabled themes will be listed, not just the default theme).
7. Scroll to the Visibility settings. Select the vertical tab Pages. Enable the option "Only the listed page." In the large text area below the option you just enabled, type **contact** (all lowercase).
8. Scroll to the bottom and click "Save block."

Your new message should now appear on the contact form. Navigate to this page to check your work.

Managing Content Types

For each of the six default content types (Article, Basic page, Blog, Book, Forum, and Poll), you can adjust any of the default settings to suit your needs. In this section, you will learn how to use the administrative controls for managing content types and then create your own custom content type. Each content type has three basic groups of settings: metadata, fields, and display settings. Most of a content type's features are the fields it uses, which we'll cover in the next section.

Basic Settings

For each content type there are only a few settings. To make adjustments to these settings, navigate to Administer > Structure > Content types. Then click the link "edit" next to the content type you'd like to manage. In this section, I've used the "Basic page" content type as an example.

At the top of the configuration screen are the name and description for this content type. As I mentioned earlier, you can change the names of the default content types. (For example, if you'd rather your article were a blog entry, this is the place to make the change.) The name and description are displayed when you are creating a new node and are selecting which content type you would like the node to be.

The bottom half of the configuration screen (Figure 12.6) is the workhorse for configuring content type.

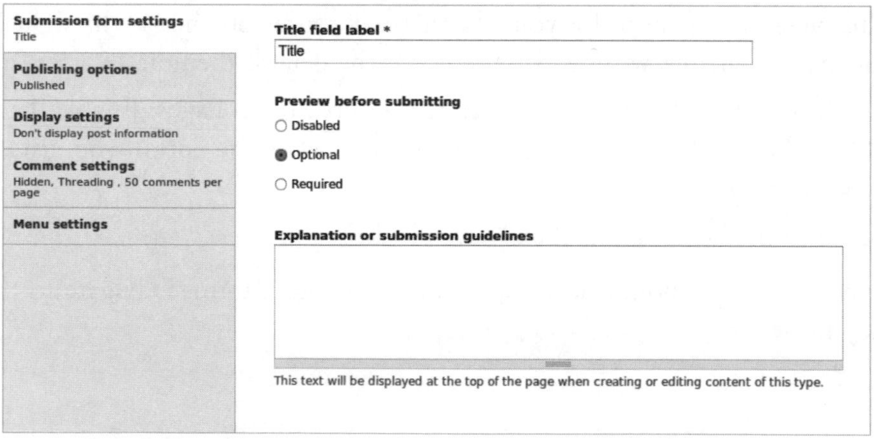

FIGURE 12.6 Configuration options for the default content type "Basic page"

Along the left is a set of vertical tabs that summarize the setting name and the current attributes that are set. By clicking each of the tabs on the left, you can change the following settings.

- **Submission form settings.** This alters the Title field label (for example, to "Tree species") and adds helper text to those creating new content on your site.

- **Publishing options.** This provides default options for the following: Published, Promoted to front page, Sticky at top of lists (used mostly in forums), Create new revision (handy for tracking changes over time to a particular page).

- **Display settings.** The display settings allow you to enable or disable the "submitted by Username on date" text when displaying content. If your content includes date-based information (such as promoting an upcoming event), it is a good idea to remove the publication date of the node to avoid confusion.

- **Comment settings.** Select from Hidden/Open/Closed. If Hidden or Open is selected, you can also choose how many comments are shown on a page, whether the comments have titles, and whether comments will be threaded (indented) according to the reply order.

- **Menu settings.** Select the menus this content type can be added to. For example, you may have a custom content type for documentation that should never be available from the Main menu, only from the User menu.

You can adjust any of these settings for existing content types, and you can create your own content types too.

Creating Custom Content Types

To create your own custom content type, you will need to know the following for every type of content you want to create.

- The properties of each field (for example, will data be captured best as a terse text description, or will you need to use a controlled vocabulary and preset the options in a selection list?)

- The grouping of individual fields within the content type, especially for long forms and complicated content types

- Optional fields vs. required fields

- The default settings for each of comments and publishing settings

With this information in hand, you are ready to create new types of content, and their associated input forms, in your Web site. The example in this chapter is the content type Portfolio (content pattern resource)—I chose it because it can be extended to include a wide range of field types.

> **Do You Really Need a New Content Type?**
> Generic content types are reusable, but I really like making "Blog entries" out of Blog content types. If you're a stickler for names too, consider renaming a generic content type so it matches your needs. For example, the content type Article can be renamed "Blog entry."

To create the shell for your new content type, complete the following steps.

1. Navigate to Administer > Structure > Content types. Click the link "Add content type."

2. Fill in the Name and Description fields for your new content type using values that are appropriate for your custom content type.

3. Adjust the default settings as follows:

   - **Name.** Portfolio.

   - **Description.** A summary of my work.

   - **Title field label (part of "Submission form settings").** Project.

   - **Publishing options.** Published, disable "Promoted to front page."

   - **Display settings.** Disable the setting "Display author and date information."

   - **Comments settings.** Closed.

   - **Available menus (part of Menu settings).** Navigation (disable the option for the Main menu).

     Leave all other settings as the default options.

4. Scroll to the bottom of the configuration screen and click "Save content type."

You will be returned to the summary of all content types after successfully creating your new content type. You are now ready to extend your new content type by adding fields.

Working with Fields

In Drupal we customize content types by adding fields. Each time you add a new field, a new form element will be added to the node-editing screen. Your content type fields can be virtually anything you need them to be. You might want to upload a picture, enter sizing information for a sweater you knit, capture your thoughts about the day's weather, rate a movie you're reviewing, or do just about anything else. Fields can be added to any content type in Drupal. First I will show you how to manage existing fields, and then you will learn how to add new fields to an existing content type.

Manage Display

Every field for each content type has its own display settings. I think it's easier to learn how to customize existing fields before trying to add your own. Within the display settings you can change the order of each field and where and how the field's label is displayed. There are also field-specific settings, such as the number of characters to show in a summary or the size of the image. To configure the display settings for your content type, navigate to Structure > Content types. Then click the link "Manage display" for your content type of choice. Figure 12.7 shows the default settings for the content type Article.

From top to bottom there are three fields that can be customized: Image, Body, and Tags. The Label column shows us that only Tags, which displays at the bottom, has a label displayed, and, by default, it is displayed above the linked tags. The label can be any of Above, Inline, or Hidden for any field you add to your content type.

In the third column are the settings for this particular field type. Most fields will have at least two formats that can be used to display the field (the default format, or hide the field from this display). Some formats can be further configured (as shown for

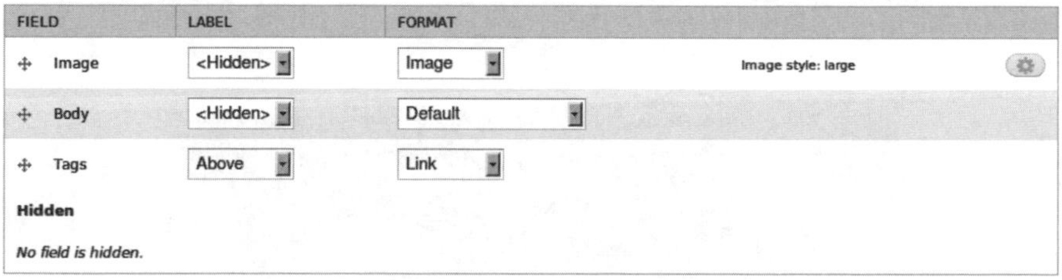

FIELD	LABEL	FORMAT		
✛ Image	\<Hidden\>	Image	Image style: large	⚙
✛ Body	\<Hidden\>	Default		
✛ Tags	Above	Link		
Hidden				
No field is hidden.				

FIGURE 12.7 Display settings for the Article content type showing the three fields whose display properties can be adjusted

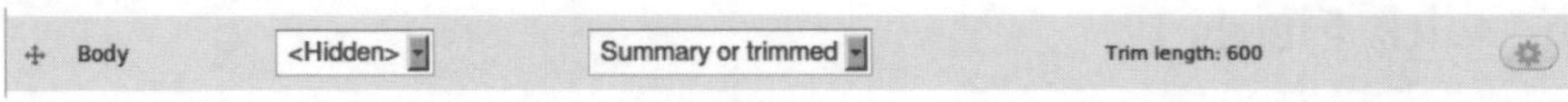

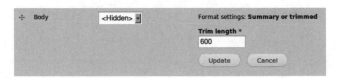

FIGURE 12.8 Changing the format of any field may reveal new configuration options—look for the cog on the far right.

the image), whereas others have no additional configuration options (as shown for the Body field). However, when you change the format, new configuration options may appear. For example, if you were to change the Body format to Summary or Trimmed, a new configuration option would be displayed (Figure 12.8).

Clicking the configuration cog on the far right opens the inline configuration options for this format (Figure 12.9). If you choose to make adjustments, you will need to click the inline "update" button *as well as* the "save" button at the bottom of the configuration screen.

Display format options for common fields include the following.

- Number of characters to display on trimmed/summary text
- Size of an image (but not alignment, which must be done with CSS)
- Link the node title to its full node
- Remove HTML/formatting from this text before displaying it

Drupal provides several default displays that can be configured individually. At the bottom of the Manage Display tab is a closed fieldset labeled "Custom display settings." Clicking this title will allow you to add custom settings for more *view modes*. (Don't confuse this with Views, which you will learn about in Chapter 13.) If you add any view modes, they will become available at the top right of the screen (below the tabs). By default only Default and Teaser are selected for custom settings. Look just beneath the tabs across the top of the administrative overlay, and you will see this secondary navigation area (Figure 12.10).

FIGURE 12.9 Adjust the format options inline for the number of characters displayed in a summary. Don't forget to update and then save to preserve your changes.

FIGURE 12.10 Two rows of tabs at the top right of the overlay: The second row allows you to choose which view mode you want to configure.

In most cases you can also change the characteristics of the individual fields. Sometimes you will be limited in the changes you can make because it will affect the way information is stored—including the loss of data if you're manipulating an existing content type. Let's customize the content type node and rename the field label Body to a more appropriate title, such as "About this project."

1. Navigate to the tab labeled "Manage fields" for your content type: Administration > Structure > Content types > Portfolio > Manage fields.
2. Next to the field Body, click the link "edit."
3. Under "Portfolio settings," change Label from Body to "About this project."
4. Scroll to the bottom of the screen and click "Save settings."

Your content type is now updated.

This technique can also be used to manage the display of comment-related fields. Use the tabs labeled "Comment fields" and "Comment display" to customize their settings.

Types of Fields

If you've ever worked with a database, you know there are specific ways that databases like to store information. You can think of these types of fields as a child's sorting block—only circles fit into the circle hole, and only triangles fit into the triangular hole. By using the right type of field, you can perform minor miracles on your data, such as adding numbers, calculating what day of the week May 2 will be this year, forcing minimum or maximum lengths of text, and so on. When Drupal is first installed, there are 13 field types available for use. They give you the ability to work with the following.

- **Choices.** Radio buttons, check boxes, select lists, and on/off single check boxes
- **Files.** Any file type including special handlers for images
- **Numbers.** Decimal, Float, Integer

- **Taxonomy.** Terms
- **Text.** Single-line text input, multiple-line text area, and long text with a summary

> **More Media Handler Modules Are Available**
> If you need media handlers for video and audio, check out the Media module (`http://drupal.org/project/media`). Although it was only in beta when this chapter was first written, it looks like a very promising module. Don't forget to grab a copy of the required Styles module too (`http://drupal.org/project/styles`) if you want to give this module a whirl.

In addition to these field types, I find the following very useful in building many Web sites.

- **Date (`http://drupal.org/project/date`).** This module comes with several formats for dates as well as a pop-up jQuery date picker..
- **Link (`http://drupal.org/project/link`).** Create and customize links to off-site Web pages.
- **References (`http://drupal.org/project/references`).** The References project contains two submodules: Node reference (used to make nodes related to one another) and User reference (used to make nodes related to users).

With all of these field types enabled, you will have a total of 19 different field types, which allows you to create just about any content type you can imagine.

Of course, with that challenge, you're probably going to spend the next 20 minutes thinking of even more field types just to prove me wrong. Maybe you need to have people rate content (see `http://drupal.org/project/fivestar`), add geographic locations (see `http://drupal.org/project/location`), or mathematically manipulate fields (see `http://drupal.org/project/computed_field`). We're only covering the most common field types in this book, but if your needs are great, do explore beyond the basics! I personally find the reviews on `www.drupalmodules.com` very useful for making informed decisions when there are many similar modules available.

Field Type Modules

Almost everything you need to create custom content types is available from Drupal core. Each field type is controlled by its own module. You may need to install some modules to add specific field types.

All of the following modules are enabled by default in a clean installation of Drupal. If any have been disabled, navigate to Administration > Modules and enable them.

- **File.** Enables the field type File.
- **Image.** Enables the field type Image.
- **List.** Enables the field types Boolean, List (float), List (integer), and List (text).
- **Options.** Used by other field types to create the necessary form elements for field types where you can choose between options.
- **Text.** Enables the field types necessary to make text-based content on your site. This is the building block of most nodes.

In addition to these core modules, download and enable my favorite noncore field types.

- **Date** (`http://drupal.org/project/date`). Enable the modules Date, Date API, and Date pop-up for date-based content such as events.
- **Link** (`http://drupal.org/project/link`). Enable the module Link to make links fields that link to external Web sites.
- **References** (`http://drupal.org/project/references`). Enable the modules References and Node Reference.

You are now ready to add fields to a content type. You can either extend an existing content type or create a new content type. Either way, you can add fields only to something that already exists.

Adding Fields

When a content type is first created, it contains only two fields—Title and Body. Adding more fields forces content authors to enter precise bits of information and ensures your content is complete and correct. As an added bonus, you can retrieve and sort nodes based on any fields. Need to sort alphabetically by town name as well as street name? No problem! You will learn about sorting lists of content in Chapter 13. Each time you add a new field to your content type, Drupal automatically updates the node-editing form, allowing you to retroactively add field values to existing nodes.

> **Extending Existing Content Types**
> You can add content fields to both core and contributed content types. For example, if you want to extend the core content type "Basic page" to include images, you could use the instructions included in this section.

Before adding fields to your content type, create a summary of what you want to add. Write down the unique properties of each field. This will help you choose the right field type. We are working on a sample content type, Portfolio, which will have fields described in Table 12.1.

Once each of these fields has been added, the summary of your portfolio content type will look like Figure 12.11. You will be adding these fields throughout this section.

To add a new field, regardless of type, you will always start with the following steps.

1. Navigate to Administer > Structure > Content types. For the content type you'd like to customize, click the link "manage fields."

2. A list of fields will appear for this content type. Near the bottom of the screen is a set of fields labeled "Add new field." Enter a value for the label (human-readable, displayed to users) and field name (machine-readable, not displayed).

3. Select the relevant *field* (type of data to store) from the drop-down list and relevant *widget* (form element to edit the data) from its drop-down list.

4. Scroll to the bottom of the screen and click Save to proceed to the configuration screens for your new field.

TABLE 12.1 Field Attributes for the Content Type Portfolio

Content to Be Stored	Label	Machine Name	Type	Widget
Select list of tasks performed for this project	Type of project	project_type	List (text)	Check boxes/radio buttons
Names of modules used	Key modules	key_modules	Term reference	Autocomplete term widget (tagging)
Length of project in hours	Length of project	project_length	Integer	Text
Date project was completed	Completed	finish_date	Date	Text Field with Date Pop-up Calendar
Screen shots of finished work	Screen shots	screenshots	Image	Image
Web link to client's site	Project URL	url	Link	Link
Node reference to related projects	Related projects	related	Node reference	Autocomplete text field

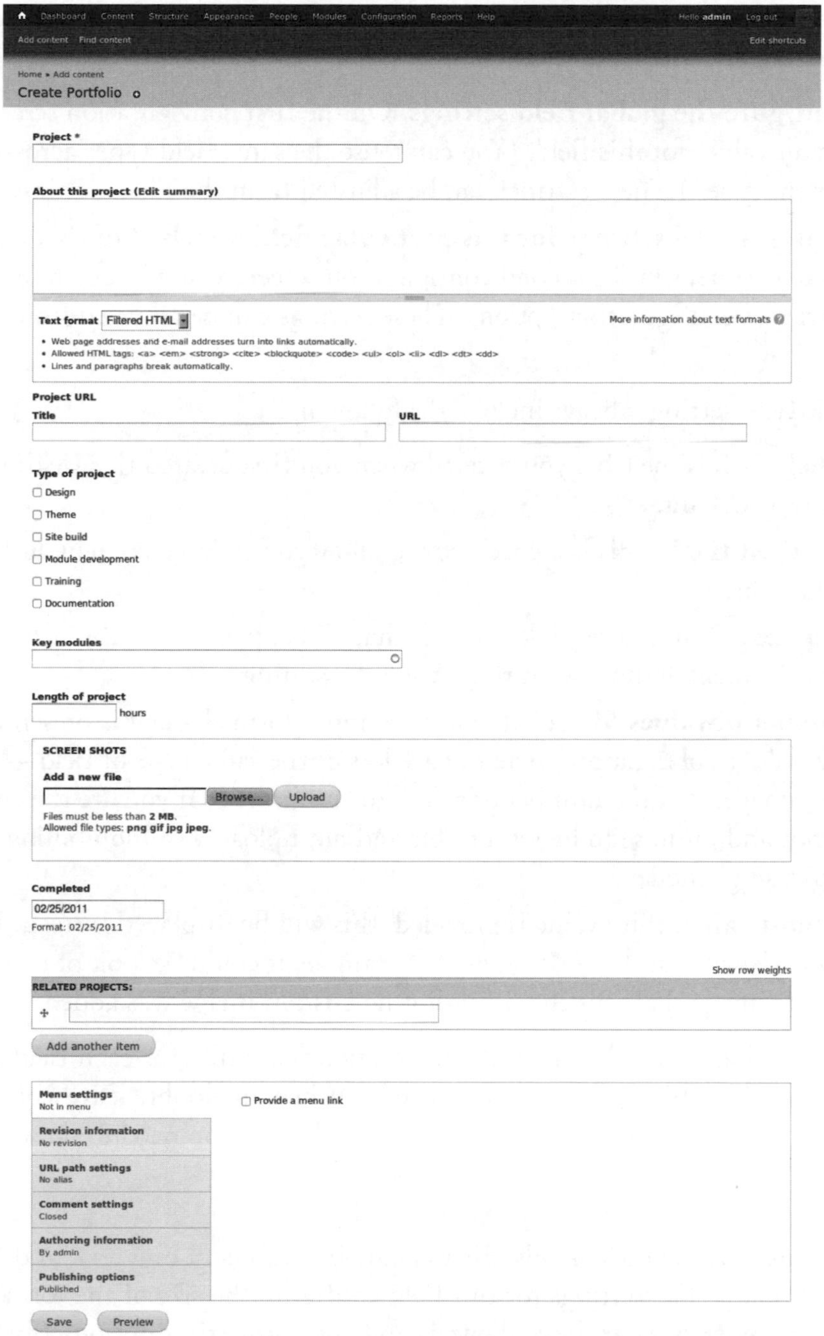

FIGURE 12.11 The Portfolio content type has been created and is ready for use. Two core fields are present (Project, About this project) as well as eight new custom fields.

Next you will configure both the global field settings and the specific field settings for this particular content type.

- **Configure the global field settings.** On the first configuration screen, set the default values for this field. (You can reuse the same field types across multiple content types.) These settings can be adjusted from the Field Settings tab.

- **Configure the settings for this particular field attached to this particular content type.** On the second configuration screen, you will be presented with a series of configuration options. These settings can be adjusted from the Edit tab.

Specific field settings always include the following.

- **Label.** This is the label you entered when you first created this field; it is provided by default.

- **Required field.** This is a check box to allow you to force content authors to add a value.

- **Help text.** This is a terse description that will appear below the field explaining to content authors what they should be adding.

- **Number of values.** By default only one input form element is presented; however, it's often appropriate to have lots of the same type of field—especially with images. Set the number of values to "unlimited" if you are the content author and promise to be responsible and not upload a million billion pictures onto a single node.

- **Default value.** If no value is provided, this will be displayed instead. Possible values depend on the field type—for example, it could be a bit of text or a generic image that tells the site visitor no custom image was added.

While creating new fields, read the instructions carefully for each field type, and choose the options best suited to your needs. When in doubt, leave configuration options as the default values. You can adjust them later if you need to do so.

Text Fields

There are three types of text fields: Text (single-line input), Long text, and Long text without summary. The settings for this field configure the size of the form field, the maximum number of characters allowed, and the formatting options (for example, plain text only). You weren't really expecting more to configure for this, were you? Let's move on to numbers.

Numbers

There are three types of number fields.

- **Decimal.** This is good for very precise numbers, especially dollar values. Thirty-two digits will be stored including those to the right of the decimal marker—and only those digits within the specified number of decimal places will be saved. For example, if a content author enters 42.024 but the decimal places setting is set to 2, the number saved will be 42.02.

- **Float.** Float stores a total of ten digits and will "float" the decimal marker, unlike decimal where the precision is fixed (for example, 8.08437, 6.07, 8.3, and 4 are acceptable float values; but as decimals with a precision of two, these numbers would be 8.08, 6.07, 8.30, and 4.00).

- **Integer.** No decimals allowed; you can enter whole numbers only.

The settings for these field types allow you to configure the following.

- **Minimum and Maximum values.**
- **Prefix and Suffix.** An example is $.
- **Decimal marker.** You can choose between a period and a comma. This is not available for Integers.
- **Precision.** This is the number of digits to store in the database. This applies to the Decimal field type only.
- **Scale.** This is the number of digits to display after the decimal marker. This applies to the Decimal field type only.

For the Portfolio content type, create a new Integer field per Table 12.1. Leave all settings as the default value except change Suffix to "hours."

Link

Useful for creating off-site links, this field type has the following settings.

- **Link title.** This can be Optional, Required, Static (for example, "read more"), or omitted.
- **URL display cutoff.** This is the number of characters to display in the URL before truncating the field and adding an ellipsis.
- **Link target.** This allows you to open link in a new window or in the current window.

- **Rel attribute.** This is most commonly set to "nofollow" to prevent search engines from following the URL (and leaving the site).
- **Additional CSS class.** This is useful if you want to style off-site links to have a fancy icon.

For the Portfolio content type, create a new Link field per Table 12.1. Leave all settings as the default values.

List and Boolean

Lists allow the content author a choice between many items, whereas Boolean fields allow the user to toggle between two possible answers (yes/no; cat/dog; Leafs/Canadiens; Kirk/Picard) or a single on/off switch ("I agree to the following terms and conditions").

When choosing a type of list, you can choose between a select list *or* check boxes and radio buttons. If a single value is allowed, the select list will be a drop-down menu (Figure 12.12) or a set of radio buttons (Figure 12.13). If more than one value is allowed, the select list will be expanded (Figure 12.14) to allow the content author to choose several options (perfect for very long lists) or a set of check boxes (Figure 12.15).

Select, single item
- None -
Select, single item
- None -
- None -
Design
Theme
Site build
Module development
Training
Documentation

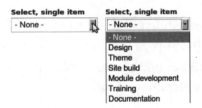

FIGURE 12.12 Select list, one value permitted; displayed closed (left) and open (right)

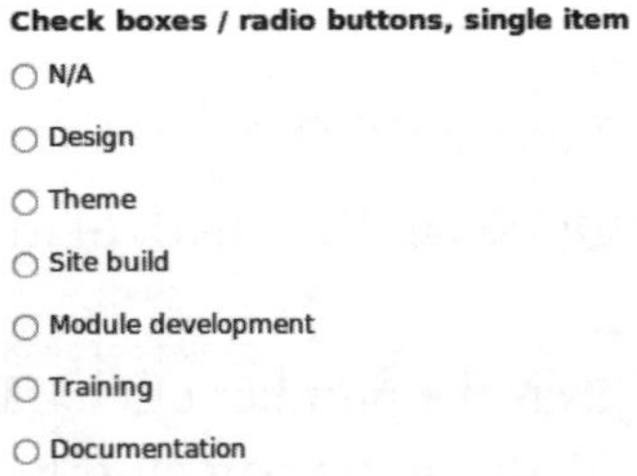

Check boxes / radio buttons, single item
N/A
Design
Theme
Site build
Module development
Training
Documentation

FIGURE 12.13 Radio buttons, one value permitted

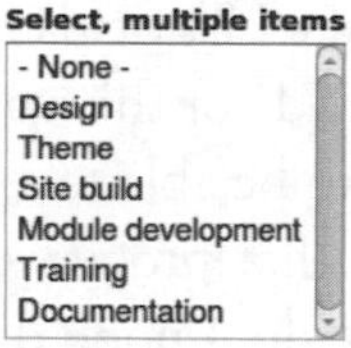

FIGURE 12.14 Select list, unlimited values permitted

Check boxes / radio buttons, unlimited item

☐ Design

☐ Theme

☐ Site build

☐ Module development

☐ Training

☐ Documentation

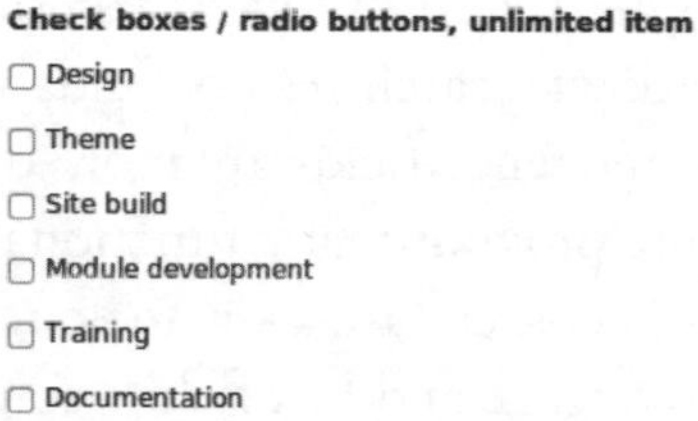

FIGURE 12.15 Check boxes, unlimited values permitted

For the content type Portfolio, create a new List (text) field per Table 12.1. Leave all options as the default values except the following.

- **Allowed values list (each item must be on its own line, omit the commas, as shown in Figure 12.16).** Design|Design, Theme|Theme, Build|Site build, Modules|Module development, Training|Training, Documentation|Documentation
- **Number of values.** Unlimited

Term Reference

This field type allows you to assign tags (taxonomy terms) to your nodes. You can either use a set of predefined terms or make them up as you edit the node (free tagging).

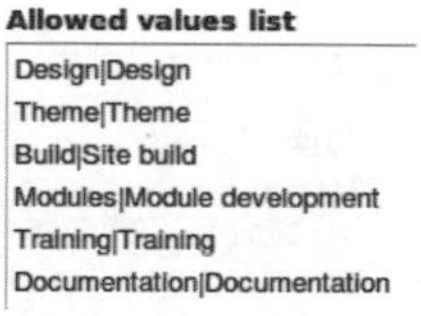

Allowed values list

Design|Design
Theme|Theme
Build|Site build
Modules|Module development
Training|Training
Documentation|Documentation

FIGURE 12.16 Allowed values come in pairs: the machine stored value (first)|the human display text (second).

Term reference fields behave much like List fields from within the node-editing screen; however, they are quite different outside of this context.

List fields are useful if you want to be able to assign a property to an item but don't need to perform tasks according to that property. It is generally easier to apply field styles to List fields so that the individual node display looks consistent and polished without having to muck around with CSS.

If you want people to be able to group similarly tagged items, use the Term reference field. Content groupings are found in image galleries and product catalogs. You can also use terms to narrow down search results fields with Drupal's built-in search engine. In other words, Term reference fields are more difficult to deal with visually, but they provide you with more programmatic functionality especially when it comes to building sites where groups of content are a key to your site navigation. Figure 12.17 shows the output from Term reference and List fields. You can disable the links used in Term reference fields, but there's no way to enable links for List fields.

Clear as mud? Let me share this little secret if you're not sure how to proceed: A lot of the time it's the right choice to use List fields, especially on small Web sites. It's slightly less work to set up a List field, so I usually pick this option; however, more than once I've really regretted my decision to go the quick-and-dirty route. If you choose poorly too, check out the module Views Bulk Operations (`http://drupal.org/project/views_bulk_operations`). With some fancy magic you can create a list of all items with a specific List property and update them *all* to apply specific taxonomy terms with the click of a button. If only the rest of life had that kind of safety net too!

Adding a Term reference field to a content type is really easy, but you must have already created the vocabulary you want to use. Three widget types are available for the Term reference field: select list, check boxes/radio buttons, and the Autocomplete term widget (tagging). The display options for select lists, check boxes, and radio buttons we covered in the section "List and Boolean." These display options force content authors to choose from an existing set of terms within a specific vocabulary.

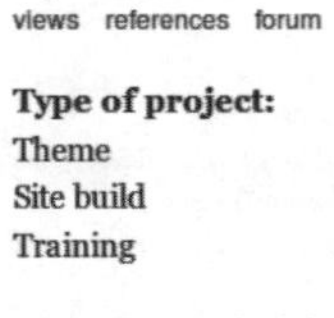

Key modules used:
views   references   forum

Type of project:
Theme
Site build
Training

FIGURE 12.17 Term reference (top) and List (bottom) fields with default styling provided by the Bartik theme

FIGURE 12.18 The Autocomplete widget allows you to create new terms on the spot. Drupal will look for existing terms with the same name. The circle on the far right will spin as Drupal searches for possible matching terms.

Autocomplete is a new type of widget. This option allows you to invent new terms on the spot! Multiple terms can be added by separating each term with a comma. As you type, Drupal will look for terms that start with those letters (Figure 12.18). This is the autocomplete part of free tagging. Each new term you enter is automatically added to the list of terms for that vocabulary.

For the content type Portfolio, create a new Term reference field with the Autocomplete widget per Table 12.1. Leave all options as the default values except the following:

- **Vocabulary.** Tags
- **Number of values.** Unlimited

References

The field "Term reference" allows you to make connections between nodes and taxonomy terms. References work much the same way except it is used to make connections between nodes and between nodes and users. References should be used for content patterns that have related content. References uses the same selection widgets as Term reference (select list, check boxes/radio buttons, and autocomplete text field).

Global settings include the following.

- Content types that can be referenced

Field specific settings include the following.

- **Autocomplete matching.** Choose between Starts with or Contains (default)
- **Size of textfield.**

For the content type Portfolio, create a new Node reference field with the Autocomplete widget per Table 12.1. Leave all options as the default values except the following.

- **Content types that can be referenced**: Portfolio
- **Number of values**: Unlimited

Files

To allow content authors to upload and display images for each node, choose File for both the type and widget of the new field. Image fields have the following settings that can be configured.

- **Enable display field and Files displayed by default.** The display option allows users to choose whether a file should be shown when viewing the content.
- **Allowed extensions.** This is a list of permissible extensions. By default only TXT files are allowed.
- **File directory.** This is a subdirectory of the global files directory to place these images into. If the global files directory is `sites/default/files` and you choose "mp3s" for this field, the files will be available from `sites/default/files/mp3s/`.
- **Maximum upload size.** This is the maximum size for uploaded files. If left empty, the maximum size allowed by your PHP configuration file will be used.
- **Enable description field.** This allows content authors to provide a terse description of the contents of the file, instead of just displaying the file name.
- **Upload destination.** Override the global settings for the upload destination (this will default to a single option of the public files directory if you have not configured your site to support the delivery of private files).

Images

To allow content authors to upload and display images for each node, choose Image for both the type and widget of the new field. Image fields have the following settings that can be configured.

- **Allowed extensions.** This is a list of permissible extensions. By default only PNG, GIF, JPG, and JPEG are allowed.
- **File directory.** This is a subdirectory of the global files directory to place these images into. If the global files directory is `sites/default/files` and you choose "portfolio" for this field, the files will be available from `sites/default/files/portfolio`.
- **Maximum image resolution.** This is the largest height and width of the file content authors may upload.

- **Minimum image resolution.** This is the minimum required dimensions for uploaded images.
- **Maximum upload size.** This is the maximum file size for uploaded files. If left empty, the maximum size allowed by your PHP configuration file will be used.
- **Enable alt and title fields.** This can improve accessibility and search engine rankings. Label your images with `alt` and `title` attributes.
- **Preview Image style.** A small summary image (typically referred to as a *thumbnail*) is provided when you are editing your node. This is the size (image style) that will be used.
- **Upload destination.** This will default to a single option of the public files directory if you have not configured your site to support the delivery of private files.

For the content type Portfolio, create a new image field per Table 12.1. Leave all options as the default values except the following.

- **File directory.** Portfolio.
- **Enable alt and title fields.** Enable both check boxes.
- **Number of values.** Unlimited.

Date

Nearly a decade ago I had a contract to build a Web-based calendar. I had no idea dates were so complicated. We made something workable, but it was a fraction of the elegance that Karen Stevenson and the Date module contributors have built into this module. Relatively speaking, the Date module makes adding date-based fields to your site a breeze.

When you create a new Date field, you can choose between the following formats: Date, Datetime, and Datestamp. If you're just making regular calendar events, Date should be sufficient for most sites. Date (ISO standard) allows Drupal to quickly and easily store both complete and incomplete dates. According to the module maintainer, Karen Stevenson, this makes it marginally faster than other formats that require more computation.

There are three display widgets for the Date field: Select list (Figure 12.19), Text field with custom input format (Figure 12.20), and Text Field with Date Pop-up Calendar (Figure 12.21).

FIGURE 12.19 Date field, select list widget

FIGURE 12.20 Date field, Text list with custom input format widget

FIGURE 12.21 Date field, Text field with Date Pop-up Calendar widget

The global settings for the Date field include the following.

- **To Date.** If your event lasts for a specific period of time, you can include an end date as part of the field. All day events and content types that are simply displaying a date (such as our Portfolio) can omit the end date. The options include Never, Optional, and Required.

- **Granularity.** You can store any of the following options but must include at least a year: Year, Month, Day, Hour, Minute, Second.

- **Time zone handling.** This is used only for dates that include the hour of the day and finer granularity. You can choose between the site's time zone, the date's time zone, the user's time zone, UTC, and no time zone conversion (required for dates that do not include an hour).

The field-specific settings include the following.

- **Default Display.** The options are Short, Medium and Long dates. These options can be customized at Administration > Configuration > Date and time.

- **Default value.** This is the date that appears by default in the input box. Your options are Now, Blank, and Relative (as in "time ago").
- **Input format.** A variety of date formats are available. I like ISO dates (YYYY-MM-DD) and dates in English (May 2, 1977). You should like them too. But if you don't, that's okay. We can still be friends.
- **Years back and forward.** This is the number of years to go back and forward in the selection list. By default you are given three years back and three years forward. If the date will always be in the future, you can change this to show only dates in the future.
- **Time increment.** Increment the minutes and seconds by this amount. The default value is 1, but additional sanc options include 10 and 15.

For the content type Portfolio, create a new date field with a pop-up widget per Table 12.1. Leave all options as the default values except the following.

- **Default Display.** Year, Month, Day (unselect Hour and Minute)
- **Time zone handling.** No time zone conversion
- **Default display.** Short

Assuming you've added each of the fields specified throughout this section, you should now have a custom content type, Portfolio, that has eight fields with the machine names: `title`, `body`, `field_project_type`, `field_key_modules`, `field_project_length`, `field_finish_date`, `field_screenshots`, and `field_url`.

Node-Editing Form Field Order

At this point, you are ready to arrange the form fields for your new content type. You can also choose to adjust the display for each of the fields and group similar fields so the form is easier to complete. The settings for the order, display, and groupings can be configured for each of your content types. You can adjust the order of the node-editing form and node display pages separately. To change the order of the form elements for your content type, navigate to Administration > Structure > Content types. Beside the content type you would like to alter, click the link "Manage fields."

On the summary page for field management, you will see a screen that is similar to Figure 12.22. If you have JavaScript enabled, you will see a small crosshairs beside each content field. To change the order of the fields, click the crosshairs and drag the field to its new location. Once you have rearranged the fields, you must commit the changes to the database by clicking the button Save at the bottom of the page.

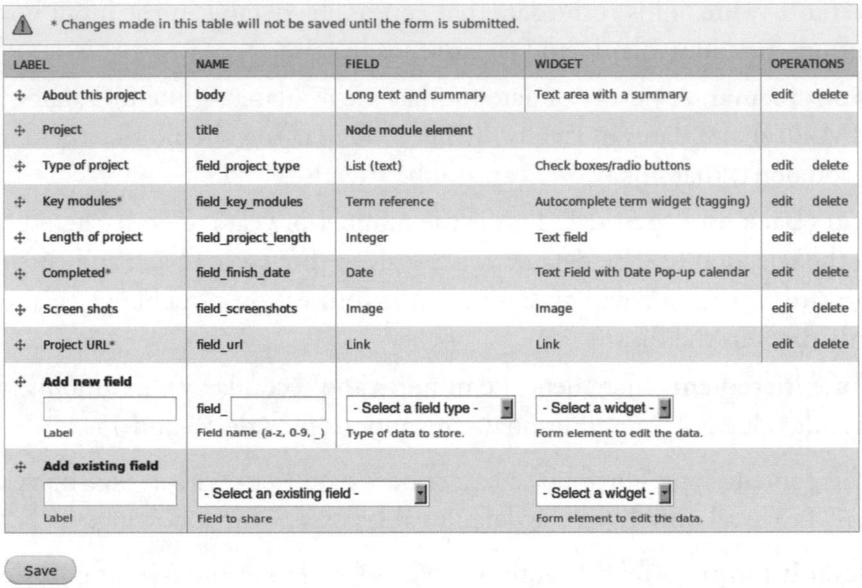

⚠ * Changes made in this table will not be saved until the form is submitted.

LABEL	NAME	FIELD	WIDGET	OPERATIONS	
⊹ About this project	body	Long text and summary	Text area with a summary	edit	delete
⊹ Project	title	Node module element			
⊹ Type of project	field_project_type	List (text)	Check boxes/radio buttons	edit	delete
⊹ Key modules*	field_key_modules	Term reference	Autocomplete term widget (tagging)	edit	delete
⊹ Length of project	field_project_length	Integer	Text field	edit	delete
⊹ Completed*	field_finish_date	Date	Text Field with Date Pop-up calendar	edit	delete
⊹ Screen shots	field_screenshots	Image	Image	edit	delete
⊹ Project URL*	field_url	Link	Link	edit	delete
⊹ **Add new field**	field_ [_____]	- Select a field type - ▾	- Select a widget - ▾		
[_____] Label	Field name (a-z, 0-9, _)	Type of data to store.	Form element to edit the data.		
⊹ **Add existing field**	- Select an existing field - ▾		- Select a widget - ▾		
[_____] Label	Field to share		Form element to edit the data.		

(Save)

FIGURE 12.22 After changing the field order, you must commit your changes by clicking the button Save.

You can adjust the default display for each field by clicking the "Display fields" tab from the content type–editing screens. Each field type has different display settings that can be adjusted for the teaser and full node. You can also choose to display the label beside the data when the content is viewed or decide to hide the label completely. The ability to make these minor adjustments from Drupal's administrative interface means a lot less work is required to create custom template files for each content type. This was covered in greater detail in the section "Manage Display."

Field Groups

In Drupal 6 the CCK suite of tools included the module Fieldgroup, which allowed you to group content fields on the content-editing screen. This is now available as a separate module, Field group (`http://drupal.org/project/field_group`).

Once the module is installed and enabled, you can create new groups by navigating to Administer > Content management > Content types and selecting the option "manage fields" next to the content type you want to alter. To add a new group, you must complete the following fields.

- **Label.**
- **Machine name.**

- **Widget.** Fieldset (Figure 12.23). Horizontal tabs (Figure 12.24), Accordion (Figure 12.25), and Vertical tabs (Figure 12.26) all require at least two groups which fields are placed into. If there are no groups provided for Vertical tabs, fields will appear in the vertical tabs provided by Drupal (Figure 12.27).

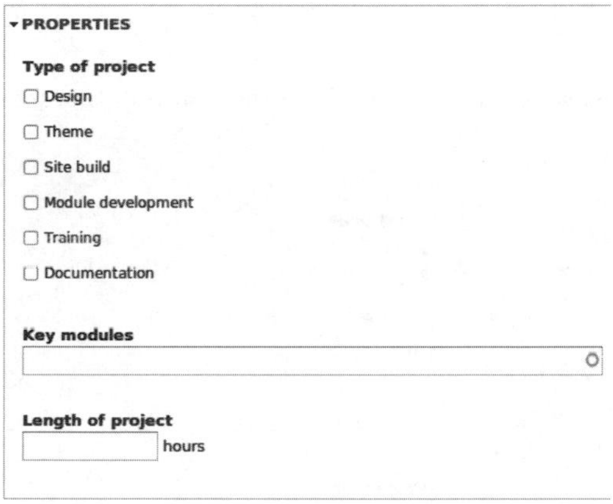

FIGURE 12.23 Fields grouped into a collapsible fieldset named Properties

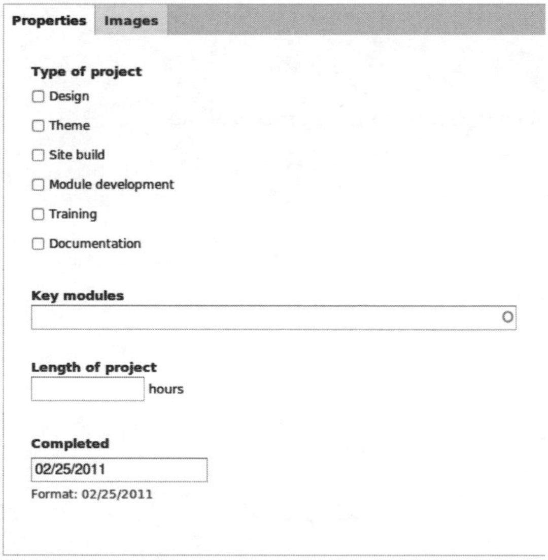

FIGURE 12.24 Fields grouped into horizontal tabs

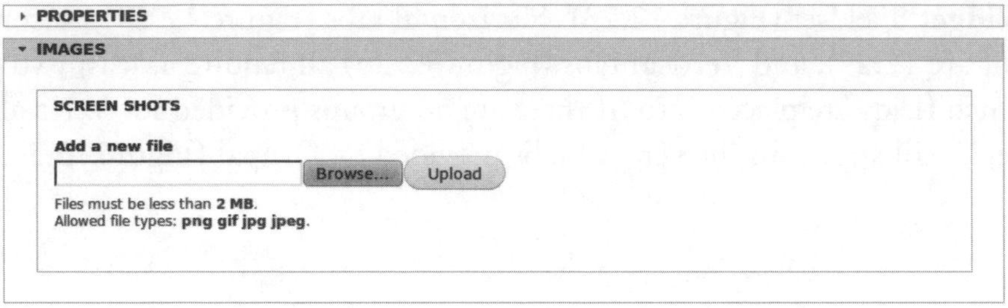

FIGURE 12.25 Fields grouped as an Accordion (unlike Fieldset, only one set can be open at a time)

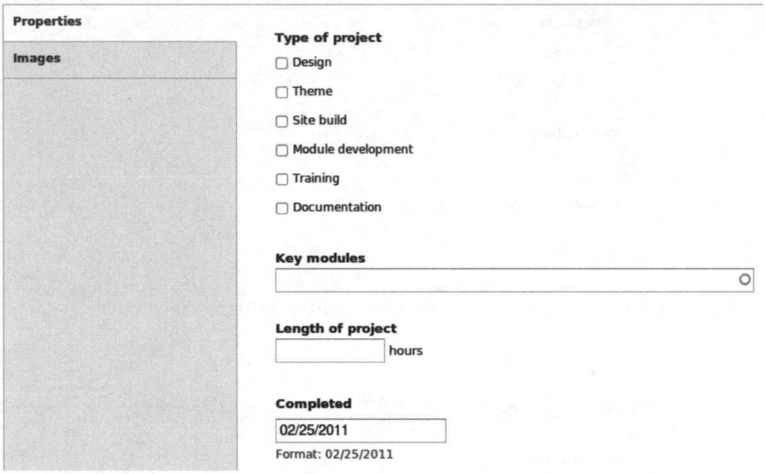

FIGURE 12.26 Fields grouped into a custom set of vertical tabs

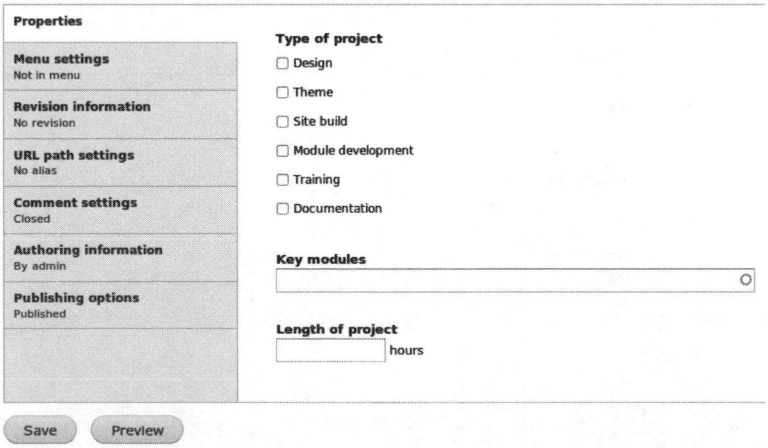

FIGURE 12.27 Fields grouped into a single vertical tab, Properties, and inserted into Drupal's vertical tabs

LABEL	NAME	FIELD	WIDGET	OPERATIONS	
✛ Project	title	Node module element			
✛ About this project	body	Long text and summary	Text area with a summary	edit	delete
✛ Project URL	field_url	Link	Link	edit	delete
✛ **Components**	group_components	Vertical tabs group ▾	**classes**	⚙	delete
✛ **Properties**	group_properties	Vertical tab ▾	**tab** open **classes**	⚙	delete
✛ Type of project	field_project_type	List (text)	Check boxes/radio buttons	edit	delete
✛ Key modules	field_key_modules	Term reference	Autocomplete term widget (tagging)	edit	delete
✛ Length of project	field_project_length	Integer	Text field	edit	delete
✛ Completed	field_finish_date	Date	Text Field with Date Pop-up calendar	edit	delete
✛ **Images**	group_images	Vertical tab ▾	**tab** open **classes**	⚙	delete
✛ Screen shots	field_screenshots	Image	Image	edit	delete

FIGURE 12.28 To add a field to a group, you must slide the field slightly to the right to show that the field belongs with that specific group.

The new group will appear at the bottom of the list of fields. Drag it to the appropriate location within the list of fields. To add a field to a group, you must slide the field slightly to the right to show that the field belongs with that specific group (Figure 12.28).

Summary

Throughout this chapter, you learned how to create the most common content patterns we see on the Web today, including basic content, events, and resources. With your content types in place, you can start filling your site with content. In the next chapter, you will learn how to make your content findable with custom navigation and the ever-popular module Views. Before moving on, be sure to fill your Web site with content so that you have something to find with your new navigation system.

Chapter 13

Lists of Content

When I say navigation, you think of...probably a whole lot of different things. A navigation system includes a primary menu, subsection menus, breadcrumbs, menu trees, tabs, accordion menus, inverted *L*s, and a lot of other terms you may not be familiar with yet. Drupal has a plethora of navigation options available to you. From the Menu module that allows you to create as many custom menus as you need to its breadcrumbs, a lot of helpers are built right in. Sometimes these modules will do exactly what you want without any additional customization.

Menus

Drupal menus are one of the most misunderstood concepts in building a Drupal site. Over and over again I've seen people create entire menu trees and wondered why no corresponding page was created. A menu item does not create a Drupal node. It merely provides a reference point to something that does (or does not) exist. Think of it as a bookmark. Just because you write a topic on a slip of paper doesn't mean that a corresponding book with relevant page is suddenly available on your nightstand. (Although if you do get this to work, *please* let me know.) Because of this misunderstanding of how menus work, I find that newcomers to Drupal often "lose" content when they forget to create menu items for new nodes.

Let's begin at the beginning.

By default there are five menus you can place menu items into.

- **Main menu.** The Main menu is used on many sites to show the major sections of the site, often in a top navigation bar.

- **Management.** The Management menu contains links for administrative tasks.

- **Navigation.** The Navigation menu contains links intended for site visitors. Links are added to the Navigation menu automatically by some modules. This menu appears in the Bartik region "Sidebar first" by default. With the new administrative toolbar and customizable shortcut bar, I find menu to be redundant and do not use it.

- **User menu.** The User menu contains links related to the user's account, as well as the "'Log out'" link.

Bartik displays the links in the Main menu as tabs across the top left of the page (Figure 13.1).

Adding Items to Menus

To add a menu item for a node on your site, you can use one of two methods.

- Edit a specific node and adjust its menu settings.

- Use the menu administration system to add a menu item (this is the one that typically gets people into trouble as they try to create bookmarks to pages that don't exist).

To add subsection menu items, you use either of the same techniques described earlier but change "Parent item" to the menu item in which your new subsection ought to be included. For example, suppose you have a set of primary links containing Mammal, Amphibian, and Reptile. To place Kitten as a subsection of Mammal, you would set "Parent item" to Mammal when adding the menu information for the Kitten node.

FIGURE 13.1 In Bartik, Main menu items are displayed as tabs in the top left of the page.

Changing the Order of Menu Items

When you add a new menu item, it won't always appear in the correct sequence. You can change the order of your menu items by completing the following steps.

1. Using the administrative toolbar, navigate to Structure > Menus.
2. Next to the menu you want to adjust, click the link "list links."
3. Using the crosshairs next to each menu item, click down and drag the links to their correct location.
4. Scroll to the bottom of the screen and click "Save configuration."

Custom Menus

You can also create custom menus with additional navigation. One of my favorite menus to add to a site is a set of "utility links." These links may include Contact, Search, Login, and any other items that are not really part of the main Web site. To add a custom menu to your site, complete the following steps.

1. Using the administrative toolbar, navigate to Structure > Menus.
2. Click the link "Add menu."
3. Enter a title and a short description of the types of links that ought to be added to this menu.
4. Scroll to the bottom of the screen and click Save.

You can now start adding links to your new menu using the instructions outlined in "Adding Items to Menus."

If you want to be able to add nodes to this menu directly, you must add the menu to the list of available menus by completing the following steps for each content type that should be able to be listed in this menu.

1. Using the administrative toolbar, navigate to Structure > Content types.
2. Next to the content type you want to configure, click on the link "edit."
3. Click the vertical tab labeled "Menu settings."
4. Under the heading "Available menus," enable your new menu.
5. Under the heading "Default parent item," adjust the drop-down menu so that the correct default menu is selected. By default <Main menu> is selected.
6. Scroll to the bottom of the screen and click "Save content type."

Your new menu is now available from the node-editing screen for whichever content type you just altered. You may repeat these steps for any additional content types.

When you are ready to display the menu on your site, complete the following steps.

1. Using the administrative toolbar, navigate to Structure > Blocks.

2. Find your new menu in the list of Disabled blocks (near the bottom of the page).

3. Drag your menu to the appropriate region (where you want it to be displayed). You can just change the region in the drop-down box; however, if you have multiple blocks in the destination region, it might not appear in the right order.

4. Scroll to the bottom of the screen and click Save blocks.

> **Turn Off the Heading**
> If you don't want the name of the menu to be used, you need to override the module default by setting the block title to <none>. To do this, hover your mouse over the block you want to change. A small cog will appear on the top-right corner of the block. Click it and choose "configure block." The administrative overlay will pop up, and you will be able to alter the block's title.

Once you've saved your new menu link, you can adjust the order of the items in the Main menu by dragging each of the items to a new position in the list as described in the section "Changing the Order of Menu Items." Don't forget to scroll to the bottom of the screen and click "Save configuration" before closing the overlay.

Secondary Navigation

Unfortunately, there are two ways to approach the concept of secondary navigation. These links can be either the subsections of the primary navigation *or* a completely different set of links, unrelated to the primary links (for example, the utility links described previously or legal links for terms of service and privacy policy).

Drupal allows you to choose how you want to configure your secondary navigation. By default the primary and secondary links use two different menus as source material. Use the following steps to change the default behavior and show subsection links instead of a different menu.

1. Navigate to Structure > Menus.

2. Choose the tab Settings.

3. Change the option "Source for the Secondary links" so that it matches the menu that is set in "Source for the Main links."

4. Scroll to the bottom of the page and click "Save configuration."

The page template variable for the secondary links will now display the sub links from your Main menu.

Unlimited Depth to Menu Navigation

The Primary and Secondary links feature allows you to display only two levels of navigation. Even the most basic of Web sites need more flexibility than this. The contributed module Menu block (http://drupal.org/project/menu_block) provides configuration blocks of menu trees from any menu, to any depth.

Once you've downloaded and installed the contributed module Menu block, you must choose which menus will be available for sub-subnavigation goodness.

1. Navigate to Structure > Menu block.

2. For each menu that needs subnavigation support, click the check box Available.

3. Scroll to the bottom of the screen and click "Save configuration."

You are now ready to add a Menu block to your site.

1. Navigate to Structure > Blocks.

2. Click the tab "Add menu block." Enter relevant settings for the following.

   - Menu
   - Starting level
   - Maximum depth

3. Scroll to the bottom of the page and click "Save block."

You have created a new block that can be placed into any region of your Web site and will display the appropriate menu items for the page your Web site visitor is viewing.

Useful Menu Modules

The following contributed modules further extend Drupal's core menu system. You might find them useful. Shoutouts to John Albin Wilkins, author of the Menu block module, for his dedication to making navigation easier in Drupal. This list is adapted from his list of useful menu modules.

- **DHTML menu (`http://drupal.org/project/dhtml_menu`).** This makes any of Drupal's standard menu trees have dynamically expanding menu items. This integrates automatically with Menu block.

- **Superfish (`http://drupal.org/project/superfish`).** This provides blocks of fly-out menus. Unlike Nice menus, Superfish does not rewrite the HTML for the menu tree.

- **Nice menus (`http://drupal.org/project/nice_menus`).** This provides blocks of fly-out menus. This module rewrites the HTML for the menus.

- **Menu position (`http://drupal.org/project/menu_position`).** This allows you to dynamically add the current page to the menu system at the requested spot.

- **Navigation 404 (`http://drupal.org/project/navigation404`).** When a page is "not found," Drupal will skip the rendering of navigation links in your Web site (for performance reasons). This module puts 'em back. See the related 404 Blocks module too (`http://drupal.org/project/blocks404`).

Breadcrumbs

Breadcrumb navigation is a series of links that show you where you are in the site relative to the home page. Breadcrumbs are exceptionally difficult to get right because they build on where you have been, and rarely do site visitors today enter the Web site from a site's home page. The Custom Breadcrumbs module (`http://drupal.org/project/custom_breadcrumbs`) allows administrators to set up parameterized breadcrumb trails for any node type. This allows the following style of breadcrumbs: Home > User Blog > 2005 > January. You will also need the helper module Token (`http://drupal.org/project/token`).

In the contributed module Custom Breadcrumbs, support has been added for views, panels, taxonomy, and paths. This gives you an incredible amount of control for the most common ways we display content and lists of content in our Drupal sites.

To create a custom breadcrumb for your site, download and install Custom Breadcrumbs and then follow these steps.

1. Navigate to Structure > Custom Breadcrumbs.
2. Click the relevant tab across the top of the administration screen to create a new custom breadcrumb (for example, Node).
3. Enter the following information.

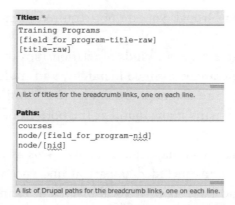

FIGURE 13.2 Match the titles to the paths for your custom breadcrumbs.

- **Breadcrumb Name.** An administrative name
- **Node type, View or Path.** This setting will change based on the tab you selected previously.
- **Titles.** This is a list of titles to be displayed as breadcrumb links. You can use tokens, which are listed at the bottom of the configuration screen.
- **Paths.** This is a list of corresponding paths for each of the titles you've entered in the previous field. See Figure 13.2.

4. Click Save.

Categories: Taxonomy, Vocabulary, and Terms

Humans seem to have an insatiable need to classify things. We build libraries with books sorted by topic, we use Latin naming conventions to sort plants and animals into families, and we use categories to sort our blog posts. This science of naming and classifying things is known as *taxonomy*. Within Drupal, the term *taxonomy* refers to any form of organization based on terms, the vocabularies they compose, and any hierarchical structuring of them.

The content type Article comes with one vocabulary that allows you to add new terms each time you create a new article. This is known as *free tagging*.

A taxonomy typically has a hierarchical structure, like a family tree—there are terms at the top of the tree structure that are relevant to many things, but as you descend the structure, the terms become narrower and apply to a smaller subset of the items being described. In Drupal, you are not required to create a hierarchy of your taxonomy terms.

Figure 13.3 shows three different kinds of relationships that taxonomy terms (categories) may have: no hierarchy, a single hierarchy, and multiple hierarchies. Notice that only the second and third diagrams are similar to a "family tree," with fewer items appearing at the top and many items found at the bottom of the "tree." Free tagging has no hierarchy.

Within each vocabulary you may have as many terms as you like. In Figure 13.3, the diamonds represent terms included as part of one vocabulary. Each discrete set of terms, however, should have its own vocabulary. For example, in addition to the vocabulary used for the content type Article (Tags), the case study in Chapter 10 used separate vocabularies to categorize types of businesses, types of products, and regions.

You can easily create hierarchical relationships between taxonomy terms; however, you will need Drupal modules that effectively deal with the relationships to really take

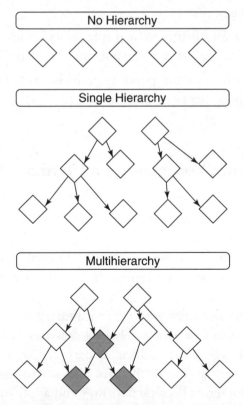

FIGURE 13.3 Taxonomy terms may have no hierarchy, a single hierarchy, or multiple hierarchies.

advantage of the structure you create. Chapter 10 gives an example of how one site used a simple hierarchy in taxonomy terms.

Creating Vocabularies

To create a new vocabulary for your site, complete the following steps.

1. Navigate to Structure > Taxonomy.
2. Click "Add vocabulary" (top of the page).
3. Add a name for the vocabulary (for example, Type of Products).
4. Click Save.

You should now see "Vocabularies" listed.
At this point, you should add new terms to your vocabulary.

1. Click "add terms."
2. Type in the name of the term you want to add (for example, Fruit). You may also add a URL alias for this term. Chapter 10 explains how to do this automatically with Pathauto instead.
3. Click Save.

Finally, you need to add your vocabulary to a specific content type.

1. Navigate to Structure > Content types.
2. Next to the content type you want to configure, choose "manage fields."
3. Beneath the label "Add new field," enter information for the following options.
   - **Label.** Choose an appropriate heading, such as `Categories`.
   - **Field name.** Choose an appropriate machine-readable name, such as `categories`.
   - **Type of data to store.** Choose Term reference.
   - **Form element to edit the data.** Choose Select list *or* Check boxes *or* Auto-complete term widget.
4. Click Save to proceed.
   You will now proceed through a configuration wizard to configure the field settings for your vocabulary as it applies to this content type.
5. Select the vocabulary you would like to apply to this content type.

6. Click "Save field settings" to proceed.

7. Read the settings field carefully to configure this field. Depending on which of the widget options you selected, you may add settings for each of the following.

- **Label.** This is preset to the label you entered previously.

- **Required field.**

- **Help text.**

- **Default value.** Choose what terms should be preselected. You can leave this blank.

- **Number of values.** Set this to "unlimited" for check boxes or 1 for radio buttons.

- **Vocabulary.** This is preset to the value you entered on the previous screen.

8. Click "Save settings."

Your new vocabulary will now be available when you add or edit new nodes for the specified content type. You will be able to apply any of the "terms" you entered to each of your nodes. Drupal will automatically make links on the relevant nodes that allow people to view all content that has been assigned this term. For each content type, you can adjust the order of display under the tab "Manage display."

Linking to Taxonomy Terms from the Main Menu

You can create menu links to any content on your site, including individual taxonomy terms. Complete the following steps to add a link to your favorite term.

1. You will need to know the URL for the taxonomy term to which you want to link. Navigate to Administration > Structure > Taxonomy > list terms. Click the tag to which you want to link (for example, "kittens" or "Chapter 1").

2. From the location bar in your browser, copy the Drupal path for the destination page to which you want to link. This will include everything after the domain name and subdirectory for your site install. For example, the base path for your installation might be `http://example.com/drupal/` or just `http://example.com/`. When you remove the base path you are left with the path, which is what you want to copy.

3. Navigate to Administration > Structure > Menus.

4. Next to the label for "Main menu," click the link "add link."

5. On the editing screen for the menu item (Figure 13.4), add the menu link title and the path (the URL you copied previously). Adjust the weight of the menu item if you know what it should be.

6. Scroll to the bottom of the configuration screen and click Save.

Once you've saved your new menu link, you can adjust the order of the items in the Main menu by dragging each of the items to a new position in the list. If you make changes, don't forget to scroll to the bottom of the screen and click "save." You can now close the overlay and see your new menu item.

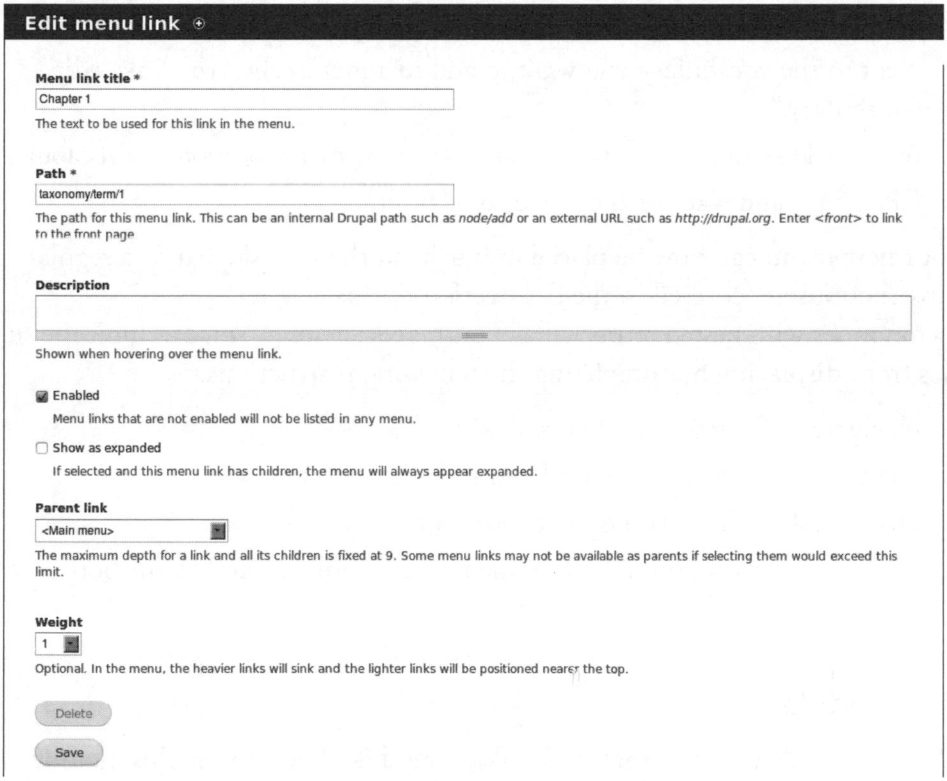

FIGURE 13.4 The editing screen to add a new menu item to the Main menu of your site.

Taxonomy Menu

The contributed module Taxonomy Menu (`http://drupal.org/project/taxonomy_menu`) makes it a snap to add taxonomy-based navigation to your site, as you learned in Chapter 10.

To create a new taxonomy-based menu, complete the following steps.

1. Navigate to Structure > Menus > Add menu.
2. Add a relevant title, such as Vocabulary: (and then the name of your vocabulary).
3. Add the description "Menu items for <vocabulary name>."
4. Click Save.

Place the vocabulary into your new menu.

1. Navigate to Structure > Taxonomy.
2. Next to the vocabulary you want to add to a menu, click the link "edit vocabulary."
3. In the field setting Taxonomy Menu, change the menu location to <Vocabulary: >.
4. Click Save and wait for the menu to be built.

Your new menu can now be placed as blocks in the first sidebar as a regular menu (the instructions are covered in the first section of this chapter).

Taxonomies with nested terms will get outrageously long. You can limit the subcategories from displaying by completing the following instructions.

1. Navigate to Structure > Menus.
2. Next to the relevant menu click the link "list links."
3. Disable all the links you do not want to display.
4. When you have adjusted each of menus appropriate, scroll to the bottom of the screen and click "Save configuration."

Views Module

The Views module is the ultimate list-making module. You can use this module to create anything from a simple list of recent comments to a complex photo gallery. Chapter 10 featured a business directory with a number of views.

The Views module can be downloaded from the project page at `http://drupal.org/project/views`. To install Views, you also need the companion module CTools (`http://drupal.org/project/ctools`). Advanced Help (`http://drupal.org/project/advanced_help`) provides the framework needed to see the inline help files that are available to assist with configuring and using views.

To use Views, you will need to enable all of the following modules: Views, Views UI, and Advanced Help. CTools will be automatically installed.

> **Save Server Resources**
> Once you have created all of your views, you can disable the module Views UI. This module is needed only to build new views; it does not need to be enabled once your views are set. If you need to edit your views, you can enable the Views UI module any time to make the necessary changes.

When you create a view, you are "just" making a list of things. Start by describing your list. It will make it a lot easier to navigate the administrative interface. There are a few key concepts that you will need to build a custom list of content using views.

- For each list item, what should be displayed? For example, a node title? Full node? Only specific content fields?

- What qualifiers (limiting criteria) should be applied to items in your list? For example, only display published nodes? Only display nodes of a specific content type? These are your filters.

- How should your list be sorted? For example, alphabetically? Reverse alphabetically? Chronologically?

- Where will your list be displayed on your site? For example, as a page? As a block? As an RSS feed?

The more detailed your description of what your list looks like, the easier it is to create a relevant view.

Default Views

Navigate to Structure > Views, and you will see a number of views have been provided by the module. Each of the default views shows you a different technique you can use for your own views:

- **Archive** and **Front page** create a simple, date-based list of content.

- **Taxonomy term, Backlinks,** and **Glossary** use contextual filters.

- **Glossary** uses attachments to group nodes together (all nodes starting with *A*, *B*, *C*, and so on).

- **Recent comments** creates relationships between nodes and their authors.

- **Tracker** uses filters.

> **Clone Your Views**
> Even though you can enable and edit any default view, I highly recommend *cloning* any view before making changes to it. You can be really close to what you want and then mess everything up and, well, there's no undo. Make friends with cloning, and when you have a view that's perfect, delete the ones you don't need any more. It will save you a lot of agony. Trust me.

Views Administration Screens

When you navigate to the Views administration area, you will see a list of all views including both the default views and any views you have made to date (Figure 13.5).

The screen (Figure 13.5) includes two important links at the top (Add new view, Import) and two tabs (List and Settings). Although I rarely use any of the settings, one setting is quite useful: Under the Advanced settings you can clear cache for views.

To understand how views are built, take a look at the configuration screen for the "archive" view. You must first enable the view before configuring it.

1. On the drop-down menu at the edge of the disabled archive view, select the link "clone." The Views configuration screen will open.

2. The view name "Clone of archive" is fine. Click the link Continue. The views configuration screen (Figure 13.6) will open.

The configuration screen contains several important areas, some of which are self-explanatory. For example, to save your view, click the link at the top right of the screen. Most of your work will be done in the bottom three columns where you will configure main settings (Figure 13.7), display settings (Figure 13.8), and advanced configuration (expanded in Figure 13.9).

Views uses JavaScript to hide and display components on the configuration screen. To edit an option, you click the label, or text setting, of the component you would like

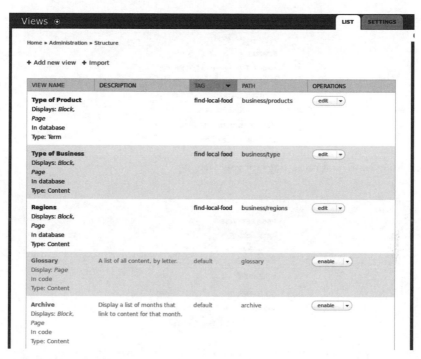

FIGURE 13.5 The Views administration area lists all views, both enabled and disabled. By default, no views are enabled.

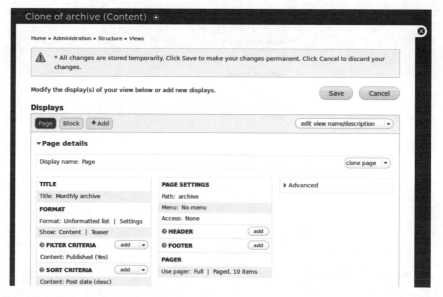

FIGURE 13.6 The Views configuration screen

FIGURE 13.7 Main configuration settings for your view

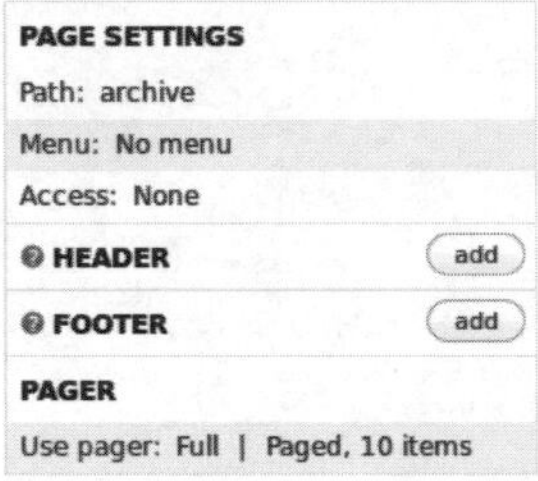

FIGURE 13.8 Display-specific settings for your view. This screen shows Page settings.

FIGURE 13.9 Advanced settings for your view

to change. For example, if you wanted to change the number of items displayed on a default archive page, you would click "Paged, 10 items" from the display-specific settings column (Figure 13.8), and the configuration screen would appear (Figure 13.10) in a modal ("pop-up") window.

At the bottom of the main Views configuration screen is a live preview for the output of your view (Figure 13.11).

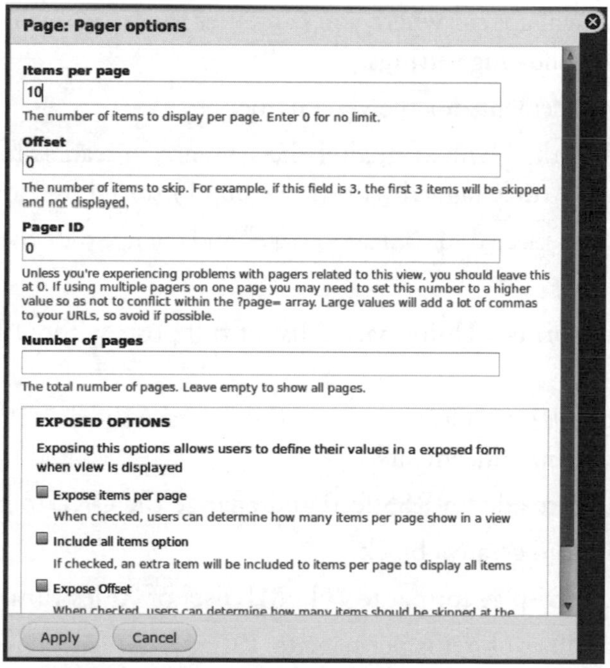

FIGURE 13.10 Configuration window for the pager

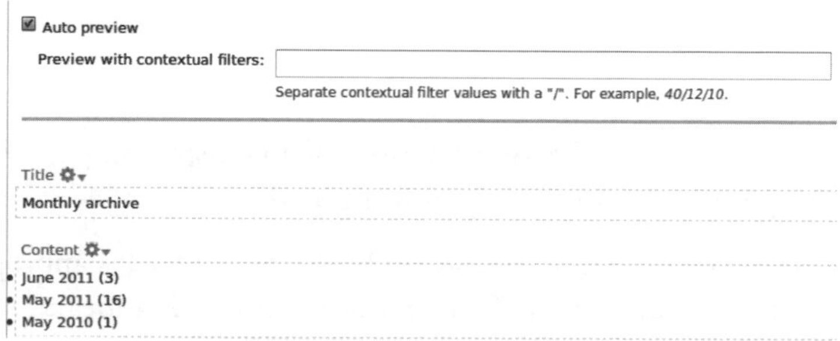

FIGURE 13.11 Live preview for the archive view

Creating a View

Previously you walked through the steps necessary to clone one of the default views. Now let's take a look at how to create a view from scratch—in this case, a "most recent" content view. Complete the following steps.

1. Navigate to Structure > Views.
2. At the top of the page, click the link "Add new view."
3. A new screen will appear where you can enter the basic settings for your new view. Use the following settings.
   - Use Announcements for the view name.
   - In the fill-in-the-blank area, alter the sentence to read as follows: Show content of type Article tagged with (leave blank) sorted by Newest first.
   - Leave the box selected for "Create a page" and change only the following settings.
      ◦ **Path.** news
      ◦ **Display format.** Unformatted list of full posts without links without comments
4. Enable the check box "Create a menu link." Leave the defaults of "Main menu" and link text "Announcements."
5. Enable the link to add an RSS feed and change the URL to news.xml.
6. Enable the link to create a block.
   - Change the Display format to "HTML list" of "titles (linked)."
   - Change number of items per page to 10.
7. Click "Save & exit."

Phew! You have created your first view that has three displays (Page, Feed, and Block)!

Adding Header and Footer Text to a View

You can easily add static text to the top or bottom of any display in your view. Navigate to the views editing screen for the view you want to alter.

1. In the central column, locate the label Header or Footer (as appropriate) and click the button "add." A modal configuration box will appear.
2. Enable the check box "Global: Text area."
3. Click "Add and configure."

4. At the top of the screen, locate which display you are changing. By default "All displays" is selected. You may not want this. If you want the text to appear only on this display, change it to "This block (override)."

5. In the text area (large box at the bottom), enter the HTML you would like to display at the top of this view. If you need to, update the input filter to Full HTML so that all of your HTML tags are preserved.

6. Click Apply. The modal box will close.

7. On the main configuration screen, at the top click "save."

Displays

When you create a view, you are building a list of content. You may have variations on how this content is *displayed* on your site. The view you created from scratch earlier adds three displays. Each display can list identical content or variations on the same content. In this section, we will create displays for the previous view with no additional modifications to the properties of the view. You will typically build displays for pages, blocks, and feeds. The glossary uses a special display, Attachment. Some modules will offer additional displays; for example, the References module includes a display for related content.

To add a new display to your view, click the "add" button. A drop-down box will appear with your available displays (Figure 13.12).

Each display has unique configuration options.

Block Display

When you add a Block display for your view, you must then place it into your Web site display. Complete the following steps.

1. Navigate to Structure > Blocks.

2. Scroll to the bottom of the page and find your new view. It should be listed according to the name you gave it in the Views administration.

FIGURE 13.12 Adding a new display for your view

3. Change the drop-down menu labeled "<none>" to "Left sidebar" (or whatever region name is most appropriate for your block.)

4. At the bottom of the page, click "Save blocks."

Your block display will now be available from every page on your Web site in the specified region. You can also limit the display of your block to match a specific Drupal path. This is configured from within the block settings.

1. Click the "configure" link next to the block you want to alter the display settings of.

2. Scroll to the vertical tabs. Click on the tab "Pages."

3. Enable the option "Only the listed pages."

4. In the text area enter the paths for the pages where you would like the block to appear.

5. Scroll to the bottom of the configuration screen and click "Save block."

To see an example of this in action, refer back to Chapter 10.

Page Display

A page is like a full node: It has its own URL. You must add a path for your display. To add a path, navigate to the editing screen for the view you want to alter, and follow these steps.

1. Locate the central display-specific settings column.

2. Locate the label Path.

3. Click the linked path name. If there is no path set, click None.

4. In the modal configuration window, enter the path you would like to use for this page display.

5. Click Apply. The modal configuration window will close.

6. Click Save at the top of the main configuration screen.

Your page display for this view is now available at the path you entered.
You can choose to add a Menu tab for your view as well.

1. Locate the label Menu.

2. Click the link "No menu." A modal configuration window will open.

3. Choose "Normal menu entry." A new set of configuration options will open. The window may not resize itself. Look for scroll bars along the sides.

4. Enter your title and parent menu for this page display.

5. Click Apply.

6. From the main configuration screen, click Save.

Your page display is now available from the appropriate menu.

Feed Display

The display for RSS feeds has three settings you should be aware of.

- **Path.** This is the URL your feed will be accessible from. It is appropriate to use the same path as the page display but with /rss.xml added to the end, as in blog and blog/rss.xml.
- **Attach to.** This is the display the RSS feed icon will be visible from. For example, if you want the feed icon to display on the block display but not the page display, you would configure that here. By default, the feed icon is not displayed.
- **Access.** This is used to limit who can access the feed by role or permission. By default feeds are available to everyone.

Each of these settings can be configured by clicking the set value (the blue link to the right of the label).

Grouping Similar Views

I like to group similar views into a single view that has multiple displays. I find it's easier to keep track of everything this way. For example, the blog page on Design to Theme (http://designtotheme.com/blog) has a full-node page display, an RSS feed, and a block with recent blog entries generated from a single view (Figure 13.13).

The features of this view include the following.

- Full text for the most recent blog post
- The ten most recent blog posts, not including the current post displayed as a list
- RSS feed icon displayed on the page

To create these three displays, I created a single view showing all published nodes of the content type Blog with a sort criteria of "Date created, Descending." Then I created three displays with the following variations.

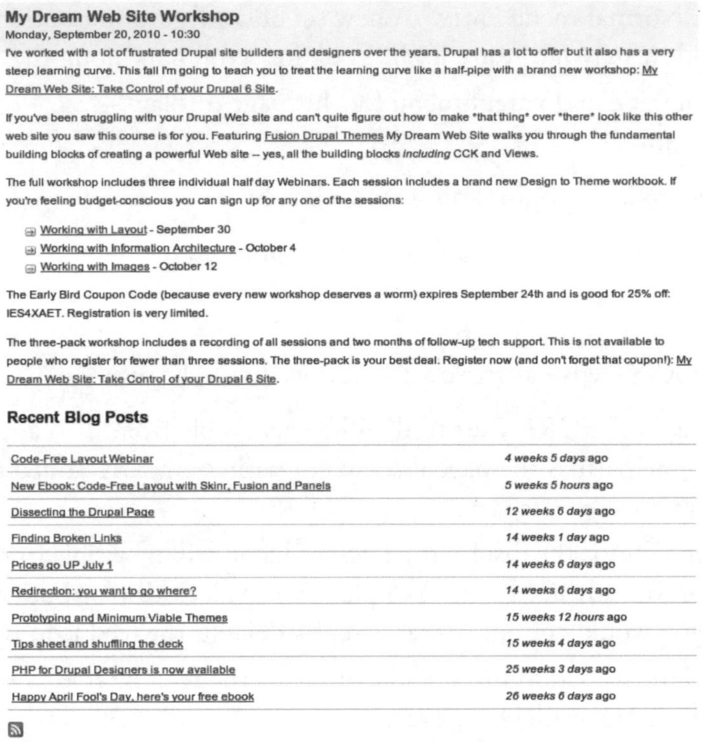

FIGURE 13.13 The Design to Theme blog has multiple displays used on a single page.

Page Display
- **Fields.** Title, Post date, Body, Add comment link
- **Items to display.** 1
- **Use pager.** no
- **Style.** Unformatted

Block Display
- **Fields.** Title, Post date (formatted as "time ago")
- **Items to display.** 10, offset 1 (omits the most recent blog post)
- **Style.** Table (with no headings)

Feed Display

- **Row style.** node (shows all fields)
- **Items to display.** 10 with 0 offset
- **Attach to.** Page display

Creating Reusable Views

You will likely use some views over and over again. The following are some examples.

- A list of published content
- A list of unpublished content waiting in a moderation queue
- A list of recent, or popular, items (for example, nodes or comments)

Creating a few generic views will help you quickly snap together new Web sites. To create a reusable view, repeat the steps outlined previously to create a view. Omit any fields or filters that make the view too specialized to be reused. For example, omit the content type from the filter.

If you want to share views between a development and live server, complete the following steps.

1. Navigate to Structure > Views.
2. Next to the generic view, click the link Export.
3. You will be redirected to a page with a textarea containing the code for your view. Select all of this text and copy it.
4. On your second Drupal installation, navigate Structure, Views.
5. Click the tab labeled Import.
6. Paste your view code into the available text area.
7. Click Import. You will be redirected to the views-editing screen where you can adjust the settings for your imported view.
8. Remember to save your changes!

Your imported view is now available on the new Web site. You will need to place any relevant block displays into your site and adjust the paths and menu items if necessary.

Filters

It is very easy to refine what items are displayed in the list. You will need to create a *filter* to do this. Here is an example that filters a list of nodes to show only the nodes that are tagged with a specific taxonomy term (you must have content with taxonomy terms applied to complete these steps).

1. Navigate to the view of nodes you want to refine (create a new one if necessary using Node as the type).
2. Next to the label Filters, click "add."
3. In the search box, type **Taxonomy**.
4. Enable the check box Taxonomy: Term (Taxonomy term ID).
5. Click "Add and configure filter criteria."
6. Choose the vocabulary you want to use (for example, Type of Products) and the selection type (for example, Dropdown).
7. Select the term you want nodes to be tagged with to be included in this list.
8. Click "apply." The modal window will close.
9. Click Save.

Your view will now be filtered to show only nodes that a term applied within a specific vocabulary. This view works well if you have multiple content types that share a vocabulary.

Site Maps

Providing a list of all pages on your site will help search engines to quickly index your entire site (without missing a page). Additional information about the SEO-friendly modules Index Page (http://drupal.org/project/indexpage) and XML Sitemap (http://drupal.org/project/xmlsitemap) is provided in Chapter 16. If you are interested in submitting your site to Yahoo! Site Explorer, you should also take a look at URL list (http://drupal.org/project/urllist).

Additional information on creating search engine–friendly site maps and submitting them to multiple search engines is available from www.sitemaps.org. Google-specific information is available from its excellent "Webmaster central" online help area (www.google.com/support/webmasters/).

Summary

In this chapter, you learned about some of the key modules that can be used to make lists of content in Drupal.

- Menu is used to link to individual paths within your site. These paths might display a node, a taxonomy term, or a view.

- Taxonomy is used to create and assign groups to content. The configuration of how the output is displayed is somewhat limited, but there are useful modules, such as Taxonomy Menu and Views, that will create lists of taxonomy terms or tagged items.

- Views is the ultimate list-making module. There are entire books written on recipes for Views. Tinker with it, try it out, and don't forget to *clone* your views so that you don't overwrite something that works with something that...doesn't quite work yet.

To see many of these modules in action, review Chapter 10.

Chapter 14

Recipes

Chapter 1 began with a list of different types of Web sites for you to emulate. In this chapter, you will mix and match the functionality provided by these types of Web sites with your own definitions for success to come up with a build plan.

Building Your Site

Use the matrix provided in Table 14.1 to help you find each type of functionality for each of the different types of Web sites. Some functionality is available to many different types of Web sites. Generally, the description for any given module (down the left column) is available under the first relevant Web site type (top row).

Your Web site may not fit into this matrix exactly. That's okay! For example, if your community site allows people to buy T-shirts, you may have a hybrid site that meshes the options from "Commerce" and "Community." Don't be afraid to mix and match. This is your Web site, and the goal is to get it running the way you want.

> **Getting Started**
> This chapter is not intended to replace the online help manuals for the individual modules. Modules are updated, and things change. To get the most complete and up-to-date information on how to configure the modules you need, you will need to do a little extra reading.

TABLE 14.1 Types of Site and Modules Used to Build Them

	Basic Site	Identity	Reported News	Community	Digital Collections	Instructional	Commerce	Portals and Aggregators
Aggregator			x					x
Analytics	x	x	x	x	x	x	x	x
Backup and Migrate	x	x	x	x	x	x	x	x
Basic page	x	x	x	x	x	x	x	x
Blog		x	x	x				
Comments		x	x	x				
Contact Module	x	x	x	x	x	x	x	x
Custom Fields					x	x	x	
Forum				x				
Images		x	x	x	x	x	x	
Member Listing				x				
Newsletter		x		x			x	
Rich Text Editor		x	x	x				
Search	x	x	x	x	x	x	x	x
Spam filter	x	x	x	x				
Taxonomy		x	x	x	x	x	x	x
Tracker				x				
Shopping cart				x		x	x	
Video (Embedded)		x	x		x	x		
Voting			x	x				

All Site Types

Every good Web site built today will have more than a few things in common. Table 14.2 outlines the modules you should be using on every site you build.

TABLE 14.2 Modules That Every Site Needs

Functionality	Core or Contrib	Enabled by Default	Project Page
Basic pages	Core	Enabled	
Contact the site owner	Core	Disabled	http://drupal.org/handbook/modules/contact/
Spam filter	Contrib	n/a	http://drupal.org/project/captcha
			http://drupal.org/project/recaptcha
			http://drupal.org/project/mollom
Backup and migrate	Contrib	n/a	http://drupal.org/project/backup_migrate
Analytics	Core and contrib	Disabled	Core: http://drupal.org/handbook/modules/ statistics/
			Contrib: http://drupal.org/project/ google_analytics
Search	Core	Enabled	http://drupal.org/handbook/modules/search
Lists of content	Various	n/a	Core: http://drupal.org/handbook/modules/ taxonomy/
			Contrib: http://drupal.org/project/views
			Contrib: http://drupal.org/project/xmlsitemap

Basic Pages

Virtually every single site on the Web has a basic page somewhere. This may be an About page or a disclaimer. I've even built Web sites so simple they had only a front page. In Chapter 4 you learned how to make basic pages and articles for your Web site. Refer to that chapter for more information on creating simple pages for your Web site.

Contact the Site Owner

Generally, you want people to be able to get in touch with you. By creating and customizing Drupal's contact form, people will be able to easily get in touch with you. Using a contact form also allows you to hide your e-mail address from robots that want to steal your e-mail address and sell it to spammers. Drupal's contact form is not enabled by default. Complete the following steps to enable and customize your site's contact form.

1. Using the toolbar, navigate to the Modules page.

2. Scroll to the module named Contact and select the check box. Scroll to the bottom of the screen and click "Save configuration."

3. When the page has finished reloading, scroll back to the module named Contact and click the link labeled Permissions.

4. Adjust the permissions so that all user roles may "Use the site-wide contact form." Click the check boxes for anonymous and authenticated users; then scroll to the bottom of the screen and click "Save permissions."

5. To add a link from the Main menu to the contact form, navigate to Structure > Menus > Main menu > Add link. Add an appropriate title. For the path, enter the value **contact**.

6. Scroll to the bottom of the screen and click Save.

A new menu item has been added to your Main menu.

Spam Filter

Whenever you add a publicly accessible form to your site, you open yourself up to spammers. There are several modules you can install to test whether a form submission is likely to be from a real person or from a robot spammer (*spambot*). These modules will add a special "CAPTCHA" test to publicly available forms that add a challenge to the form submission process. CAPTCHA is a **C**ompletely **A**utomated **P**ublic **T**uring test to tell **C**omputers and **H**umans **A**part. This definition is only really useful at cocktail parties when you want to impress your friends. The following are the most common CAPTCHA challenges.

- **Simple logic test.** For example, "What is the fifth word of this sentence?" or "1 + 3 = ____"

- **Visual recognition of numbers and letters.**

- **Auditory recognition of words.** A sound is played, and the site visitor must type the words they heard into a form field.

- **Image recognition.** A photo or illustration is displayed, and the site visitor must type the name of the object into a form field (for example, identify this image as a cat or a dog).

The most popular spam filter modules are CAPTCHA (`http://drupal.org/project/captcha`), reCAPTCHA (`http://drupal.org/project/recaptcha`), and Mollom (`http://drupal.org/project/mollom`). CAPTCHA is the easiest to install but is also the most easily foiled. reCAPTCHA (`http://recaptcha.net`) is a service that helps digitize books while fighting spambots. Each time a form is presented, two words from a book are displayed. Mollom (`http://mollom.com/`) is another service that performs a multipass check. When the form is submitted, Mollom reads the text and analyzes it to see whether it looks "spammy." If it does look like content previously flagged as spam, Mollom presents a CAPTCHA challenge to the site visitor to complete before resubmitting the form to your site. Figure 14.1 shows Drupal's contact form with the Mollom text challenge. Both reCAPTCHA and Mollom require a free user account. When I need to install a spam filter, I use Mollom, and I don't just use their service because they gave me a free T-shirt once. I use 'em because I like 'em!

To install a spam filter, choose the module that best meets your needs and complete the following steps.

1. Download, install, and enable your spam filter module of choice.
2. On the toolbar, navigate to Configuration and then your spam filter module.

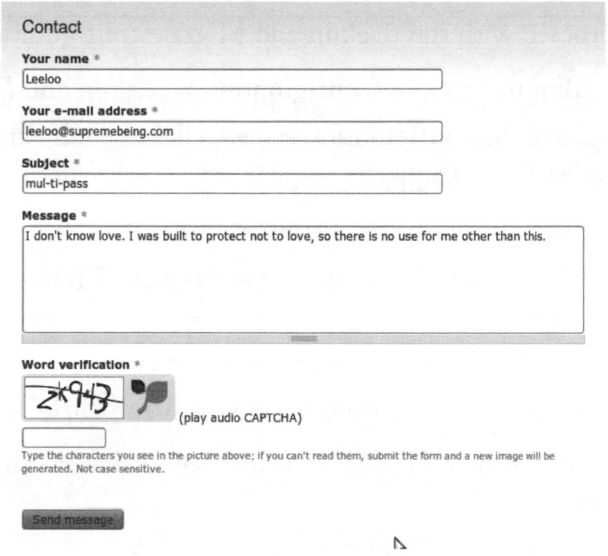

FIGURE 14.1 Mollom is a spam-filtering service that can be applied to any form on your Web site. This image shows the contact form with Mollom's text challenge at the bottom.

3. Set the forms you would like to protect with CAPTCHA, such as the contact form. Save your confirmation options.

4. If you are using either reCAPTCHA or Mollom, create an account on their site and get your "public" and "private" keys.

5. In the Drupal administration area for your spam filter, enter the private and public keys. This will allow your Drupal site to report to your spam-filtering service of choice.

Backup and Migrate

If you've heard it once, you've heard it a thousand times: Back up your work! Ronan Dowling's Backup and Migrate module makes it so easy to back up your work that there's no excuse not to do so. Install and enable this module and then configure the module to automatically back up your site's database every day. First you will need to configure a private directory where you can store backup files.

1. On the administrative toolbar, navigate to Configuration > File system.

2. In the field "Private file system path," enter a path on your server that is accessible by Drupal but not from the Web, such as /home/emmajane/backups.

3. Scroll to the bottom of the screen and click "Save configuration."

You may now proceed with the Backup and Migrate configuration.

1. Navigate to Administration > Configuration > Backup and Migrate.

2. At the top right of the configuration screen, click the tab Schedules.

3. Click the link "Add a schedule."
   - Update the schedule name to "Daily backup."
   - Change the "Number of Backup files to keep" to 7 (always keep a week's worth of backups).
   - The default settings for the remaining options are fine.

4. Scroll to the bottom of the configuration screen and click "Save schedule."

Your Web site database, including all your text-based content and module settings, will now be updated daily.

Analytics

Tracking visitors on your site is more than a little bit of voyeurism. It is critical to measuring how successful your site is at converting visitors to consumers. Out of the box, Drupal allows you to track visitor errors including top "access denied" errors and top "page not found" errors. This isn't very useful in figuring out what people are actually doing on your site, though; for that you'll need to enable the core module Statistics. This module provides a summary of the following.

- Recent hits
- Top referrers
- Top pages
- Top visitors

Once you've enabled the Statistics module, you can start to track results by going to the administrative toolbar and clicking Reports.

> **Use the Statistics Module in Addition to Your Stats Service**
> Pay special attention to the reports for pages that are "access denied" and "page not found." This information is not available to services such as Google Analytics. The "Top search phrases" report will also let you know what people aren't able to find (but want to find) within your site. You can use this information to improve the usability of your site by providing better links to the pages that are hidden. It may also give you some ideas about what kind of information you should be including on your site!

The Statistics module, however, is just a snapshot of what's happening on your site right now. For a long-term overview of how your site is performing, you will need to use a software package that is designed and optimized to look at your site over time.

One of the most popular analytics services available today is Google Analytics. The Drupal module for this service embeds a snippet of JavaScript in your pages. Each time a visitor looks at one of your Web pages, the JavaScript widget is retrieved and Google is notified of your visitor. This information is then tallied on Google's Web site and presented to you as a graphical summary of information. Figure 14.2 shows the dashboard summary for a sample Web site tracking visitors with Google Analytics.

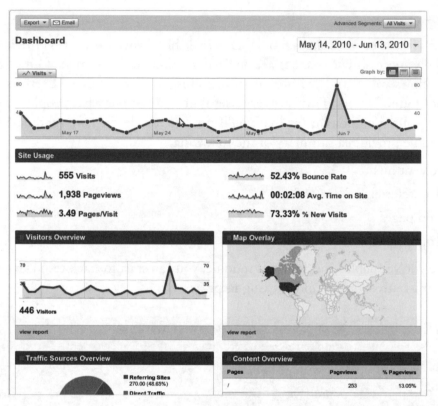

FIGURE 14.2 Google Analytics is a popular service used by companies and individuals who want to track the success of their Web site.

Like with Mollom and reCAPTCHA, you will need to create an account to use this service. To use Google Analytics to track visitors on your site, complete the following steps.

1. Create an account at `http://google.com/analytics`. Create a new Web site profile for the Web site you want to track. For each site that you set up, you will receive a unique Web property ID. This ID will be in the form of `UA-xxxxxxx-yy`, where the x's represent your account and the y's represent the specific Web site you want to track.

2. Back at your Drupal site, download, install, and enable the Google Analytics module.

3. Navigate to Administration > Configuration > Google Analytics.

4. Enter your unique ID in the UA form field. Adjust the settings according to the additional options required (I typically leave mine as the default settings). Scroll to the bottom of the configuration screen and click "Save preferences." Your Web site is now being tracked by Google.

5. Reload your dashboard at `http://google.com/analytics` obsessively to see your Web site traffic.

Google Analytics is just one of many different analytics services available. You may also be interested in KISSMetrics (`http://kissmetrics.com/`), VisiStat (`www.visistat.com/`), or Crazy Egg (`https://www.crazyegg.com/`). Or you may want to use your own server logs to analyze data. Analytic tools for server logs include AWStats (`http://awstats.sourceforge.net/`), Webalizer (`www.webalizer.org/`), and Pwiki (`http://piwik.org/`).

Search

The Search module is enabled by default in Drupal but is not available to anonymous site visitors. To configure the settings, use the toolbar to navigate to Configuration > Search settings. Here you can select the minimum number of letters per word indexed, the types of content to index, and the importance of several additional factors. To alter the location of the search box, use the following steps.

1. Navigate to Administration > Structure > Blocks.
2. Drag and drop the block labeled "Search form" to an appropriate region.
3. Scroll to the bottom of the configuration screen and click "Save blocks."

For more sophisticated searching options including faceted search, take a look at the Apache Solr Search Integration module (`http://drupal.org/project/apachesolr`). This module requires advanced server configuration that is well beyond the scope of this book. If it's well beyond your capacity too but you absolutely *must have* this functionality, take a look at the service Acquia Search (`http://acquia.com/products-services/acquia-search`).

To adjust the ranking algorithm for your site, navigate to Administration > Configuration > Search settings. On this configuration screen (Figure 14.3), the following settings will impact the ranking algorithm for your site.

- Number of comments on a node
- Keyword relevance

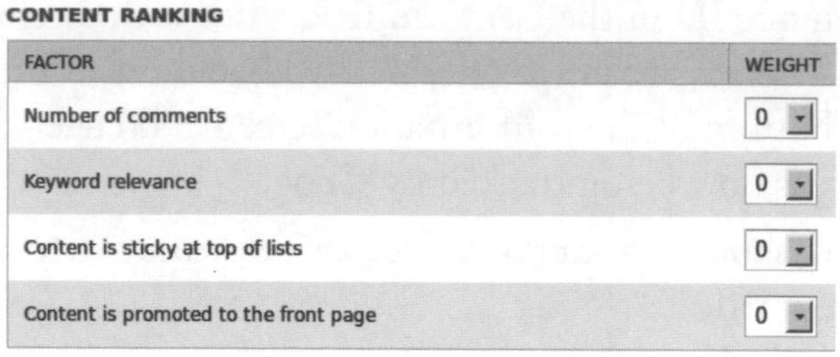

CONTENT RANKING

FACTOR	WEIGHT
Number of comments	0 ▾
Keyword relevance	0 ▾
Content is sticky at top of lists	0 ▾
Content is promoted to the front page	0 ▾

FIGURE 14.3 Configuring Drupal's built-in search engine

- Content is sticky at top of lists
- Content is promoted to the front page
- Number of views (to enable this option, see the following instructions)

By default Drupal does not factor in any of these items when finding pages that are relevant to a visitor's search terms. If these options are an indicator of content value on your site, you can enable them by setting the "weight" for each item to a number larger than zero. The ranking algorithm should be applied to new Web site searches as soon as you save your changes. Test your ranking to ensure the results are being sorted appropriately.

To use the number of page views in your ranking, you will need to enable the core Statistics module. Using the administrative toolbar, navigate to Modules. Enable the Statistics module. Once it's enabled, click Settings from the list of modules. On the page "Statistics settings," under the heading "Content viewing counter settings," enable "Count content views" by clicking the check box. Scroll to the bottom of the screen and click "Save configuration."

> **Drupal's Built-in Search Engine**
> By default Drupal's built-in indexer ignores words with fewer than three characters. This means the word *sea* can be searched for, but the word *an* will be omitted from the search index. If you need to adjust this setting, navigate to Configure > Search settings. Scroll down to "Index settings," change the minimum character length, scroll to the bottom of the configuration screen, and click "Save configuration."

The following modules may provide additional functionality to your on-site search engine if Drupal's core search is not meeting your needs. Descriptions are pulled from the Drupal project page and are not necessarily an endorsement of the project or a guarantee of success.

Custom Search

This module alters the default search box in many ways. If you need to have options available like in advanced search but directly in the search box, this module is for you.

The module adds options to do the following.

- Select which content types to search
- Select which specific module search to use (node, help, user, or any module that implements search)
- Change the default search box label
- Add a default text in the search box
- Change the default submit button text
- Use an image instead of the submit button

The project page is at `http://drupal.org/project/custom search`.

Search Lucene API

Search Lucene API adds Solr-like search functionality to Drupal. Because it is built on top of the Zend Framework's PHP port of Lucene, neither Java nor any external services are required to use the module. Out of the box, the bundled Search Lucene Content module adds advanced features that the core content search lacks such as advanced Lucene query syntax, fielded sorting of search results, and finer-grained content bias settings. Search Lucene API also has the ability to integrate with existing Drupal word stemmers such as the Porter-Stemmer project, but unlike the core search module, it correctly highlights the matches. Enabling the bundled Search Lucene Facets module adds faceted searching to your site, and the exposed hooks allow developers to add additional Lucene fields and facets with ease. Because Search Lucene API caches search results and facet displays, repeated queries are returned instantly with little resource consumption.

The project page is at `http://drupal.org/project/luceneapi`.

Apache Solr Search

This module integrates Drupal with the Apache Solr search platform. Solr search can be used as a replacement for core content search and boasts both extra features and better performance. Among the extra features is the ability to have faceted search on facets ranging from content author to taxonomy to arbitrary CCK fields. If you want to use Apache Solr but don't want to have to configure the search platform, you may be interested in Acquia's hosted version of Solr. More information of this service is available from `http://acquia.com/products-services/acquia-search`.

The project page is at `http://drupal.org/project/apachesolr`.

Visual Search

The Visual Search project is a suite of modules that allow your end users to search for content visually. This is particularly useful in e-commerce applications by giving your customers the ability to search for products by color, as well as in gallery applications.

The project page is at `http://drupal.org/project/visual_search`.

Extending Your Blog

If you are putting together a little promotional site for yourself or your business, there are a few more modules you will need to add to your site in addition to the ones all sites should have. Table 14.3 outlines the additional modules you can use for your new Web site.

Blog and Visitor Comments

By using only the content type Article, you can easily create a blog with Drupal. It has images enabled, and published content is automatically promoted to the front page of your Drupal site with comments turned on. There are blocks for "Recent content" and "Recent comments" that can be placed into your site if you want a quick snapshot of what's new. An RSS feed is available through the Syndicate block and lists all content posted to the front page. For a lot of Web sites, this combination of features will be

TABLE 14.3 Modules That Self-promotion Sites Need

Functionality	Core or Contrib	Enabled by Default	Project Page
Blog	Core	Disabled	`http://drupal.org/handbook/modules/blog/`
Comments	Core	Enabled	`http://drupal.org/handbook/modules/comment/`
Newsletter	Contrib	n/a	See inline notes
Rich Text Editor	Contrib		See inline notes

perfectly adequate. Where the Blog module really shines is for sites that have multiauthor blogs—with each author maintaining their own blog.

I'm a stickler, though. When I sit down to write a blog entry, I don't want to write an article. I want a blog post. There are two ways for me to deal with this little neurosis.

1. Rename the content type from Article to Blog by navigating to Structure > Content types. On the row for Article, click the link "edit." On the Article summary page, change Name to Blog, scroll to the bottom of the configuration screen, and click "Save content type."

2. Enable the Blog module provided by Drupal core.

If you opt to use the Blog module, you will get an extra block titled "Recent blog posts"; however, blog entries do not have the option to upload an image or be tagged with categories. If you want to enable these two fields, complete the following steps.

1. Navigate to Administration > Structure > Content types. In the row next to the content type "Blog entry," click the link "manage fields."

2. At the bottom of the field list, under the heading "Add existing field," add the label Image and change the first drop-down box to "Image: field_image (Image)." Click Save to proceed.

3. Read the configuration options, changing any options that you would like to adjust. Any changes you make will be applied to all content types using this field. Then scroll to the bottom of the screen and click "Save settings."

Repeat steps 1 and 2, but this time change the "Field to share" to "Term reference: field_tags (Tags)."

Newsletter

Many sites now offer a content–to–e-mail service for readers who want news delivered to their inbox. If you have a small audience, it may be appropriate to use a Drupal module such as Simplenews (`http://drupal.org/project/simplenews`). If you have a larger audience, you may want to use an e-mail service provider. My personal favorite is MailChimp (`http://mailchimp.com`). MailChimp has a nifty service that allows you to e-mail your RSS feed to a list of subscribers. A monthly fee applies for lists larger than 1,000 e-mail addresses. At the time of this writing, neither module had a Drupal 7 version available; however, they are both popular modules and should have something available shortly. Additional e-mail service providers include AWeber (`http://aweber .com`) and Constant Contact (`http://constantcontact.com`).

Rich Text Editor

Unfortunately, the core installation of Drupal requires you to learn a tiny bit of HTML. Fortunately, there is a contributed module in Drupal that allows you to snap in your favorite rich text editor. WYSIWYG (`http://drupal.org/project/wysiwyg`) supports any kind of client-side editor. It can be an HTML editor (aka WYSIWYG), a pseudo-editor (buttons to insert markup into a textarea), or even Flash-based applications. The editor library needs to be downloaded separately. Various editors are supported; see the project page for detailed information on how to install a rich text editor.

Portals, Aggregators, and Reported News

These three types of sites all rely on external content. The source may be a computer-generated feed of content (portals and aggregators) or a community member providing the content (user-generated content for reported news sites). See Table 14.4 for a list of modules.

Aggregator

In addition to content that is contributed directly to your Web site, your reported news site may pull content in directly from other sources of news. Any Web site that offers an RSS, RDF, or Atom feed can be syndicated.

Check the License Before Syndicating Content
Some news feeds are offered for personal use only. Be sure to check the content license before publishing the feed on your site.

TABLE 14.4 Modules That Reported News Sites Need

Functionality	Core or Contrib	Enabled by Default	Project Page
Blog	Core	Disabled	`http://drupal.org/handbook/modules/blog/`
Comments	Core	Enabled	`http://drupal.org/handbook/modules/comment/`
Rich Text Editor	Contrib	n/a	See inline notes
Aggregator	Core		`http://drupal.org/handbook/modules/aggregator/`
Video	Contrib		`http://drupal.org/project/emfield/`
Taxonomy	Core		`http://drupal.org/handbook/modules/taxonomy/`
Voting	Contrib	n/a	`http://drupal.org/handbook/modules/votingapi/`

To add external sources of content to your site, complete the following steps.

1. Enable the Aggregator module provided in Drupal core.

2. Navigate to Administration > Configuration > Feed aggregator.

3. Click the link "Add feed" and fill in the form on the subsequent page. You will need the title of the feed as well as the URL of the feed. Scroll to the bottom of the configuration screen and click Save.

4. Repeat step 3 for each site that you want to syndicate.

All syndicated content is available at `http://example.com/aggregator` and also by source as individual blocks. Figure 14.4 shows a sample of two feeds that have been imported with the Aggregator module. The author name is derived from the content feed.

User-Contributed Content

Content in a reported news site is essentially the same as content in a self-promotional blog. Unlike a self-promotion site, the content is being contributed by lots of different

FEDERAL NEWS

More than money was abused: Greens call for inquiry into G20-G8 civil liberty abuses

New report shows total oil sands emissions close to double widely used figures

On Environment Week, Government of Canada missing in action

Budget once again fails on long-term planning and vision

Media Advisory: Elizabeth May to address Federation of Canadian Municipalities AGM

More

PROVINCIAL NEWS

Second Annual Calendar Contest - Submit Your Photos Today!

Disappointing Legislative Session Ends with Partisan Rhetoric and False Choices for Ontarians

Disappointing Legislative Session Ends with Partisan Rhetoric and False Choices for Ontarians

Green Party Nominates Two-Term West Grey Councillor as Candidate for Upcoming Provincial Election

Will Ontario Follow Germany's Lead on Nuclear Power?

More

FIGURE 14.4 Content syndicated from other sites using the Aggregator module. Two feed sources are visible from the Green Party of Canada and the Green Party of Ontario.

users. To maintain individual streams of content, use the Blog module instead of the Article content type. Instructions earlier in the chapter provide information on customizing the "Blog entry" content type to include categories and images.

Additional instructions on rich text editing are also available in the section about self-promotional sites.

Video

Video on the Web is changing. When the book was written, I liked using the Embedded Media Field module (http://drupal.org/project/emfield) and the Media module (http://drupal.org/project/media) to create custom fields for embedding video into Web sites. The documentation was good, and the modules behaved the way I expected. Start here with these two modules if you too want to embed video into your site without having to worry about hand-coding HTML.

Taxonomy

This core module allows you to group content by category. It is discussed in greater detail in Chapter 13.

Voting

In the sample site in Chapter 1, news was promoted to the front page according to its popularity within the community. Drupal has a whole category of modules that allow you to evaluate or rate content (http://drupal.org/taxonomy/term/60). The most popular of these modules all use the module Voting API (http://drupal.org/project/votingapi). This module provides a standardized way of storing, retrieving, and tabulating votes. Some of the implementations include the following.

- **Fivestar.** Allows visitors to assign a one- to five-star ranking for content (http://drupal.org/project/fivestar).
- **Plus1.** Allows visitors to agree with the content that is presented in a node. There is no "negative" vote. You either agree or don't vote (http://drupal.org/project/plus1).
- **Vote Up/Down.** Allows visitors to agree *or* disagree with content. Visitors are presented with the option to add one vote to the content or subtract one vote from the content (http://drupal.org/project/vote_up_down).

You will need to choose the voting system that is most appropriate for your content and site goals. Installation instructions are available through each project's documentation page.

Community Sites

Community sites will cover much the same functionality as all the sites listed so far. Table 14.5 outlines the modules you will find useful when building community sites. Take a look at the self-promotional site and reported news site descriptions for additional key modules. If your community group wants to sell promotional items related to the group, such as T-shirts, hats, or membership dues, you should also take a look at the e-commerce site profile.

Forum

Drupal ships with a basic user forum that allows you to create topics with individual posts (and comments) within these topics. It meets the needs of most low-volume sites as well as the main Drupal.org support forum (`http://drupal.org/forum`).

Figure 14.5 shows the Drupal.org support forum. The front page of the forum lists the containers and their forum. In this example, the Support container contains eight forums (Post Installation, Before you start, Installing Drupal, and so on).

TABLE 14.5 Modules That Community Sites Need

Functionality	Core or Contrib	Enabled by Default	Project Page
Blog	Core	Disabled	`http://drupal.org/handbook/modules/blog/`
Comments	Core	Enabled	`http://drupal.org/handbook/modules/comment/`
Rich Text Editor	Contrib	n/a	See inline notes
Member Directory	Contrib		See inline notes
Forum	Core	Disabled	Core: `http://drupal.org/handbook/modules/forum/` Contrib: `http://drupal.org/project/advanced_forum` `http://drupal.org/project/group`
Tracker	Core	Disabled	`http://drupal.org/handbook/modules/tracker/`
Voting	Contrib	n/a	`http://drupal.org/handbook/modules/votingapi/`

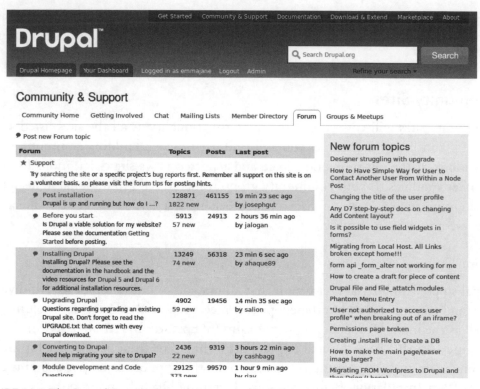

FIGURE 14.5 The Drupal Support home page groups its forums into containers.

Each forum contains user-contributed topics. Figure 14.6 shows the list of topics for the forum Upgrading Drupal. This free support forum on Drupal.org is one that you should definitely participate in! You can register for a free account at `http://drupal.org/user/register`.

To add a forum to your site, complete the following steps.

1. Using the toolbar, navigate to Configuration > Account settings. Confirm the Registration and Cancellation settings are appropriate for your site. By default visitors can create new accounts, but they require Administrator approval before being activated. Additional information about configuring your site for multiple users is available in Chapter 14.

2. With the default user settings verified, enable the Forum module.

3. Configure the default containers and topics for your forum by navigating to Structure > Forums. One container is provided by default: "General discussion." You can change the title by clicking "edit forum."

Upgrading Drupal

🗨 Post new Forum topic

Topic	Replies	Created	Last reply▴
Designer struggling with upgrade	0	15 min 32 sec ago by salion	n/a
Upgrade from 6.17 to 7 generates error after	4 2 new	5 weeks 1 day ago by mhurston	1 hour 27 min ago by Gary Coleman
Drupal still reading as 6.20 after update to 6.22	5 5 new	1 week 1 day ago by aggiechris	8 hours 47 min ago by zorax
Drupal 7 UPGRADE.txt Does Not Cover Bootstrap Issue	1 1 new	2 weeks 3 days ago by Dr. DOT	11 hours 13 min ago by vindesh
Upgrading from 6 to 7 - huge issue - stops at "user"	3 1 new	1 year 20 weeks ago by blavish	11 hours 19 min ago by vindesh
GoDaddy stuck at version 7.0, so what's the best way to manually upgrade to 7.2?	1 1 new	1 day 11 hours ago by herojig	1 day 9 hours ago by seanray
PHP Notices and warnings after upgrade from 7.0 to 7.2	3 3 new	1 week 1 day ago by Eru	2 days 2 hours ago by Eru
Drupal 6.x Upgrade - Files Only	20 6 new	1 year 45 weeks ago by Sam308	2 days 4 hours ago by VM
Drupal 6.19 to 6.20 Upgrade - Files Only	24 3 new	25 weeks 18 hours ago by Sam308	2 days 5 hours ago by Sam308
PHP requirements	0	2 days 6 hours ago by amussen	n/a

FIGURE 14.6 Each forum contains many user-contributed topics.

4. To add a new container, click the link "Add container" and enter a container name, description, and parent. You may nest this container into General discussion or create a new, top-level container by setting Parent to <root>. By default a new container is created.

5. To add a new forum, click the link "Add forum" and enter a forum name, description, and parent. You can nest your forum into other containers and forums as well.

6. On the list of containers and forums, you can adjust the order by clicking the crosshairs and dragging the forum to the correct location. To nest a forum, slide the crosshairs slightly to the right. It will indent to show the nesting of topics. Click the Save button to set your new topic order.

7. Finally, adjust the settings for your forum. In the top right of the forum administration screen, click the tab Settings. Adjust the hot topic threshold, topics per page, and default sort order for your forum.

Instructions on how to create a private member forum are covered in Chapter 9. Additional advanced forums are also available for Drupal. If the Drupal core Forum module does not meet your needs, take a look at Advanced Forum (`http://drupal .org/project/advanced_forum`) and Group (`http://drupal.org/project/ group`).

Member Directory

A member directory is essentially a list of people with accounts on your Web site. Step-by-step instructions on how to create lists of content appear in Chapter 13. A step-by-step guide on how to create a business directory is in Chapter 10.

Tracker

This core module provides you with a quick summary of all the new content that has been added to the site since you last logged in. Figure 14.7 shows my Tracker on Drupal.org. Once you've enabled this module, authenticated users can see recent content by navigating to `http://example.com/tracker`. You can add a link to the Tracker module on your shortcut menu if it's relevant for your site.

Instructional Sites and Digital Collections

These sites use highly customized content types and lists of content to present information to the visitor. Table 14.6 provides a summary of useful modules. Configuration for these modules is covered in Chapter 12 and 13.

Recent posts

All recent posts   My recent posts

Type	Post	Author	Replies	Last updated
Issue	Error generating image	emmajane	17	9 hours 38 min ago
Issue	Different user theme throws errors	redijedi	57	12 hours 23 min ago
Issue	Usage of deprecated $form_state['clicked_button'] causes bugs during AJAX submissions by non-buttons	rfay	36	1 day 2 hours ago
Issue	How do I make a taxonomy breadcrumb in D7?	emmajane	26	1 day 4 hours ago
Book page	Setup of /sites directory for multi-site	emmajane	31 1 new	3 days 1 hour ago
Issue	Hide empty admin categories	icouto	152	3 days 2 hours ago
Book page	Coding standards new	beeradb	7 1 new	3 days 5 hours ago
Issue	Separate usage of hide(), render(), and other template features from print statements to enable non-developers to create themes	chx	103	6 days 7 hours ago
Issue	Add tracking for replies	emmajane	19	1 week 1 hour ago
Book page	Webform Module new	LinL	2	1 week 1 day ago

FIGURE 14.7   The module Tracker allows you to see what new content has been added to the site since you last logged in.

TABLE 14.6 Modules That Instructional Sites and Digital Collections Need

Functionality	Core or Contrib	Enabled by Default	Project Page
Taxonomy	Core	Enabled	`http://drupal.org/handbook/modules/taxonomy/`
Fields	Core	Enabled	`http://drupal.org/handbook/modules/fields/`
Book	Core	Disabled	`http://drupal.org/handbook/modules/book/`
Images	Core	Enabled	`http://drupal.org/handbook/modules/file/`

Commerce Sites

Finally, we get to commerce sites. I like these sites because they pay me money. Literally. I've had the most success with Ubercart. And I'm not just saying that because they gave me a free T-shirt once. (There are a lot of free T-shirts in the world of software.) Just about everything I've ever wanted to deploy in an online shop Ubercart has already thought of. In addition to Ubercart, there are lots of add-on modules that extend its functionality. Ubercart can be downloaded from `http://drupal.org/ project/ubercart`. Its project site is at `www.ubercart.org/`.

In addition to Ubercart, there is also the following.

- **Drupal Commerce** (`http://drupal.org/project/commerce`) is a new module that is rethinking commerce architecture from the ground up. It was not ready for production sites when this book was written; however, there is active development on the project. Development is sponsored by Commerce Guys (`www.commerceguys.com/`). This is turning into the new "hot" commerce solution for Drupal 7 and deserves very serious consideration for new commerce sites.

- **e-Commerce** (`http://drupal.org/project/ecommerce`) is the longest-running e-commerce module. Although under active development, there was no Drupal 7 version at the time this book was written.

Configuring an e-commerce shop is beyond the scope of this book. The online documentation for Ubercart along with its support forum is sufficient for most small businesses looking to set up their first online shop. The Commerce Guys often offer public training sessions as well.

Summary

With Drupal core installed, you move into the site-building phase of your site's development. Most sites use a combination of core and contributed modules. In this chapter, you learned which modules are some of the best for a variety of different types of sites. Basic configuration information was provided for the most common modules you will use in almost any Web site you will build using Drupal.

Part V

Extending Drupal

Chapter 15

Theming

Whenever I create a new account on a social Web site, one of the first things I do is decorate my account. You too will probably want to personalize your Drupal Web site. Maybe you'll dress it up in a pirate hat or give it a duck suit, or maybe you just want to create a really great design for your new site.

Themes have the ultimate and final control over how a page is displayed. Once a theme is created, it may be applied with the simple click of a button. If you have ever used a downloaded theme, you know how impressive and instantaneous the process is to flip from your current theme to one that you downloaded and unpacked only a few moments ago.

Theming is a black art too complicated to cover *entirely* in this book, but this chapter covers all the steps needed to shake your Web site into some groovy new pants. We'll start with the basics of customizing the core theme, Bartik; give you tips on how to find great free themes for your site; and finally wrap up the chapter by creating a custom theme from a static design file.

Building Pages

In Drupal, a *theme* is the final step in the process of building a Web page for display. It converts the data from PHP objects and arrays into HTML markup and CSS style definitions. Drupal takes several steps to prepare a page for viewing in a Web browser.

1. Information is retrieved from the database using code from your installed modules.
2. The retrieved data is refined using relevant output filters. This step may include the conversion of URLs into clickable links and line breaks into new paragraphs.
3. Content is inserted into each of the relevant theme templates provided by Drupal core, contributed modules, and your custom theme.
4. Finally, the formatted page is displayed in the Web browser.

(This is a very simplified process that omits some programmatic steps where parts of pages are cached to make Drupal faster, but it's basically right.)

Drupal provides generic templates for everything that is displayed in your Web site but stored in the database. Most themes will omit at least a few customizations and will rely on the relevant Drupal core templates instead. Some themes are purely CSS enhancements with no additional code at all.

Customizing Your Site Without Code

Without touching any code, there are at least a few things you can do to customize how your Web site looks. The available configuration options are directly related to how your theme was built. For example, the primary menu of your site might have its location hard-coded into the theme or may need to be placed into a region via a customizable block. This section covers some of the most popular settings that can be changed for most themes without having to know any code.

Site Settings

When you first installed Drupal, you gave your site a name. This name is typically displayed along the top of your new Drupal site. If you'd like to adjust the name of your site, you can do so at any time.

1. From the administrative toolbar, click Configuration.
2. Find and click the link labeled "Site settings."

3. From here you will be able to adjust settings for the site name and slogan.

4. When you've finished, scroll to the bottom and click "Save settings."

Custom Logo and Favicon

The default logo is the Drupal mascot, Druplicon. To replace this icon with your own image, complete the subsequent steps. Your new logo will not be resized by Drupal, so make sure it's the right size before you upload the image.

1. From the administrative toolbar, click Appearance. For the theme labeled "default theme," find and click the link titled "Settings."

2. Scroll to the section Logo Image Settings. Deselect the check box "Use the default logo." A new configuration area will appear.

3. To upload an image from your computer, click the button Browse. You will be prompted to locate an image from your computer to upload. Select the image and click Open. (The text may differ slightly for different Web browsers.)

4. Scroll to the section titled "Shortcut icon settings." Deselect the check box labeled "Use the default shortcut icon." A new configuration area will appear.

5. To upload an image from your computer, click the button Browse. You will be prompted to locate an image from your computer to upload. Select the image and click Open. (The text may differ slightly for different Web browsers.)

6. Scroll to the bottom of the configuration screen and click "Save configuration settings."

Your new logo and favicon will now appear.

Regions for Layout

When Drupal is first installed, it appears as in Figure 15.1 to Web site visitors. Hidden on this page are 15 regions that you can use to place page elements onto your site (Figure 15.2). In Drupal-speak, a page is divided into regions. Each region may contain zero, one, or many blocks. In addition to a theme's regions, there are a number of static placeholders that are filled with very specific information including site name and logo. In Drupal 7 any region can hold your site's content; however, the region in the middle, labeled Content, is typically used.

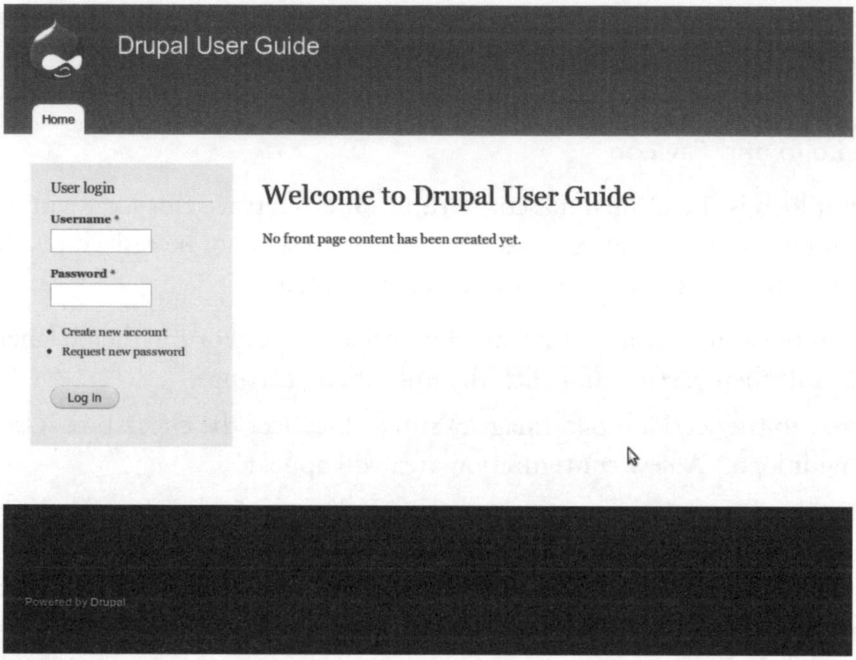

FIGURE 15.1 The front page of your new Web site actually contains 15 hidden regions.

The Bartik theme has five strips that each contains one or more regions.

- Header region (beside the logo)
- Featured region (full width of the page, above the content)
- Sidebars and content
- Second featured region (triptych; displays full width of the page below the content)
- Footer (divided into five regions: four columns across one row and a second with a second full-width region at the very bottom of the page)

Preview Theme Regions
To see what regions are available for your theme, use the administrative menu to navigate to Structure > Blocks. Click the link "Demonstrate block regions." You will be redirected to a screen that is similar to Figure 15.2. Click the tab in the top right of the screen labeled "Exit block region demonstration" to close the preview.

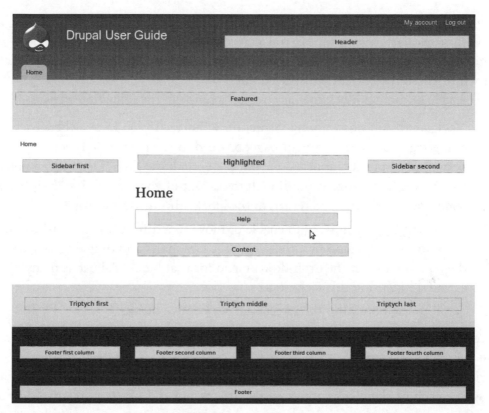

FIGURE 15.2 Bartik has 15 unique regions that you can place blocks into. By default primary links are baked into the page template, and the main page content is placed in the region Content.

A block can contain a navigation menu, a random image, a list of recent comments, or anything else that you might need. Blocks are typically defined by modules, but you can also create your own custom blocks. Each block must be placed into a region before it will become visible on the Web site.

Many modules provide their own blocks. For this reason, each time you enable a new module, you should check whether new blocks are now available. To ensure the blocks are visible to the appropriate user roles, you may need to adjust the permissions defined by the new module. For example, without adjusting the permissions for the search module, the search box is visible only to you when you're logged in. The public can't use the search form until you give them permission.

Blocks can be dynamic, or they can contain static information that does not change from page to page. One dynamic block is the "Who's online" block provided by User module. This block presents a list of Web site users who have been active on the Web site within the last few minutes. You can also create context-sensitive blocks—for example, an "Author information" block containing further information about the user who created the currently displayed node.

To enable or move a block to a new region, complete the following steps.

1. Navigate to Administration > Structure > Blocks. If you know where each of the regions appears on your page, proceed to the next step. If you don't know where a region appears on your page, click the link "Demonstrate block regions" to familiarize yourself with the layout of your site. Click "Exit block region demonstration" to return to the block administration page.

2. Locate the block you want to enable or move to a different region. Move the block to its new region by either using the crosshairs and dragging or setting the region name in the drop-down menu for that block. Adjust as many blocks as you'd like using this technique.

3. Scroll to the bottom of the screen and click "Save blocks."

Your blocks will now appear in their new regions to users and visitors with sufficient access permissions.

Figure 15.3 shows an alternate layout for the Bartik theme. It was made by changing where each of the blocks appeared on the site but did not require any additional code. Note: The Main menu has been disabled in the theme settings (hides the tabs below the logo), and the Primary menu block has been enabled and placed in the region "Sidebar second."

There are four ways you can limit the visibility of a block.

- **Per-page.** Specify which paths (URLs) this block should be displayed on. This is commonly used to show blocks only on the front page or on all pages except the front page.

- **Per-content type.** Specify which content types this block should be displayed on. An example is a summary of recent blog posts that is available only on Article pages.

- **Per-role.** Specify which user roles may view the block. An example is additional help tips for users, such as site managers, with elevated permissions.

- **Per-user.** Allow authenticated users to customize the visibility of this block in their account settings. This is ideal for blocks that give extra help tips, which advanced users may want to hide.

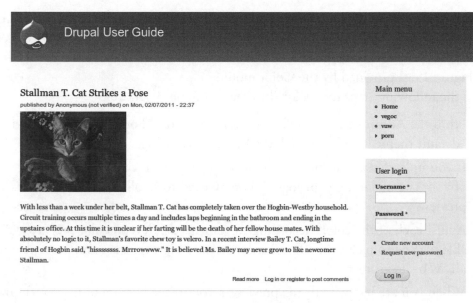

FIGURE 15.3 Placing blocks into different regions on the page gives an alternate layout for the Bartik theme.

If you would like the block to appear under specific conditions, use the following steps to adjust the visibility for each block.

1. Navigate to Administration > Structure > Blocks.

2. Next to the block you would like to modify, click the link labeled "configure."

3. Make the required adjustments according to the visibility setting options discussed earlier.

4. Scroll to the bottom of the screen and click "Save block."

Your block will now be limited in its visibility according to your new settings.

You can also set the region settings from the same screen as the visibility settings—if you want to limit the visibility of your block, set the visibility settings first and then the region.

Changing Colors

Blue is nice. The Drupal mascot, Druplicon, is great. But the default theme says something about Drupal, not about you. Let's make your site reflect you. With a few quick changes to your site, you can turn the default theme into one that reflects who you are.

Assuming you've just installed Drupal and you haven't made any additional changes, you are currently using the theme Bartik. This theme, as well as the other core theme, Garland, allows you to change the colors without learning any code via a nifty interface (Figure 15.4) provided by the Color module.

Use the following steps to recolor the default theme Bartik.

1. From the Administrative toolbar, click Appearance. For the theme labeled "default theme," find and click the link titled Settings.

2. If you uploaded a new logo in the previous step, you will now see a preview of your site including your logo. You may need to scroll down a bit to see the preview.

3. Adjust each of the colors according to your needs. Several color sets are available for you to pick from. These color sets are high contrast and accessible to all Web site visitors.

4. When you are happy with the preview, scroll to the bottom of the configuration screen and click "Save configuration."

Your site is now magically recolored. There aren't very many free Drupal themes that support this enhancement, but it sure is nice when they do!

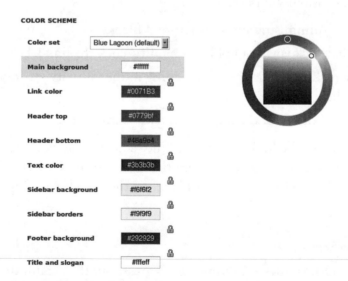

FIGURE 15.4 The Color module allows you to change the colors of some page elements in your site.

Banner Image

Bartik comes with the ability to add a logo, but what if you want an image that stretches across the header of your site? Noggin to the rescue! This contributed module allows you to upload a banner graphic to your Web site without fiddling around with code. Download and install the module from `http://drupal.org/project/noggin`. Use the instructions from Chapter 11 to install the module.

Contributed Themes

Not all themes have the same approach to getting things done. Most of the Drupal themes you find online are meant to be used as is. Without knowing any code, you will often be limited to the exact layout and colors provided by the theme.

Some themes aren't even meant to be used as a Web site design—these base themes contain shortcuts that allow theme designers to quickly convert their designs into Drupal themes. We'll use NineSixty later in this chapter. I also like the following base themes.

- **Fusion (`http://drupal.org/project/fusion`).** This adds all the features you wish you had, such as drop-down menus and pointy-clicky layout changes.
- **Zen (`http://drupal.org/project/zen`).** This has amazing documentation for wanna-be theme experts.
- **Mothership (`http://drupal.org/project/mothership`).** Markup purists may also enjoy using this theme.

Finding Themes

There are lots of gorgeous free themes available for Drupal. There are even a number of low-cost ones available. You can browse community-contributed themes at `http://drupal.org/project/themes`. This can take a long time to go through the hundreds of themes that are available. Usually you can find a gem or two, but it may take a while. Instead of looking at *all* themes, I rely on others to do the digging for me. In your favorite search engine, look for *drupal theme best of, drupal theme best,* or some variation on those words. Be sure to mix it up. Searching for *best Drupal themes* has fewer useful results than the first two suggestions I gave you...more on key word phrases in Chapter 16.

> **Paid Themes with Great Tech Support**
> If you don't have the time to wade through hundreds of free themes and want something that is gorgeous, just works, and comes with tech support, I recommend Fusion Drupal Themes (www.fusiondrupalthemes.com). They have gorgeous designs and are great to work with. Their free themes include Acquia Slate (http://drupal.org/project/acquia_slate), Acquia Prosper (http://drupal.org/project/acquia_prosper), and Acquia Marina (http://drupal.org/project/acquia_marina).

Some of the nicest Drupal 7 themes available when I wrote this book were the following.

- Mix and Match (http://drupal.org/project/mix_and_match)
- Earthish (http://drupal.org/project/earthish)
- Journal Crunch (http://drupal.org/project/journalcrunch)
- Libra Drupal Theme (http://drupal.org/project/libra)
- Antonelli (http://drupal.org/project/antonelli)
- .mobi (http://drupal.org/project/mobi)
- Abstract (http://drupal.org/project/abstract)

By the time you read this book, there will be even more.

Installing Themes

To install a theme on your site, you will need to get the files to your server. The process is basically the same as the steps to install a module (Chapter 11). In most cases, you'll need to download the theme to your desktop, unpack it, and then upload the unpacked folder (and its files) to your Web server. To install a new theme on your server, complete the following steps.

1. Navigate to the project page for the theme you'd like to use.
2. Scroll to the section Downloads. Locate the first Drupal 7 release for this theme. Ideally you will use a Recommended release (Figure 15.5). Themes written for Drupal 5, 6, and 8 will not work with Drupal 7.
3. Right-click the link that starts with "zip" and save the link location to your computer.
4. Inflate the package to reveal a theme folder. You may need special software, such as WinZip, to decompress the file.

Downloads

Recommended releases

Version	Downloads	Date	Links
7.x-2.0-alpha12	tar.gz (243.33 KB) | zip (285.34 KB)	2011-Feb-09	Notes | Edit
6.x-1.0	tar.gz (78.96 KB) | zip (90.42 KB)	2010-Nov-16	Notes | Edit

Other releases

Version	Downloads	Date	Links
7.x-1.1	tar.gz (492.13 KB) | zip (535.58 KB)	2011-Jan-05	Notes | Edit

Development releases

Version	Downloads	Date	Links
7.x-2.x-dev	tar.gz (243.29 KB) | zip (285.26 KB)	2011-Feb-07	Notes | Edit

FIGURE 15.5 There may be many releases for your theme. Be sure to choose the first Drupal 7 release listed.

5. Using FTP, upload this entire folder to your site's theme directory. This directory is the same one as the active settings file for the Web site you want to alter the appearance of. (This is probably `sites/default/themes` on your system.)

Once uploaded, your theme's files will be in the directory `sites/<site_name>/themes/<theme_name>`. You are now ready to enable and use your new theme.

Enabling and Configuring New Themes

To use your new theme, you need to enable it. Log in to your Drupal site as an administrative user and complete the following steps.

1. Navigate to Administration > Appearance.
2. Scroll down to the bottom of the screen (where all the disabled themes live), beneath your theme's screen shot, and click the link Enable.

Once your theme is enabled, you will need to configure its display and ensure blocks are appearing in the correct regions. Refer to the instructions in "Regions for Layout" previously in this chapter to adjust the placement of blocks in your new theme. Once the theme has been configured, you can set it as the default so that the public can see your newly designed site.

1. Using the Administrative dashboard, click the tab Appearance.
2. Scroll to the theme you want the public to use. Click the link "Set as default."

Your new theme will now be visible to the public.

Building Your Own Theme

So, you want to build your own theme? Great! Let's get started. In this section, you will learn how to build a static design file into a theme. You'll need to know HTML, CSS, and *not* have a phobia of PHP—you don't need to know PHP, but you do need to be able to copy snippets into your template files. If working with code gives you hives, you may want to skip the rest of this section and stick to contributed themes covered earlier in this chapter.

Theming Drupal for simple sites doesn't *need* to be complicated. I mean, if you want to do more work (or you have an intricate design), that's cool with me...but while you're over there getting mad at code, I'll be playing with the cats waiting for you to finish up. That's the beauty of working with base themes: Any code you do *not* provide will be supplied by relevant modules, Drupal core, and your base theme (NineSixty in this case).

Using a Grid System

In this next section, you will learn how to build simple three-column Drupal theme. I will use the Domicile theme as an example (Figure 15.6). This gorgeous three-column design was created by Betty Biesenthal at Design House (www.design-house.ca). The files for the theme you're going to build are available at http://drupal.org/project/domicile.

The designer used the 960.gs, 12-column grid layout for her design. This makes it a lot easier to re-create the design in Drupal. With the columns turned "on," we can see clearly how the design is split into its separate regions (Figure 15.7).

In addition to the banner and the footer, which each stretch across all 12 columns, there are three regions on the page. One of which is broken into an additional two columns (Figure 15.8).

Our front page needs the following regions.

- Banner (top). The banner image will be placed via the site logo. No additional content may be placed in this area, so we'll omit creating a Drupal region to avoid confusion later.
- Navigation sidebar (left).
- Feature column (middle).
- Content column (right). This is the only region that is required. It must be named "content."
- Copyright notice (footer).

FIGURE 15.6 The design for the theme, Domicile, was created by designer Betty Biesenthal (www.design-house.ca).

FIGURE 15.7 Domicile theme with the grid overlay turned on. This screen shot was taken from the graphics application Gimp.

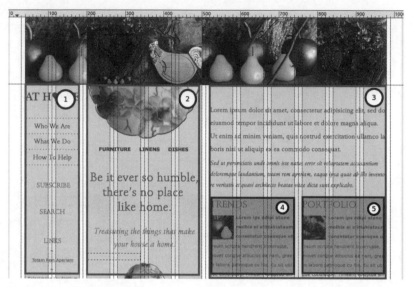

FIGURE 15.8 Regions in the Domicile theme

This is all the information we need to start building our Drupal theme. Additional information on working with CSS grid frameworks is available in Appendix D.

Theme Shell

Working on your local computer to start, complete the following steps to create your *minimum viable theme* (MVT, a theme that just barely works).

1. Create a new folder named `domicile` for your theme in the same parent directory as `ninesixty`. For example, these two folders may both be on your desktop to start but will be uploaded to your Web server.

2. In the folder `domicile`, create a new empty text file with the name `domicile. info`. You must use a text editor, not a word processor, when editing this file.

3. Into the info file you just created, add the definitions for `name`, `description`, `screenshot`, `core`, `engine`, `base theme`, `stylesheets`, and `regions` to your theme.

```
name = Domicile
description = A three-column design by Design House.
screenshot = screenshot.png
```

```
core = 7.x
engine = phptemplate
base theme = ninesixty


; Stylesheets.
stylesheets[all][] = styles.css


; Regions
regions[nav_left]          = Navigation (left)
regions[feature_middle]    = Feature column (middle)
regions[content]           = Content column (right)
regions[copyright_footer]  = Copyright notice (footer)
```

Additional information about the info file is available from `http://drupal.org/node/171205`. Lines starting with semicolons are comments for human purposes only. They are not used by Drupal.

Page Template

For this theme, we will create only one page template file. Read this entire section before writing your code. Some of the code is duplicated between steps to show you where to place the next snippet.

Create a new text file in your theme's folder named `page.tpl.php`. Open the new file with a text editor (for example, Notepad or BBEdit, *not* Microsoft Word), and add the following HTML (without the line numbers, of course).

```
1. <div id="page" class="container-12 clearfix">
2.   <div id="banner" class="grid-12 clearfix"> </div>
3.   <div id="main" class="grid-12 clearfix">
4.     <div id="nav" class="grid-2 alpha"></div>
5.     <div id="feature" class="grid-4"></div>
6.     <div id="content" class="grid-6 omega"></div>
7.   </div>
8.   <div id="copyright" class="grid-12 clearfix"></div>
9. </div>
```

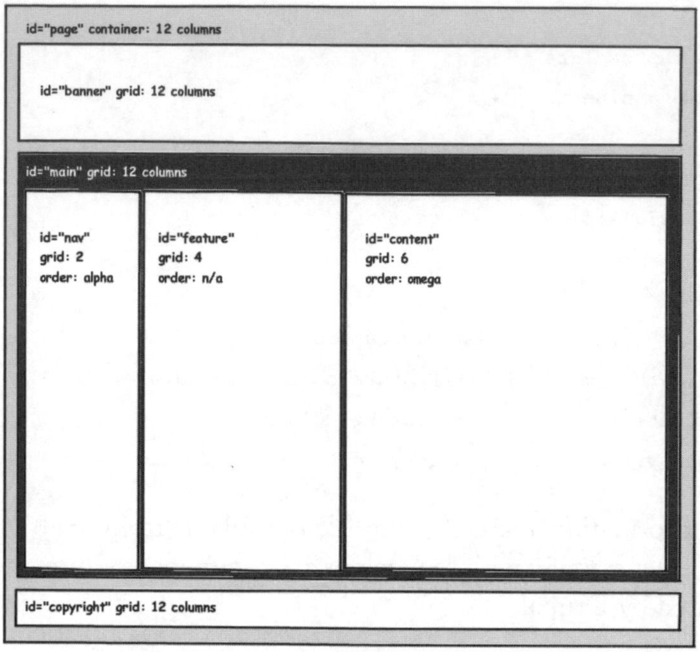

```
id="page" container: 12 columns

  id="banner" grid: 12 columns

  id="main" grid: 12 columns

    id="nav"         id="feature"        id="content"
    grid: 2          grid: 4             grid: 6
    order: alpha     order: n/a          order: omega

  id="copyright" grid: 12 columns
```

FIGURE 15.9 Domicile theme wireframe showing seven unique HTML divs

This makes up the basic shape of your page, as shown by the wireframe in Figure 15.9.

To the basic HTML framework we need to add the PHP snippets responsible for displaying the content for each of the regions: banner, navigation, feature, content, and copyright.

In the next snippet, we add the banner image and the link back to the home page (bold text is the link; italicized text is the banner image). On the second line of the previous HTML snippet (`<div id="banner" class="grid-12 clearfix"> </div>`), insert the following code between the open and close `<div>` tags.

```
<a href="<?php print $front_page; ?>"
  title="To <?php print $site_name; ?> home page">
  <img src="<?php print $logo; ?>" alt="<?php print $site_name; ?>" />
</a>
```

From the fourth line of the HTML snippet, add the following PHP to print your navigation region (the bold region name was defined in your theme's .info file).

```
<?php print render($page['nav_left']); ?>
```

If you want to know more about this new Drupal function, render, please read http://api.drupal.org/api/drupal/includes--common.inc/function/ drupal_render/7. This is *not* required reading!

On the fifth line, add the PHP snippet for the feature region.

```
<?php print render($page['feature_middle']); ?>
```

On the sixth line, add the PHP snippet for the content region.

```
<?php print render($page['content']); ?>
```

On the eighth line, add the PHP snippet for the copyright/footer region.

```
<?php print render($page['copyright_footer']); ?>
```

The completed snippet will now look like the following (bold text shows the inserted PHP snippets).

```
1.  <div id="page" class="container-12 clearfix">
2.    <div id="banner" class="grid-12 clearfix">
       <a href="<?php print $front_page; ?>" ↵
          title="To <?php print $site_name; ?> home page">
          <img src="<?php print $logo; ?>" ↵
             alt="<?php print $site_name; ?>" />
       </a>
      </div>
3.    <div id="main" class="grid-12 clearfix">
4.      <div id="nav" class="grid-2 alpha">
          <?php print render($page['nav_left']); ?>
        </div>
5.      <div id="feature" class="grid-4">
          <?php print render($page['feature_middle']); ?>
        </div>
```

```
6.    <div id="content" class="grid-6 omega">

        <?php print render($page['content']); ?>

      </div>
7.  </div>
8.  <div id="copyright" class="grid-12 clearfix">

        <?php print render($page['copyright_footer']); ?>

      </div>
9.  </div>
```

Navigation

We're going to use Drupal core's menu blocks to place our navigation for the primary and secondary menus. This means the variables won't be placed into the file page. tpl.php, and you must remember to place the blocks into the appropriate regions after the theme has been enabled.

If you want to prevent the menus from appearing on the theme settings configuration page, you must set the features you *do* want to show. The following is an example.

```
features[] = logo
features[] = name
features[] = favicon
; Disabled:
; features[] = main_menu
; features[] = secondary_menu
; features[] = slogan
```

Drupal core adds a skip-to-content link for accessibility purposes in the template file html.tpl.php. You do not need to add this link to your templates.

Content

Finally, we can add the fixed markup to your page template to flesh out the content region. There's a lot to add. The content region of a page typically contains eight separate items.

- **Title, title prefix, and title suffix.** When you are viewing a *node*, this set of variables displays the Title field.

- **Tabs.** This is where an authenticated user will be shown the View and Edit tabs for content and user profiles. This variable must be rendered (extracted from the rest of the page) before printing.

- **Messages.** Notifications about your most recent action will be displayed here. This also includes administrative notices if a module that you've installed has a newer version available.

- **Help.** Extra tips that are available for this module will be displayed here. It's more common to see these tips in the administration area of your Drupal site.

- **Page content.** Everything except the title of a page will be displayed in this area. If you are looking at a single node, the display for the individual fields is controlled by the template file `node.tpl.php`. This variable must be rendered (extracted from the rest of the page) before printing.

- **Feed icons.** This is the orange RSS icon for those who want to subscribe to your site. This variable must be rendered (extracted from the rest of the page) before printing.

You will be replacing the following line in the file `page.tpl.php`.

```
<div id="content" class="grid-6 omega">
  <?php print render($page['content']); ?>
</div>
```

> **Note: I've Omitted the Breadcrumbs**
> Drupal breadcrumbs make me angry when trying to combine them with redundant navigation systems (commonly seen when using Taxonomy), so I generally omit them from all sites to avoid pain down the road. Yes, even when using the Custom Breadcrumb module, there is no way to get context on which navigation system you used to arrived at a specific node without a lot of voodoo. Trust me.

Here is the new "content" snippet that prints variables for `$title`, `$title_prefix`, `$title_suffix`, `$tabs`, `$messages` (notification that your comment was saved), and `$feed_icons`. The variables for content and help are actually page regions. They must use the special Drupal function `render` before they can be printed.

```
<div id="content" class="grid-6 omega">
 <?php print render($title_prefix); ?>
 <?php if ($title): ?>
 <h1 class="title" id="page-title"><?php print $title; ?></h1>
 <?php endif; ?>
 <?php print render($title_suffix); ?>
 <?php if ($tabs): ?>
 <div class="tabs"><?php print render($tabs); ?></div>
 <?php endif; ?>
 <?php print $messages; ?>
 <?php print render($page['help']); ?>
 <?php print render($page['content']);?>
 <?php print $feed_icons; ?>
</div>
```

Graphics

With the basic shell in place, it's time to extract the graphics from the design file and place them into the appropriate Drupal template file. As in most themes, Domicile has graphics in the page template only.

1. Create a screen shot that you can use to preview and select this theme. It can be either an overview of the front page or just a highlight. The image should be 294×219 pixels. Name this file `screenshot.png`. This file name must match whatever file name you specified in your theme's info file.

2. From the design file, crop images that will be used into their individual pictures.

    a. Banner

    b. Site name or logo if you are using a nonstandard font

    c. Static decorations (plates in the middle column)

The images for Domicile were cropped according to Figure 15.10.

Each of these graphics will appear throughout the site; however, I want to make it possible for the site owner to swap out the banner image from time to time without having to ask me to make a change to the site. The banner will be uploaded through the Drupal user interface. The remaining three graphics will be hard-coded into the theme.

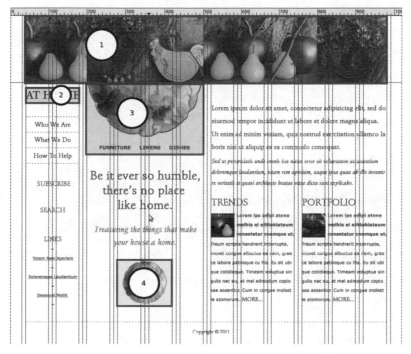

FIGURE 15.10 Crop areas for each of the four images used in the Domicile theme

1. The site title graphic (image 2) should be hard-coded inside the Navigation `<div>` but above the Navigation region.

2. The top feature decoration (image 3) should be hard-coded inside the Feature `<div>` but above the Feature region.

3. The bottom feature decoration (image 4) should be hard-coded inside the Feature `<div>` as well but below the Feature region.

In your template file `page.tpl.php`, locate the snippet for your navigation and feature regions.

```
<div id="nav" class="grid-2 alpha">
  <?php print render($page['nav_left']); ?>
</div>
<div id="feature" class="grid-4">
  <?php print render($page['feature_middle']); ?>
</div>
```

Replace that snippet with the following.

```
<div id="nav" class="grid-2 alpha">
 <a href="<?php print $front_page; ?>"
  title="Back to <?php print $site_name; ?> home page">
 <h1 id="site-name"><img src="
  <?php print $base_path . $directory; ?>/site-name.jpg"
   alt="At Home" /></h1>
 </a>
 <?php print render($page['nav_left']); ?>
</div>
<div id="feature" class="grid-4">
  <div class="decoration">
   <img src="<?php print $base_path . $directory; ?>
    /feature-decoration-top.jpg" alt=" " />
  </div>
  <?php print render($page['feature_middle']); ?>
  <div class="decoration"><img src="
   <?php print $base_path . $directory; ?>
    /feature-decoration-bottom.jpg" alt=" " /></div>
</div>
```

Update the `alt` attribute on the feature decoration if the content of the graphic is important to your site. Adding text replacements will improve your accessibility to search engines and visitors using adaptive technologies.

> **Use Flexible Path Names**
> The source of the images uses the special Drupal variables, `$base_path` and `$directory`, so that you can install the theme on any Web site without having to change the template files.

The complete source code for the template file `page.tpl.php` is available in Appendix E.

Launch Your MVT

Your theme isn't finished yet. Right now it's an MVT that will display basic shapes and content. You will use this MVT to see what else needs to be refined and to obtain the CSS selectors you'll need to make everything look "just so."

Upload Your Theme Files

You will need to upload your files and the base theme you downloaded earlier using the same steps as when you uploaded a contrib theme earlier in this chapter. Note the locations for your base theme and your new custom theme.

1. Download a copy of the base theme NineSixty (`http://drupal.org/ project/ninesixty`). This base theme allows us to make cross-browser friendly columns with minimal fuss.

2. Uncompress the base theme NineSixty. You will not edit or place any additional files into this folder. It will be used by Drupal as a reference for any template you do not want to alter in your own theme.

3. Upload the base theme `ninesixty` and all of its contents to the folder `sites/ all/themes`. This base theme is now available to any Drupal site that shares this code base.

4. Your new theme folder `domicile` and all of its contents should be uploaded to the folder `sites/default/themes`. If you have more than one Drupal site running on this server, you may need to change `default` to a more specific site name.

The goal is to have this theme available *only* to the site to which it belongs. You don't want Vinny's Harley being used on Sue's T-shirt Web site!

Enable Your New Theme

Log in to your Drupal site as an administrative user and complete the following steps.

1. Using the administrative dashboard, click the tab Appearance.
2. Scroll down to the bottom of the screen (where all the disabled themes live), beneath your theme's screen shot, and click the link "Enable and set default."
3. After the screen refreshes, click the settings link for your theme.
4. Scroll to the fieldset "Logo image settings." Unselect the check box "Use the default logo." A new set of settings will be revealed.

FIGURE 15.11 The MVT for Domicile still needs work, although the basic shapes are in place.

5. Click Browse, and find your banner image for this theme on your hard drive.

6. Scroll to the bottom of the screen and click "Save configuration."

Your new banner will be uploaded, and your site's home page should now look like Figure 15.11.

Most of the heavy lifting is now done. It's now time to fill up your site with content to see how the theme fits together. Refer to the CSS file in Appendix E to see how CSS was used to style the fonts and get the teaser list (highlights at the bottom of the front page) to sit side by side.

Site Configuration to Finish Your Theme

When creating a theme, you must decide what to put into the theme's files and what to use the Drupal administrative interface to build. The more you put into the theme files, the less work it takes to install the theme; however, the more you put into the code of your site, the harder it is for someone to edit site design elements. There are no hard rules about what goes where. It will take a bit of trial and error to see how you like to work best. This section covers the site-building tips you will need to implement to make your theme look like the finished theme in Figure 15.6.

1. The front-page quote is a custom block, so add a custom block to the front page with your quote of choice. Wrap the two separate quotes in HTML and add a class that you can use for styling. Here's an example.

```
<blockquote class="large-bold">Be it ever so humble,
  there's no place like home.</blockquote>
<blockquote class="medium-ital">Treasuring the things
  that make your house a home.</blockquote>
```

And in your theme's style sheet, add the following.

```
#feature blockquote {
  text-align: center;
}


.large-bold p {
  color: #996633;
  font-family: serif;
  font-size: 200%;
}


.medium-ital p {
  color: #999999;
  font-family: serif;
  font-size: 150%;
  font-style: italic;
}
```

2. The primary navigation will use the menu blocks provided by Drupal core instead of page template variables. Navigate to the list of blocks (Structure > Blocks) and drag the block Main menu into the Navigation (left) region.

3. The block Main menu will have a header turned on by default. You don't want your navigation area to have a heading called "Main menu," so we'll need to turn it off. Navigate to the block settings page and set the title to <none> (including the angle brackets).

4. Add a custom menu for the utility links (Search and Subscribe). The styling has been added in the CSS file. You will need to adjust the selectors in the CSS file if you use a menu link other than "Utility Links."

5. Add the content you want to appear in the copyright/footer to a new, custom block. Add appropriate font styles to your CSS file.

6. Use the content type Article to create the summaries on the front page with images.

7. Create a new image display format that is scaled and cropped to 60×60 square. Apply this display format to your Article content type.

Variations on a Theme

By changing the images, this theme can get a radically different tone. Figure 15.12 shows two variations created by my students, Donna Benjamin and Teri Gibson.

FIGURE 15.12 By varying the images used in a theme, the tone can be radically transformed.

Summary

In this chapter, you learned how to customize your Web site and create your own Drupal theme. You were exposed to the bare minimum of what it takes to create a theme. If you want to learn more about theming Drupal, check out the free, community-maintained Theming Guide (`http://drupal.org/documentation/theme`). When working with themes, remember the following tips.

- Isolate each page element that you want to change and work on only one thing at a time. Trying to change *everything* at once leads to frustration. Break apart your tasks so you can complete them one at a time.
- The smallest of changes can make a very big difference. Try changing the banner image and background colors of a contributed theme to get a whole new look for your Web site.
- Theming a Drupal site is more than just the template files. Create the shape of your theme, but use the Drupal administrative interface to help you place elements within your theme.

Chapter 16

Search Engine Optimization

With its scary acronyms and marketing gurus, search engine optimization (SEO) can seem like some kind of magic potion that gets poured onto corporate Web sites. Fortunately, SEO doesn't need to be hard or complicated or expensive. In this chapter, you will learn the fundamentals of how to get your site ranked higher than your competitors. You will learn the key Drupal modules needed to customize the content, page titles, and markup that will get your site search engine ready.

Getting Started with SEO

Let's start with an example. I recently purchased a new computer and needed to install my graphics toolkit. I use free software almost exclusively, so installing new software is a matter of doing a quick search on the Web and downloading my tools. I use Gimp for most of my work but occasionally use Inkscape when I need to modify vector-based illustrators. I did a quick search for the following terms.

- *free graphics application*
- *free graphics software*
- *free graphics program*
- *free graphics editor*

GIMP (www.gimp.org) ranks well in all four search phrases, but only the first link yields a top-ten result for Inkscape (www.inkscape.org). GIMP is a more popular software package. It has more incoming links and is generally more visible on the Internet. Inkscape, however, has made one fatal flaw in its Web site that is preventing it from achieving a strong search engine ranking: All of its page titles are the same! ("Inkscape. Draw Freely.") A single template had been used to create all the pages on the site, leaving no clues for the search engine indexer to determine what each page is about. Throughout the rest of this chapter, you will learn how search engines work and how you can avoid making some of the common mistakes found on the Internet that will prevent your site from getting a good ranking. As you'll see, Drupal takes care of a lot of the heavy lifting for you.

One of my favorite SEO specialists, Darryl Peddle, defines SEO as "the process of enhancing both the content and the reputation of a Web page in order to improve search engine rankings and meet your top prospects at their immediate point of need." Broken out, this gives you four key areas.

- **Content.** This is the quality of the words and phrases you use on your site, including the semantic value you give that content through the use of HTML markup. For example, headings are more important that plain text, and page titles are more important than headings.

- **Reputation.** This is the quality of incoming links including the key phrases used in the link text as well as the popularity of the sites that link to you.

- **Top prospects and qualified buyers.** Who's got the potential to buy your product, sign up for your mailing list, or become a raving fan? You want to create content to attract the people who will do the most good for your business.

- **Site content and visitor needs.** This is the pairing of your "most wanted outcome" with your visitor's "point of need." If your visitor needs a tutorial to help them assemble their new bookcase and you give them an article on feng shui and how to place the bookcases in the right energy center, there is a mismatch between what you want and what your visitor wants, and no one will go home happy.

Seeing Your Site Through a Search Engine's Eyes

Every single page of your Web site should have a purpose with an intended audience and a most wanted outcome. Whether you're trying to attract users or developers, take a good look at every page on your Web site, and ask yourself the following questions.

- What's the point of this page? Who needs to read it, and what should they do after reading it?
- What are the key phrases or keywords for this page?
- What's the Wordle (`www.wordle.net/create`) for this page (Figure 16.1)?
- Does the Wordle have the key phrases it needs for the right type of visitors to find this page?
- What are key search phrases that visitors are currently using to get to my site? (There's more about this later, but if you aren't tracking users on your site yet, skip back to Chapter 11 and learn how to install Google Analytics so that we have some data to examine by the time you're done reading this chapter.)

Next you'll need to examine your competition to find out how to outrank them. Find out what keywords your competitor sites are using. You can "view source" of individual pages to look for the meta tag that holds the keywords for that page, or you can have Google scrape out the keywords they think are important using one of its free tools.

FIGURE 16.1 The Wordle for the blog of the popular SEO company Volacci

- Keyword Tool for Google AdWords (`https://adwords.google.com/select/KeywordToolExternal`)

- Microsoft adCenter Excel plug-in; requires Excel 2007 (`http://advertising.microsoft.com/canada/en/learning-center/downloads/microsoft-advertising-intelligence`)

- Wordtracker (`http://freekeywords.wordtracker.com/`)

Not only will these tools help you get a list of terms for your site, but they'll also tell you how popular the term is and how heavy the competition is for the keyword.

> **Choose Good Keywords to Get More Traffic**
> SEO isn't a game of trying to beat the search engines; it's about beating your competition for keywords that your top prospects are using. Start by including key word phrases in your Web site that are high on search volume but low on competition according to Google's Keyword Tool. Once you've mastered these terms, you'll be better prepared to go head to head with your competitors for more valuable (and more popular) key search phrases.

Making Your Site Better

You should now have a huge list of all the key phrases your site should be using, so it's time to fix things up. Here's a quick summary of how to convert that list into higher search engine rankings that will help you attract more top prospects at their point of need. Later in this chapter you will learn Drupal-specific techniques to apply these key concepts.

- Add keywords from your list to relevant pages.

- Fix up the title of your pages so that they're unique and contain keywords.

- Add markup to content to improve the semantic value of your keywords. Break your page into content that has headings and otherwise emphasizes important text.

- Make your site faster. Where relevant, reduce the number of files that are being loaded, compress your images, and use Drupal's built-in caching system when you can. Not only are people impatient, but search engines are now using page load time to rank sites.

- Monitor your using an analytics program for search phrases people are using (and are not using) to find your site.

Give it a week or two and then retest your search engine ranking for the key words and phrases that are important to your top prospects.

With these few simple tips, any open source project can help propel its Web site to a higher ranking in the search engines. It'll help you attract new users and keep your existing users happy that they've been able to quickly find that tutorial they need to solve whatever problem they're dealing with right now. Now that I've tricked you into thinking this SEO stuff is doable, let's go deeper to find out how SEO really works.

How Search Engines Work

There is a lot more to that thing we call a "search engine" than just a form with a "search" button. A search engine is built from four main components: crawling, indexing, ranking, and user searches (Figure 16.2). Each of these parts is performed by a different bit of code. Before you can find a Web page in a search engine, it must have gone through the first three steps in the search collation process. Web sites are visited by both humans and robots. The robots built by search engines are responsible for "crawling" around on the Internet, following links, and reporting content back to the main search engine system.

This description covers organic search engine listings. It does not cover the paid search engine ads that appear when you complete a search on a search engine. Optimizing for paid ads is a completely different kettle of fish involving herrings that aren't relevant to building a Drupal site.

This is why it is so important that your Web site can be used without fancy plug-ins and extra software installed. Search engine robots are dumb robots. The best they can do is click a link and see what is on the other side. They can't invent URLs they don't know about, and they can't open pop-up windows. So, this crawler worms its way around the Internet finding pages and telling the indexer about these pages.

FIGURE 16.2 Search engines are made up of four main parts: crawlers, indexers, ranking algorithms, and user searches.

> **Search Engines Make a Database of Your Database**
> As the crawler finds pages, it tucks them into a new database that will be used by the indexer and the ranking algorithms to help people find content on your site. Essentially, a search engine creates a database of your database. In the new database, the words on your page are sorted according to the HTML tags around them and their frequency on the page.

The indexer then reads the page and thinks really hard about all the information that's contained on the page. It looks for headings, page titles, and any other "semantic" information that it can find about the page. Semantic information is added by the HTML code of the page. On a well-designed page, the HTML tags will tell the indexer additional information about the page, such as "this word is a heading" or "this word has been emphasized" or "this phrase is a link to another page." The indexer also looks for things to ignore. This may include style sheets and JavaScript and tiny words that have no real meaning such as *a*, *the*, and *Joomla!* Just kidding about that last word. It has meaning.

The next part of the search engine process is for the search engine to apply a "rank" to a page based on some magic voodoo sauce that the search engine company has invented. These search algorithms typically change at least once a month and affect how a page ranks against others with similar content. The ranking system typically applies more importance to content headings than plain paragraph text and applies more importance to page titles than subheadings.

Once each page has been assigned a ranking for each of the key terms it contains, it is entered into the public search form. The public search form is what you see when you use Google or Bing or Yahoo! You may have noticed that search results for a blog will sometimes have an old entry in the description than what is currently available on the front page. That's because of the process the search engine uses to build its index. If a site is updated frequently, the search engine crawler may return daily to look for new content; however, if the site is inactive, the crawler will visit less frequently.

> **Keep Your Site's Content Up to Date in Search Engines**
> Want to make sure that your site is always up to date in search engines? Add at least one new page to your site weekly. The more often you update your site, the more often the search engine crawler will visit your site.

Fixing Your Site: The Factors Drupal Can't Affect

In our definition of SEO, there were four important pillars that you needed to consider when optimizing your site for search engines: content, reputation, top prospects, and the needs of the visitors. Drupal can help you optimize your site's content. But it can't force people to link to you, it can't ask incoming visitors what their intentions are, and it can't make you coffee. Here's a quick primer on improving the three pillars of SEO that Drupal *can't* help you with.

Reputation

Every incoming link to your site is like a vote for your content. The more links you have, the higher your reputation will be. Links from pages that are related to the content on your site will reinforce the key phrases you have used on your site. In other words, people who write about the same thing you do and link will increase your search engine reputation more than unrelated content. An easy way to add incoming links from related pages is to comment on someone else's blog or answer a question in Yahoo! Answers (`http://answers.yahoo.com/`).

High-quality, reputation-building links use link text that matches the keyword "themes" on your site, not your business name (theme as in thematic, not as in the designs that you install to change how Drupal looks). In other words, a link that looks like this:

```
Amye's site has a really <a href="http://example.com/seo-top-ten-tips">great
tutorial with useful SEO tips</a>.
```

is more valuable than a link that looks like this:

```
For more information go to <a href="http://example.com/">Amye's site</a>
```

In the second example, the search engine indexer knows that you think Amye's page is related to the terms *tutorial*, *SEO*, and *tips*. Similarly, a link to your site with the anchor text, "great horse blankets" is also more relevant coming from *Horse & Rider Monthly* than *Jake's Chihuahua Haven*, unless of course Jake has higher page rank. Relevance is important to your reputation. In building your site's reputation, themed links that use relevant key words are more valuable than nonthemed links.

> **Optimize for the Right Words in Your Link Text**
> In Google do a quick Web search for the term *click here*. The number-one search result is Adobe Acrobat's download page. For years Adobe told Web people to link to its site using a very specific phrase with a link that read "click here" to download and install its software. Although it hasn't hurt their search engine rankings, it's unfortunate Adobe accidentally optimized its site for such a poor keyword phrase.

In addition to sprinkling your own links to your own site on the Internet, another great way to get incoming links is to ask people to write a review of your product from their blog. Do you have favorite blogs that already write about topics and products related to yours? Drop them a private e-mail and ask if they would be interested in writing a review of your product in exchange for a free one.

Marketing

In almost every single case where a Web site has failed online, the owner has done nothing to promote their site. They haven't advertised the new site in-store or on their mailing list. They aren't a member of any social media sites such as Twitter or Facebook where they can make an announcement about their new site. When visitors do come to the site, there are no sections that are obviously updated on a regular basis such as monthly newsletters or a blog. No wonder they're not getting any sales.

You can start promoting your site today, even if it won't exist until tomorrow. Once the site is built, you will need to give people a reason to come back and visit often. Think about what kinds of promotional tactics have worked on you. Emulate the successful campaigns, and learn from the annoying and weak ones.

There are lots of free ways to promote your business online. First and foremost, include your URL in all outgoing e-mails. It's amazing how many people forget to do this one little step. Your mail program will have a function called a *signature* that you can use to automatically append all outgoing e-mails with your name, contact information, and URL. Set it and forget it! Any print materials that you create should also include your URL. This includes business cards, fliers, postcards, buttons, stickers, and posters. Participate in online communities; Facebook, Twitter, and LinkedIn are great places to expand your network.

Ask your customers to sign up for a mailing list, and send them periodic updates. Remember to follow the law and respect your customer's right to privacy. Do not share or distribute your mailing list to anyone; always have a way for subscribers to opt out of your mailings, and collect personal information only with your customer's consent.

If you have a retail location, the easiest way to do this is to have a clipboard where individuals write in their own e-mail and their name. This way, you know for sure that the individual wanted to be on your mailing list.

Make an event out of your Web site. Throw yourself a party and invite the media. Make sure you can make a story out of the event. It's not just a Web site; it's... (you fill in the blank here).

Do you have a blog? You should add one to your site if you want to improve your search engine rankings. If you write a high-quality blog, chances are good that other people will start linking to your content from their Web sites. But you don't have to rely entirely on what other people link to. You can link to your own articles from your own site too. By using high-quality link text in your blog entries and referring to other pages on your site, you can actually improve your off-site reputation with your own content.

The Internet is also full of these aggregator sites known in the software world as *planets*. They are places where community members republish their RSS feed in one common place. If you participate in any online communities, check to see whether they offer a "planet" or an "aggregator" where you can publish your blog too. This is a very easy way to put your high-quality links onto an external Web site that links back to you. Drupal's planet feed is available at `http://drupal.org/planet`.

Attracting Top Prospects and Qualified Buyers

Remember in Chapter 5 when you were supposed to decide what your goals were for your Web site? And then in Chapter 6 when you figured out what customers were going to do on your site? If you've completed all the exercises from these chapters, it should be no problem to create content that contains the keywords that your top prospects will be using when searching for sites like yours. If you don't know who your best customers are and what they are most interested in buying from you, it doesn't matter how many people visit your site. They won't stick around, and you will have an exceptionally difficult time converting visitors into customers (your site does have measurable goals, right?).

Providing the Right Type of Content at the Visitor's Point of Need

In addition to attracting the right type of visitors, you need to make sure that you help visitors find the right kind of content. Someone searching for *cheap mothers day flowers* probably doesn't really care about the difference between the significance of giving a red or white rose. Make sure your site has a clear call to action on each page with links leading to alternate content where appropriate. A set of links may include About Roses, Buy Roses Now, and Rose Photo Gallery.

Best Practices for Creating SEO-Friendly Content with Drupal

Even though SEO sounds super technical and has more acronyms than a high-school yearbook, it doesn't (always) need to be hard. In this section you will learn the easiest ways to make your site SEO friendly using only Drupal core modules. (I will recommend a few contributed modules too for those of you who don't believe it could possibly be this easy.)

> **Want to Be an SEO Ninja?**
> If you want to be a search engine ninja, you need to install the module SEO checklist. This module was created as a companion to Ben Finklea (Volacci)'s excellent book *Drupal 6 Search Engine Optimization*. Even though it's just a checklist, the module helps you identify each of the steps you need to take to make an awesome search engine–friendly Web site. The module references specific pages in Ben's book, which tell you why it's important to configure that particular module.
>
> An additional helper module is The Drupal SEO Friend module (`http://drupal.org/project/seo_friend`). It is meant to be used alongside existing Drupal SEO modules, such as SEO Checklist and SEO Compliance Checker, to make them more effective.

Use Unique Page Titles

In Drupal the node title is used as the primary heading and page title for each page of your site. The page title is the text that appears in the `<title>` tag, is displayed by search engine result pages, and is the title that is visible when someone bookmarks a page on your Web site. If you are writing keyword-rich node titles, give yourself a pat on the back and take the rest of the afternoon off. Without any additional customization Drupal is going to make sure you have unique page titles.

The Curse of the Home Page Title

Are you using "Welcome" as the title for the front page of your site? Be honest. Yes? Put this book down *right now* and go edit the front page of your Web site. We can't be friends until this is fixed, so go do it *now*. For the love of Drupal: Make every single node on your site something meaningful or at least slightly catchy. If you're having a hard time thinking about what else to call that front-page text, here are a few suggestions.

- Making the Web a better place.
- Real Drupal themes. Right now. No problem.

- We are SEO experts.
- What do you need help with?

Bonus tip: These are all tag lines from famous Drupal companies. Do you know who they are?

Advanced Page Titles

The contributed module Page Title (`http://drupal.org/project/page_title`) allows you to create page titles that differ from the title of the node (Figure 16.3). This is especially useful for the front page of your site where the visible tag line (node title) is inappropriate as a page title.

The module Page Title relies on the module Token (`http://drupal.org/project/token`). Be sure to download this module too. Once you've downloaded and enabled the modules Page Title and Token, use the administrative toolbar to navigate

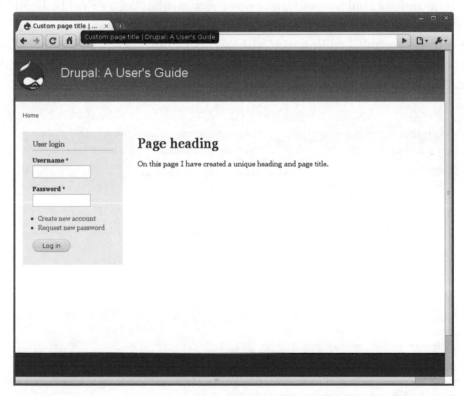

FIGURE 16.3 The page title (top left of the screen shot) differs from the node title (middle of the page) thanks to the module Page Title.

to Content. From there select the tab "Page titles." You will be presented with a config-
uration screen that allows you to set the patterns to be used for each of your page titles.
The first two page types (Default and Frontpage) show you how to assemble a pattern.
The list of available "tokens" is available at the bottom of the configuration screen.

> **Tokens Are Like Variables**
> A *token* is essentially a piece of placeholder text that will be converted into an
> actual Drupal value when the page is built. If you speak geek, this is sort of like
> a "variable." If you don't speak geek, it's a little bit like a "Save the date" card for a
> wedding. It's saying to Drupal, "Something important is going to happen here when
> the time comes."

If you're feeling brave and automation-happy, go ahead and insert replacement patterns. If you're only feeling human, scroll down to the bottom of the configuration
screen (Figure 16.4). For each of the Content types on your Drupal site as well as the
user profile and vocabulary, you can opt to create custom page titles "by hand" using
Drupal's administrative editing screens.

Once you've enabled editing, you will have a custom field available each time you
create new content, a user profile, or a vocabulary per your Page Title module settings.
Figure 16.5 shows the custom editing screen for page titles on a Basic page.

PAGE TYPE	TOKEN SCOPE	PATTERN	SHOW FIELD
Pager Suffix	Global	This pattern will be appended to a page title for any given page with a pager on it	
Comment Reply	Node	This pattern will be used for comment reply pages, where the reply is directly to a "node"	
Comment Child Reply	Node Comment	This pattern with be used for comment reply pages where the reply is to an existing "comment" (eg a comment thread)	
User Profile	User	This pattern will be used for any user profile pages	☐
Content Type - *Article*	Node	This pattern will be used for all *Article* node-type pages	☐
Content Type - *Basic page*	Node	This pattern will be used for all *Basic page* node-type pages	☐
Vocabulary - *Tags*	Taxonomy	This pattern will be used for all *Tags* term pages	☐

FIGURE 16.4 To enable editing of page titles in Drupal's administrative editing screens, select the check
box beside each of the relevant content types.

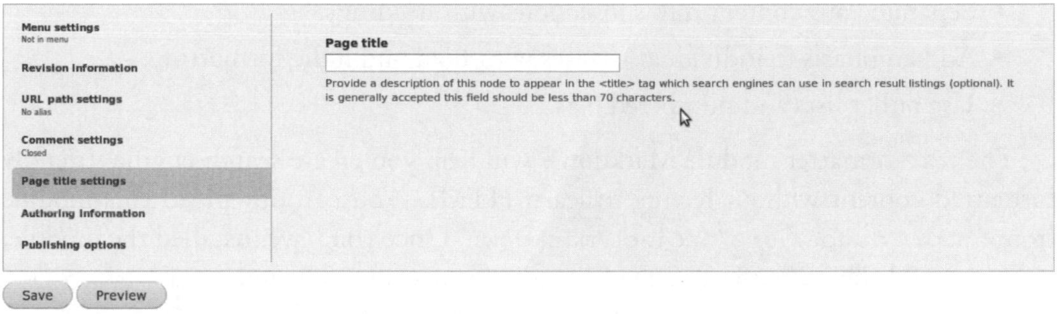

FIGURE 16.5 The Page Title settings are available in the bottom vertical tabs menu at the bottom of the administrative editing screen.

Minimum Word Count, Maximum Topic Count

Make sure every page has at least 250 words of unique content but not more than one major theme. If visitors could easily use more than three completely unique key word themes to find your page, break the content into smaller pages. For example, if a visitor could arrive at your page by searching for *history of roses, where to buy cheap valentine's day flowers,* and *care of rose bush,* you're doing it wrong. These are three completely unique themes that each deserves their own page. Of course, these pages could all be linked to one another, but the content is too broad to ensure a successful pairing of your visitor's immediate and precise needs with so much content.

> **Add Custom Meta Tags**
> Keep an eye out for the module Meta Tags (formerly Node words). This excellent module allows you to set custom per-page meta tags for your Drupal site. When you are able to set custom meta tags for the description attribute, you can create custom text that will appear in search engines and can be used to "sell" (or convince) visitors to click the link from the search engine to your site. There wasn't a Drupal 7 version at the time the chapter was written, but one is planned. See the project page at http://drupal.org/project/metatags for more information.

Structure Your Content

On the Web you want to create easy-to-scan content that your visitors can skim without missing important bits of information. A paragraph of text is difficult to read, but a few simple tricks will make your content much easier to scan.

- Separate your content into subsections with headings.
- Add emphasis to individual phrases with bold and italic formatting.
- Use bullet lists and numbered lists.

The text formatter module Markdown will help you create search engine–friendly formatted content without having to learn HTML. You can download this module from `http://drupal.org/project/markdown`. Once you have installed the module, you must add the formatter to one of the text formats on your site.

1. Navigate to Administration > Configuration > Text formats.
2. Next to Filtered HTML, click the link "configure."
3. On the configuration screen for Filtered HTML, enable the filter for Markdown.
4. Scroll down to the Filter settings. Click the vertical tab "Limit allowed HTML tags."
5. To the list of allowed HTML tags, add `<h2>` `<h3>` (remove `<h1>` if it is listed).
6. Scroll to the bottom of the configuration screen and click "Save configuration."

To use the markdown text format, follow the quick tips displayed under the text-editing screen (Figure 16.6); the resulting page appears as Figure 16.7.

My favorite Markdown formats are as follows:

- ***Single asterisks*.** Emphasis. Displays as italicized text
- ****Double asterisks**.** Strong. Displays as bold text.
- **1. Item.** Ordered list. Displays as an indented, numbered list.
- *** Item.** Unordered list. Displays as an indented bullet list.
- **## Sub-Heading.** Heading level two. Displays as big, bold text.
- **### Sub-sub-Heading.** Heading level three. Displays as big-ish, bold text.

In-Site Linking

There are three ways to improve in-site links for search engines, including the links in the content for each of your pages ("link text"), the links in your navigation system (including menus and breadcrumbs), and finally helper link pages such as site maps. This section covers all the ways you can improve in-site linking for search engine optimization.

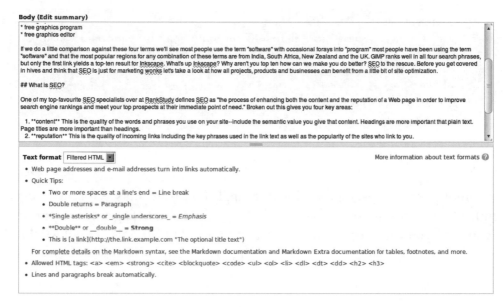

Body (Edit summary)

* free graphics program
* free graphics editor

If we do a little comparison against these four terms we'll see most people use the term "software" with occasional forays into "program" most people have been using the term "software" and that the most popular regions for any combination of these terms are from India, South Africa, New Zealand and the UK. GIMP ranks well in all four search phrases, but only the first link yields a top-ten result for Inkscape. What's up Inkscape? Why aren't you top ten how can we make you do better? SEO to the rescue. Before you get covered in hives and think that SEO is just for marketing wonks let's take a look at how all projects, products and businesses can benefit from a little bit of site optimization.

What is SEO?

One of my top-favourite SEO specialists over at RankStudy defines SEO as "the process of enhancing both the content and the reputation of a Web page in order to improve search engine rankings and meet your top prospects at their immediate point of need." Broken out this gives you four key areas:

1. **content** This is the quality of the words and phrases you use on your site--include the semantic value you give that content. Headings are more important that plain text. Page titles are more important than headings.
2. **reputation** This is the quality of incoming links including the key phrases used in the link text as well as the popularity of the sites who link to you.

Text format Filtered HTML ▾   More information about text formats ❓

- Web page addresses and e-mail addresses turn into links automatically.
- Quick Tips:
  - Two or more spaces at a line's end = Line break
  - Double returns = Paragraph
  - *Single asterisks* or _single underscores_ = *Emphasis*
  - **Double** or __double__ = **Strong**
  - This is [a link](http://the.link.example.com "The optional title text")
  - For complete details on the Markdown syntax, see the Markdown documentation and Markdown Extra documentation for tables, footnotes, and more.
- Allowed HTML tags: \<a> \<em> \<strong> \<cite> \<blockquote> \<code> \<ul> \<ol> \<li> \<dl> \<dt> \<dd> \<h2> \<h3>
- Lines and paragraphs break automatically.

FIGURE 16.6 The text-formatting tips available below the text-editing window provide help on how to use the Markdown text format.

the following terms:

- free graphics application
- free graphics software
- free graphics program
- free graphics editor

If we do a little comparison against these four terms we'll see most people use the term "software" with occasional forays into "program" most people have been using the term "software" and that the most popular regions for any combination of these terms are from India, South Africa, New Zealand and the UK. GIMP ranks well in all four search phrases, but only the first link yields a top-ten result for Inkscape. What's up Inkscape? Why aren't you top ten how can we make you do better? SEO to the rescue. Before you get covered in hives and think that SEO is just for marketing wonks let's take a look at how all projects, products and businesses can benefit from a little bit of site optimization.

What is SEO?

One of my top-favourite SEO specialists over at RankStudy defines SEO as "the process of enhancing both the content and the reputation of a Web page in order to improve search engine rankings and meet your top prospects at their immediate point of need." Broken out this gives you four key areas:

1. **content** This is the quality of the words and phrases you use on your site--include the semantic value you give that content. Headings are more important that plain text. Page titles are more important than headings.
2. **reputation** This is the quality of incoming links including the key phrases used in the link text as well as the popularity of the sites who link to you.
3. **top prospects** Who's got the potential to become a user, a developer or a raving fan that gives presentations at user groups? You want to create content to attract the people who will do the most for your project.
4. **match visitor needs to site content** This is the pairing of your "most wanted outcome" with your visitor's "point of need." If your visitor needs a tutorial to help them with their user group demo and you

FIGURE 16.7 The Web page rendered with the Markdown filter

> **Too Many Links Can Be a Bad Thing**
> A page should not have more than 100 outbound links. Any more can invite a black mark for page rank. To prevent a link from being followed, use the attribute `rel` with the value `nofollow`. This attribute is useful for pages that aggregate content from sources such as Twitter and blog feeds. If your site has a site map, you can also safely put `nofollow` directives on your site's navigation links to reduce the overall per page link count.

Link Text

When linking between pages, the same rules apply for in-site links as for incoming off-site links: Use descriptive text. If you are linking between two pages of content within the "content," you will need to know how to create an HTML link. Use the following format.

```
<a href="URL">Link text</a>
```

For example, if I wanted to link to the URL `http://fusiondrupalthemes.com/join-fusion-pro`, my HTML would look like the following.

```
<a href="http://fusiondrupalthemes.com/join-fusion-pro">Get big discounts on
Fusion Pro Themes</a>.
```

If you prefer pointy-clicky-fizzy-make-feel-good editing, you'll want to pick up a copy of the module WYSIWYG (`http://drupal.org/project/wysiwyg`) as well as your favorite HTML editor. Each editor is a little bit different. I've used TinyMCE and FCKEditor with great success in the past. Once you've installed WYSIWYG, use the administrative toolbar to navigate to Configuration > Wysiwyg profiles. Follow the on-screen instructions for your editor of choice.

Menus

To improve your in-site links, you may want to review your menu items for SEO purposes. Each content-based menu item can be configured both from the node-editing form and from the menu configuration screen. In the menu configuration screen, you are given the option to add extra "descriptive" text that will appear as a tooltip when the visitor hovers over the menu item. Some people find these highly annoying (especially if you have fancy drop-down menus on your site). If you do want to configure this text, use the administrative toolbar to navigate to Structure > Menus. Your public menus are contained in the "Main menu" and "Secondary menu" sets of links. Follow the on-screen instructions to adjust the settings for each menu item.

Breadcrumb Navigation

Breadcrumbs are hard to get right when you're building sophisticated sites with Drupal. If you are building a simple site using mostly Drupal core modules, you will probably be okay with Drupal's built-in breadcrumb navigation. If, however, you find it lacking, you will almost certainly want to try one (or more) of the following modules.

- Menu breadcrumbs (http://drupal.org/project/menu_breadcrumb)
- Custom breadcrumbs (http://drupal.org/project/custom_breadcrumbs)
- Taxonomy breadcrumbs (http://drupal.org/project/taxonomy_breadcrumb)

Menu breadcrumbs will build a breadcrumb trail based on the structure of the menu tree for the page you are currently viewing. If Drupal core's breadcrumbs aren't meeting your needs, this module is the most likely to solve your problems on a simple Web site. Typically installing the module and setting the target menu is sufficient to get everything working perfectly.

The next place to look is custom breadcrumbs. This module hooks into both core and contributed modules to provide you with unique configuration options for each different type of module. By default you may configure the breadcrumbs for each content type on your site.

Finally, if you are using Taxonomy on your site and the first two contributed modules aren't meeting your needs, you may want to try the Taxonomy Breadcrumb module (http://drupal.org/project/taxonomy_breadcrumb).

Site Map

Providing a list of all pages on your site will help search engines quickly index your entire site (without missing a page). Additional information about the SEO-friendly modules Index Page (http://drupal.org/project/indexpage) and XML Sitemap (http://drupal.org/project/xmlsitemap) are provided in Chapter 11. If you are interested in submitting your site to Yahoo! Site Explorer, you should also take a look at URL list (http://drupal.org/project/urllist).

Additional information on creating search engine–friendly site maps and submitting them to multiple search engines is available from `www.sitemaps.org`. Google-specific information is available from its excellent "Webmaster central" online help area (`www.google.com/support/webmasters/`).

SEO-Friendly URLs

And finally, the holy grail of SEO: URLs with keywords separated by hyphens. (Did you hear the chorus of angels just now as you read that? Nifty, eh?) Using only Drupal core, you can hand-build each of the URLs to each of the pages on your site. This is fine for sites that have fewer than 20 pages or are updated not more than once a day. To create a custom URL, follow these steps.

1. Navigate to the page you want to fix.
2. Click the tab Edit.
3. Scroll to the set of vertical tabs at the bottom of the screen and click "URL path settings."
4. Type in the new URL alias for this page. Use keywords related to the title of the node, and separate each keyword with a hyphen, for example `seo-best-practices-drupal` or `scotch-tastes-nice`. If the page is in a subsection of the site, you can separate the key ideas with a /, for example `workshops/seo-basics-drupal` or `scotch/balvenie`.
5. Scroll to the bottom of the editing screen and click Save.

Your node will now be available by node ID (for example, `node/2`) and by its new URL alias.

Automating SEO-Friendly URLs

For sites that have more content and are updated more frequently, you'll want to look into automating the process of building your SEO-friendly URLs with Pathauto (`http://drupal.org/project/pathauto`). Once installed, this module can be configured by using the administrative toolbar and navigating to Configuration > URL aliases > Automated alias settings (tab, top right).

Five configuration fieldsets are available. The defaults for General and Punctuation settings are already configured to use the best options for search engine optimization. You are welcome to peek at them, but you shouldn't need to alter them. The default settings provided for Taxonomy terms and User paths are also acceptable as is. You will, however, need to set up your default alias patterns for Node path. I typically set up my aliases as follows.

- **Default path pattern.** [node:title] (remove content)
- **Pattern for each content type.** [node:type]/[node:title]

If the content type warrants it, I will sometimes use a keyword instead of the automated content type. For example, if my content type is "workshop" but I want to use "workshops" in the URL because I think it reads "better," I would use the following pattern for the workshop content type: workshops/[node:title]. Note that I'm using a word instead of a replacement pattern to build the URL. This is allowed!

> **Consistency Is Important**
> Be neat and tidy and set up matching menu hierarchy, custom breadcrumb trails, and URL aliases. It'll make it easy to remember when you're creating e-mail campaigns or in-site links or you need to explain to someone over the phone how they navigate to a specific page.

Advanced URLs

Every page on your site should have a minimum of 250 words. But with all these automated aliases set up, you're sure to have a few different URLs that can be used to access *identical* content. Content duplication is bad news. Fortunately, there are two modules to help you fix this problem. (Yes, there are a lot of Drupal modules to help you with SEO; however, I'm still looking for a module that will make me a sandwich. I'm hungry.) These two modules are as follows.

- Global Redirect (http://drupal.org/project/globalredirect)
- Path Redirect (http://drupal.org/project/path_redirect)

The module Global Redirect finds the one canonical URL for each page on your site and redirects all other variations on that URL to the right page. If you have a habit of renaming URLs, you'll need Path Redirect. This module allows you to redirect people from the old URL to the new one. This means you don't need to have two (or more) URL aliases for each of your Web pages. Path Redirect is also a great way to deal with any broken incoming links. If a super-popular blogger reviews your product but links to the wrong page (*gulp*bad*), you can quickly create a redirect to point people to the place they were supposed to go to (*phew*).

Customize the File robots.txt

The Drupal module RobotsTxt (`http://drupal.org/project/robotstxt`) allows you to create and edit the `robots.txt` file dynamically from the Web UI. This file can be used to send specific instructions to Web crawlers about which pages should be indexed and which should be ignored.

When All Else Fails: 404 Helpers

Instead of showing a standard "404 Page not found," install the contributed module Search 404. This module performs a search on the keywords in the URL. For example, if a user goes to the URL `http://example.com/does/not/exist`, the module will search for the key words *does not exist* and display the results to the visitor. You can download the module from `http://drupal.org/project/search404`.

The module Link checker (`http://drupal.org/project/linkchecker`) extracts links from your content and periodically tries to detect broken hypertext links by checking the remote sites and evaluating the HTTP response codes. Broken links are listed both as a report (Toolbar > Reports) and on the content page. Individual Web users can also get a report for pages they've created from their account home page.

Web Statistics: Measuring Your Work

By measuring your baseline, you will know how effective every change is that you make to your Web site. Performing weekly searches for your key terms will show you how you rank against your competitors. But just looking at search engine results won't tell you the whole picture of how successful your site is. To see how your search terms are really performing, you need to look at what happens after visitors arrive at your site.

The Basics of Web Analytics

You've probably heard the terms *web stats* and *hits* and *page views* thrown around. Let's start with the basics of what this stuff actually means. There are two styles of Web analytics software: log file interpreters and page tagging systems.

Regardless of how the data is collected, Web analytics systems will give you a summary of the following.

- How many unique computers visited your Web site
- How many of these might have been return visitors

- What the most popular pages are on your Web site
- Where did the visitor come from (the *referrer*)?
- What were the keyword phrases the visitor was looking for
- The most popular "entry" and "exit" pages visitors used

Log File Interpreters

Each time a file is requested, a note is added to text file. Let's pretend you have a Web page with three images. Each time a visitor loads the page, four entries are added to a log file—one for the HTML page and one for each of the images. In addition to which file was requested, the time is recorded as well as the Internet address of the computer that visited your site.

At a time that is convenient (typically daily, weekly, or monthly), the log files are run through an interpretation software package, and Web statistics (usually with pretty pictures) are spit out the other end.

Advantages of using log file interpreters include the following.

- Faster page load times
- No vendor lock-in (you own your data)
- Visitor privacy

Log file interpreters also give you information about pages that *weren't* found on your site. This includes broken links between pages caused by typos or missing URL aliases and pages that are missing (maybe the incoming link is broken, or you're no longer offering a service or product that used to be featured on your site). Using the reports from a log file interpreter, you can fix things that are broken on your Web site.

There are four main disadvantages to using raw log files for Web analytics.

- **False positives.** A false positive is when a computer, which is not a real person, requests one of your pages. For example, a search engine will "crawl" your site, asking for the latest version of your pages so that it can update your search engine listing. This happens automatically and is typically a good thing for your site; however, it does mean your site statistics will show the search engine as a (human) visitor to your site. This problem is easily mitigated by identifying the "user agents" of search engine crawlers and telling your analytics application to ignore those visitors.

- **Masked IP addresses.** An IP address is the unique address of an individual computer on the Internet. Each time you connect your computer to the Internet, your Internet service provider (ISP) automatically issues your computer a unique number for that session. This means that your computer shows up as a unique visitor in the Web server's raw log file. In an office building, library, school, or other networked building, the entire *building* may show up as a single computer to the rest of the world. When this happens, it is because the system administrator for the network has "masked" the individual network addresses of each computer. There are good reasons for doing this on a network, but we don't need to worry about them at this point. At this point, we only need to be aware that 500 page views from a public library are more likely to be 5 users looking at 10 pages, rather than one person looking at 500 pages.

- **Cached pages.** "Caching" (pronounced "cash-ing") is usually a good thing for everyone. If you hit the back button on your Web browser, you don't really need to download the entire page again; you just need to see exactly what you saw a moment ago. However, hitting the back button displays the "cached" (or local) version of the page. There is no call to the server, and no record is made of the page being viewed. Large companies (including schools and libraries) will often run a caching system that stores frequently requested pages. The cache is usually updated every few minutes, and no one is the wiser for it; however, it does mean that with ten individuals in a school all accessing a Web site, fewer results may be registered in the server's log file.

The second and third are much more complex problems that have no easy solution for a small-scale web site. Unless you are running a very large-scale site, you can pretend the second and third options don't even exist; however, you should be aware that your statistics are not perfect, and there's really not much you can do about it and that's okay. Your competitors are in the same boat.

Page Tagging Systems

Web analytics systems that operate as a service, like Google Analytics, are typically using a page tagging system and are not interpreting your raw log files. After creating a Google Analytics account, you place a snippet of code into the template of your Web site (or in Drupal's case you install a module that then places a snippet of code into the bottom of your page template). Each time a page is requested, the snippet loads a tiny file from Google's Web site, and Google puts a note in *its* log file on your behalf. To see your traffic statistics, you must log into the Google Analytics Web site to see the reports Google has generated on your behalf.

The advantages of page tagging systems include the following.

- All page views are counted (even when the page is cached).
- When JavaScript is used as the "web bug" (or page tag), additional information can be sent to the analytics tool.
- No specialized knowledge is required to install, configure, and generate reports from a log file interpretation software package.
- They include reporting of on-page activity such as how much of a movie was played before the pause button was pressed.

The disadvantages of page tagging systems include the following.

- Visitors must have JavaScript enabled.
- Visitor data is shared with another company. Some Web users feel this is a violation of their privacy and will disable their computer from allowing the information to be reported.
- It results in slower page load times, which can negatively affect your page rank.

Hybrid Solutions

To overcome the limitations of each system, companies that are committed to the accuracy of their reporting tools will often use a combination of both page tagging and log file analysis tools.

Analytics Software

A lot of different applications are available to help you study the people who visit your site. Google Analytics (`http://drupal.org/project/google_analytics`) is definitely one of the most popular services available online today. It integrates with its AdWords service.

There's a world of alternatives, though. Some of analytics programs listed here integrate well with Drupal; some are stand-alone systems that you use to interpret the log files your Web server has been collecting. If you are looking for more information than what Google Analytics is providing or you just want to try something a little different, check out the following options.

Log File Analytics Software Packages

These are software packages you install on your server. Some Web hosting companies will already have one of these software packages installed and ready to go.

- Piwik (http://piwik.org/ and http://drupal.org/project/piwik)
- AWStats (http://awstats.sourceforge.net) and JAWStats (www.jawstats.com/)
- FireStats (http://firestats.cc and http://drupal.org/project/firestats)
- Grape Web Statistics (www.quate.net/grape)
- Open Web Analytics (www.openwebanalytics.com/)
- TraceWatch (www.tracewatch.com/)
- Webalizer (www.mrunix.net/webalizer and http://drupal.org/project/webalizer_integration or http://drupal.org/project/webalizer)

Page Tagging and Analytics Services

These are like Google Analytics, but they are not made by Google (unless of course Google buys them between now and when you read this chapter).

- Yahoo! Web Analytics (http://web.analytics.yahoo.com/)
- Argyle Social (www.argylesocial.com/)
- Going Up (www.goingup.com/)
- Compete (www.compete.com/)
- CrazyEgg, heat map visualization for click tracking (www.crazyegg.com/)
- KISSmetrics (www.kissmetrics.com/)
- Mint (www.haveamint.com/)
- Mochibot, for Flash applications (www.mochibot.com/)

Analytics Widgets

This list includes browser toolbars and desktop applications.

- Alexa, made famous for its "Alexa Traffic Rank" (www.alexa.com/)
- SEOMoz Term Target; requires a free account and helps you track how well your key words are performing in search engines (www.seomoz.org/tools)
- Woopra (www.woopra.com/)

Tracking and Interpreting the Results

Knowing what your site's goals are will help you pick the right metrics to follow. Not all visitors are created equal, and not all information is important. Using your analytics software, you should be tracking not your total monthly traffic but specifically the following.

- **Bounce rate.** How many people took one look at your site and hit the back button?

- **Average page views per visit.** Once people get to your site, do they stick around?

- **Total revenue and profit.** Who cares if you have a lot of traffic if no one is buying stuff?

- **Profit per order.** Can you get your customers to buy two things instead of one?

- **Referring URLs.** Where is your traffic coming from? Was it worth it to leave all those comments on blogs and social media sites?

- **Conversion rates.** Are people performing your "most wanted outcome" for each page? Who is sending you visitors that "convert"?

- **Exit pages.** It's sad when people leave. What pages are failing you, and how can you fix them?

- **Search phrases and keywords.** Have you optimized your site enough for your keywords? How's the quality of visitors for each of those keywords? Do they convert into sales? Or was optimizing for *cheap flowers* just getting you a lot of...ahem...cheap boyfriends?

Each time you look at your site's stats over time, you will get a look at how your site is doing. Try to improve the reported stats for each of the first six items in the previous list. Improving your "worst" exit pages will help keep visitors on your site and give you a second (or third or fourth) shot at converting a visitor into a customer. Examine the search phrases that are sending traffic to your site. Are they being used by your top prospects? Or have you optimized your site for low-quality prospects? Find the search terms that are performing well (converting visitors into customers), and try to improve your search engine ranking for these terms using the techniques you learned in this chapter.

Summary

Now that wasn't so hard, was it? In this chapter, you learned that SEO is about making high-quality content. You don't even have to like magic sauce to be awesome at SEO. This chapter gave you the basics of how to create high-quality content that search engines (and visitors) will love. It showed you some of the tools you can use to measure the effectiveness of the changes you make to your site, and it gave you a peek into how search engines actually work. SEO is pretty easy, but it will help your business only if you are vigilant and continue to work at improving your site's content to match what your top prospects are looking for. In summary, SEO will do the following.

- Increase the number of visitors to your site by improving your search engine ranking
- Bring high-quality visitors to your site who are interested in the topics, products, and services you offer
- Increase your sales by attracting high-quality visitors
- Increase your business's reputation through participation in online communities (you did this as part of the link building step)
- Improve the usability of your site by forcing you to carefully examine each of the navigation elements on your page
- Improve the legibility of your pages by breaking them into easily digested chunks with headings and emphasized keywords

Go forth and rank higher!

Chapter 17

Accessibility

I'm sitting in a little coffee shop in Owen Sound, Canada, across from city hall. From where I'm sitting, I can see the ramp leading into city hall and the curb cuts at the corner, and on my way here I waited at a set of lights that tweets when it's safe to walk, in tune to the direction of traffic. Even in this tiny city three hours from anywhere, the physical world is becoming more accessible. The little features we've come to expect in the built world are visibly obvious. As I watch a mum push a stroller up onto the sidewalk, I can see that the accessibility enhancements help everyone. But on the Web, things aren't always this easy or this obvious. In this chapter, you will learn how to make your Web site more accessible to everyone on the Internet.

If you think this chapter isn't for your audience, take note: Improving the accessibility of your site will also improve your search engine rankings. The crawlers that read in the content of your site have many of the same limitations that are imposed onto humans using assistive technologies, not to mention it may be required by law for your site to be accessible.

This chapter covers the following topics.

- Who needs an accessible Web site?
- How assistive technologies make computers more accessible

- Why you need to build accessible Web sites
- Drupal core
- Tips for choosing accessible themes and contributed modules
- Accessibility guidelines
- Measuring the accessibility of your site

Why Bother?

It just makes good business sense to make your sites easy to use for as many people as possible. More physical shops are making their business as accessible as possible: adding ramps, lowering counters, and providing accessible toilets. In many cases, it's government regulations that are prompting the changes, but it also makes good business sense. Why would you possibly want to put a barrier up that would prevent someone from entering your store and buying products from your shop?

Baby boomers, children born shortly after World War II, are getting older, but they definitely aren't spending any less time online. They aren't as old as my friend Ruth, but they are connecting with grandkids on Facebook or buying vacations to Spain (and probably other places too). Building accessible sites that are easy to read, easy to navigate, and easy to use just makes sense.

> **Building Accessible Sites Is Good for Business**
> According to the U.S. Department of Labor, there are more than 50 million Americans with disabilities. These individuals have a spending power of $175 billion. Billion. With a *B*. Want a piece of *that* pie? I bet you do.

Sometimes business owners need more than an incentive of increased customers to build accessible Web sites. Sometimes the government has to get involved. Around the world governments are starting to mandate that government-funded Web sites be accessible. In the United States, the Rehabilitation Act was amended to require federal agencies to make their electronic information technology accessible to people with disabilities. And in Australia the Sydney Organising Committee for the Olympic Games was found to have engaged in unlawful conduct by providing a Web site that was, to a significant extent, inaccessible to the blind. More about this court case is available from `www.tomw.net.au/2001/bat2001f.html`.

Web sites that are built with accessibility in mind from the beginning are less expensive and more user friendly. Retrofitting a Web site to make it accessible costs more because every page and every piece of media on the site must be edited a second time to add the enhancements. Although it might not add a lot to a small site, having to edit hundreds (or even thousands) of pages will definitely cost you more time and money.

Who Needs an Accessible Site

If you spend enough time meeting new people, you'll eventually collect enough friends that you'll want to make every site you build as accessible as possible. Feeling excluded is one of the worst sensations in the world. Knowing you're excluding someone must be the second-worst feeling in the world. This is the part of the book where I lay on a bit of guilt, tell you about my friends, and ask you to include them in every future Web site that you build. It's not only good for business, but it's good for your karma too.

Eli is (mostly) blind, and it's getting worse. He can only see a sliver of light out of the corner of one eye. He uses a guide dog to get around but loves it when the pretty ladies help him navigate the busy market on Saturday mornings. (I asked him once how he knew who the pretty ladies were, and he just smiled at me.) Eli broke his back a couple of years ago while chopping wood when he slipped on a log and fell. He's doing much better, and this month there's a show of his pottery at one of the local galleries. Eli loves to bike. He rides a tandem with his wife.

Chris has cerebral palsy. He can't straighten his fingers, and he shuffles when he walks. Chris is a beat boxer, which is a kind of vocal percussion. First he makes basic noises in sequence to give him a rhythm and then adds in additional sounds to make the most incredible music. Although he can't decide whether he wants to be a Web developer or a professional beat boxer, Chris spends a crazy amount of time online. He loves watching videos of other beat boxers and planning how to build the next killer app.

Shane is color-blind. He can't tell the difference between red and green. When he was little, he wanted to become a fighter pilot. He was in Air Cadets and got a glider's license and then a pilot's license. Shane played on the high-school soccer team and ran cross-country with the track team. If Shane hadn't told you that he was color-blind, there's no way you would have known. Traffic lights are stacked from top to bottom (or left to right depending on where you are), and it's hard to pick awkward color combinations when you only ever wear jeans and polo shirts.

Angela is losing her hearing. Years of construction work without protective head gear have finally taken their toll. Unfortunately, Angela is also an avid birder. She used to use her hearing to spot the birds before she could see them. Although she has a hearing aid, she hates using it—something about pride. Every year Angela flees the cold Canadian winters along with the birds and heads down to Texas.

Ruth is 103. She's as sharp as a tack, but she doesn't hear or see quite as well as she used to. She gets the retirement home to drop her off downtown where she does her banking and some shopping before being picked up again. Ruth gets around town with a walker. She likes the benches along main street where she can stop and rest as she moves between stores. She's an avid writer and poet. This fall she'll be publishing another collection of short stories. In her last book she talked about what it was like back when there were still horses and carriages. Ruth is a wealth of stories and has outlived many generations younger than her.

A number of years ago I had the best teaching experience of my life. It was a college course on Web design, and I had two students, both named Josh, enrolled in the class. Josh #1 has Asperger's Syndrome. He is wonderful in the visual realm. If he can see it, he can understand it. He had a note taker in class to help convert the oral part of my lessons into written form. Josh #2 has Attention Deficit Hyperactive Disorder (ADHD). He is wonderful in the oral realm. If he can hear it, he can understand it. He used a screen reader with a karaoke bouncing ball to help convert the written word into information he could hear. To write his exams, he'd use his screen reader so that he could hear his answers and make sure they were right. That class was the best teaching experience of my life. The two Joshes forced me to balance my time in each of the senses. Based on which Josh had their hand up to ask a question, I knew exactly when to switch from demonstrations to "lecturing," and vice versa.

Assistive Technology

Assistive technology is the general term given to both hardware and software devices that help people with their daily lives. It includes everything from hearing aids to screen readers. To help people use computers and the Internet, a wide range of hardware and software is available.

Input Devices

When you have limited mobility, keyboards can be impossible to use. If you can't straighten your fingers, how do you press individual keys? If you have no mobility in your arms, how do you click a mouse? Input devices used by people with mobility impairments include the following.

- Keyboards with larger, more widely spaced keys.
- Key guards that fit over a regular keyboard and help prevent the unintentional pressing of keys.
- Mice adapted with a foot pedal or Sip/Puff switches (mouth controlled). There are even mice that are controlled by a user's head movements.
- Joysticks.
- Embossed keyboards (the bumps on the "home" keys).
- Touch pads, touch screens, and graphic tablets.
- Text-to-speech software.
- Computer setting adjustments to control the speed of a mouse and the sensitivity of the keyboard.

Chris uses a key guard that sits overtop a regular keyboard. It allows him to intentionally press each of the keys he wants to hit instead of mistyping as he works to straighten his fingers.

Output Devices and Enhancements

If you can't see, how do you know what's on the screen? If you can't hear, how do you know what Obama said in his weekly address to the nation? The following output devices help computer users receive information through an alternate format.

- Text-to-speech screen readers (some have the visual tracking like Josh's, and some do not).
- Refreshable Braille display. These displays are like a mini portable piano keyboard; 40 to 80 "cells" at a time, the computer screen is converted into Braille that can be read.
- Screen magnifiers.
- Customization of computer settings to adjust colors and sizes of navigation widgets, shortcut icons, and fonts.

More information about the assistive technologies used to navigate the Web is available from the University of Toronto's Adaptive Technology Resource Centre (http://atrc.utoronto.ca/index.php?option=com_content&task=blogsection&id=4&Itemid=9). When I was working in Toronto, the ATRC very generously allowed me to test my sites on their devices and watch people navigate the systems I'd built. What a humbling experience.

Building an Accessible Site

Unfortunately, creating a 100 percent accessible Web site isn't an achievable goal—we take a giant leap forward to make the Web accessible for one type of disability, and we sometimes end up taking a step backward for someone else. Web technology, assistive technology, and Web browsing strategies are constantly changing. The guidelines we use to create accessible sites are often out of date against the latest trends on the Web. Web accessibility is in a state of transition. This chapter can't possibly make you an expert, but it will ideally open your eyes to some of the basic changes that you can make, and that will help a lot of your Web site visitors.

Unless you're a developer, there's very little you can do to change the way that Drupal makes Web pages. You will be limited to improving the accessibility of the content within the Drupal framework. Fortunately, Drupal core is already one of the most accessible content management systems available today. Its developers have committed to meeting the international guidelines on accessibility. You can read the full accessibility statement at `http://drupal.org/about/accessibility`. If you would like to participate in the ongoing efforts to keep Drupal accessible, you can participate with the online accessibility community on the Drupal Groups Web site (`http://groups.drupal.org/accessibility`).

Most Drupal sites, however, also use a noncore theme and at least a few contributed modules. The administration of these contributed projects may not be accessible to both Web site visitors and content authors. To create an accessible Web site for all site visitors, you will need to carefully review each module you install both as an authoring tool and for the content it outputs to your public Web site.

Drupal Core

By creating a Web site using only Drupal's core modules, you will be creating a nearly accessible Web site without any additional work. There are, however, some known issues. For a complete (and up-to-date list), please visit `http://tinyurl.com/drupal7-accessibility-issues`.

Contributed Modules

Contributed modules enhance the functionality of your Web site. Whether you are using a contributed module to build better navigation, create image galleries, or improve your search engine rankings, you will need to carefully examine the output of each module you install to ensure it does not degrade the accessibility of your Drupal site.

Evaluating Modules

The easiest way to evaluate a module is to check the project page and see whether the developer has committed to one of two initiatives: the Drupal Accessibility eXperience (D7AX) or the Drupal Core 7 accessibility eXperience (DC7X). If these tags are not available on the module page, you can check the list of known Accessibility Issues in Contributed Modules to see whether the module you want to use is listed (`http://drupal.org/node/425494` and `http://groups.drupal.org/node/66323`).

Evaluating Modules
Test only one module at a time so that you can correctly identify any underlying problems.

Configuring Modules

After installing a new module, check the settings to ensure they are as accessible as possible. This includes the input and the output for the module. Simple configuration tips are as follows.

- Create and apply appropriate profiles for modules such as WYSIWYG editors. The editor should be disabled by default for those who cannot take advantage of it. If you don't know who all of your site visitors will be, disable the enriched features by default.

- Ensure there is only useful, semantic markup introduced by the new module. Run an automated accessibility check on the output of the module. Some modules have an administrative interface for the HTML (for example, Views), but most modules will need to be fixed from the theme layer.

If you can't make the module accessible on your own, report an accessibility error to the project with details on how to fix the problem. Even though most projects are maintained by volunteers in their spare time, they are generally helpful and will fix problems for you when they can. Instructions on how to report problems are included later in this chapter.

Modules That Enhance Accessibility

A few modules will actually enhance the accessibility of your site: Text Size and Page Style. These modules provide even more control to the Web site visitor by allowing the visitor to control the appearance of the text and colors of the site. On the one hand, your site may not look the way your designer likes it; on the other hand, it allows a visitor to create a site that they can use.

Text Size (`http://drupal.org/project/textsize`) displays an adjustable text size changer or zoom function. The zoom function applies to text, variable media objects, variable pixel images, and vector images. It does not apply to nonvariable objects with fixed pixel sizes such as JPEGs and PNGs. JavaScript is not required for this module, but cookies must be enabled. Figure 17.1 shows each of the different block options for this module. By default text links are used.

Once the module is installed, you will need to place the Text Size block into an appropriate region on your site. These settings are often displayed in the top-right corner of the header region; however, your site's design may have a more appropriate location. To use one of the alternate display options, use the administrative toolbar to navigate to Configuration > Text Size. You will be able to configure the following settings.

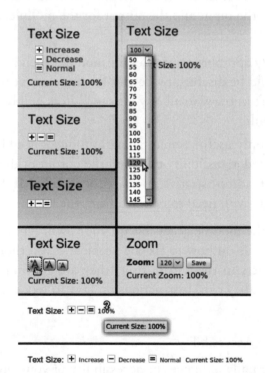

FIGURE 17.1 Multiple configuration options are available for the module Text Size including text-only links, text and images, or a drop-down menu to select the text size.

- Block title (Text Size or Zoom). You can also override this setting on the block administration page.
- Block type (Text links with CSS images, Image links, or Select menu).
- Root element to use for the resize process. Body is selected by default, but most block-level elements, along with a CSS ID or class, can be used.
- Increase and decrease steps as a percentage font size.
- Minimum, maximum, and "normal" text sizes.
- Cookie expiration date.

The Page Style module (`http://drupal.org/project/pagestyle`) allows site visitors to switch between a set of predefined, high-contrast style sheets (for example, Black on White, White on Black, or Yellow on Blue). The module Switchtheme (`http://drupal.org/project/switchtheme`) allows site visitors to switch between enabled themes (for example, Bartik and Garland).

Themes

A lot of power is given to theme builders. They are able to override any decision that has been made by a module builder on how the content of your site *looks*. This includes both the visual output and the HTML ("code") output. Accessible themes give control to the Web site visitor instead of your designer on three important points: font size, color contrast, and moving parts.

- **Font size.** Make sure your theme allows Web site visitors to use their preferred font size. Check the source of the CSS file and look for the unit used to define font sizes. Generally speaking, %, em, and keywords (xx-small to xx-large) are good; px is bad.
- **Color contrast.** Look for themes that have a high-contrast color palette and do not use color alone to convey meaning. This means pairing colors that are light and dark as well as different hues (or colors). Any icons that are used should use different shapes, not just color, to convey meaning. Additional tips on choosing high-contrast colors are included in the section "Testing Themes for Color Contrast."
- **JavaScript and other moving parts.** Those awesome carousels of content that automatically rotate from one screen of text to the next? Zzzt. It's inaccessible. That doesn't mean you can't have any type of interaction, though. Just make

sure that the user can control how things move from one element to the next. Be especially careful with things that blink. An object that blinks more than three times per second can trigger a seizure.

> ⚠ **JavaScript and Accessibility**
> Although most assistive technology works with JavaScript enabled, JavaScript *can* interfere with the assistive technology. This book will not be teaching you how to write JavaScript, so we won't get into the nitty-gritty details of how to make it accessible either.

In addition to giving your Web site visitor control over font size, color contrast, and moving parts, accessible themes will also provide "hidden" meaning to content in several key areas.

- **Alternative text for images and other non-HTML content.** Look at the HTML source for the file `page.tpl.php` and see whether you can spot `alt` attributes on images.

- **Allow users to skip repetitive elements on the page.** An important "skip to content" link is included in the template file `html.tpl.php` in Drupal core. Make sure your theme has not removed this link and actually links to the content section of your page.

Additional information on creating accessible themes is available from the Drupal-specific Accessibility Checklist in the Theming Guide (`http://drupal.org/node/465106`).

Previewing Themes

Drupal themes can be previewed on a number of live sites. The most popular preview site is Drupal Theme Garden (`http://themegarden.org/`). D theme for da Web (`http://d-theme.com/`) also allows visitors to use automated testing tools to check for WCAG 2.0 and Section 508 compliance. (Scroll to the bottom to find the links to each of the testing tools.)

> ✏ **Wish That Theme Was Accessible?**
> If there is a theme you like the design of but it is not accessible, submit an issue on Drupal.org and let the project know what needs to be fixed to comply with accessibility guidelines.

Not all contributed themes have been upgraded to Drupal 7 at this time; however, the following projects have made a commitment to accessibility in the past. This list highlights a range of different styles of themes.

- Celju (http://drupal.org/project/celju)
- Fusion, base theme for nearly 12 other plug-and-play themes (http://drupal .org/project/fusion)
- Genesis, base theme (http://drupal.org/project/genesis)
- Pluralism (http://drupal.org/project/pluralism)
- Pixture Reloaded (http://drupal.org/project/pixture_reloaded/)
- Tendu, base theme for BiDi languages (http://drupal.org/project/tendu)
- Zen, the ultimate base theme (http://drupal.org/project/zen)

In addition to these free themes, Top Notch Themes has made a public commitment to have all of its premium themes Section 508 compliant. These themes can be previewed at www.fusiondrupalthemes.com.

Testing Themes for Color Contrast

There are two styles of color testing tools for themes: those that test images (great for testing your files when they're still in the design phase) and those that test completed Web sites (great for retrofitting Web sites and checking CSS files). The following are a few of the automated testing suites available.

- **AccessColor** (www.accesskeys.org/tools/color-contrast.html)
- **Check my Colours** (www.checkmycolours.com)
- **Coblis,** a color blindness simulator for images (www.colblindor.com/ coblis-color-blindness-simulator)
- **Vischeck** (www.vischeck.com)
- **WebAIM Color Contrast Checker** (http://webaim.org/resources/ contrastchecker)

Making Drupal Even More Accessible

If you find an accessibility issue with Drupal core or one of the contributed projects, it is important that you let someone know. If you don't already have an account on Drupal.org, you will need to create one at http://drupal.org/user/register. Once you've created your account and have logged in, complete the following steps to register the accessibility problem you've found in a contributed module or theme.

1. Navigate to the project page for the module or theme for which you need to report an issue.

2. Look for the issues sidebar for this project and click the link "open issues."

3. In the issue search form, enter some keywords for your issue to see whether the issue has already been reported. If it has not been reported, proceed to the next step. If it has been reported, you can click through to see what progress is being made on fixing the issue.

4. If your issue has not been reported, click through to the link "Create a new issue." The link will take you to a URL that uses the format `http://drupal` `.org/node/add/project-issue/`*project_name.*

5. Complete the form to the best of your ability. Include a screen shot if it's relevant. Open the fieldset Tag toward the bottom of the form and add the tag "accessibility."

6. Scroll to the bottom of the screen and click Save.

You can monitor the progress on any issues you've opened (or left comments on) by navigating to `http://drupal.org/project/issues/user`.

To report a problem against Drupal core, go to `http://drupal.org/node/add/` `project-issue` and choose "Drupal core" from the list of projects.

Creating Accessible Content

Building an accessible site is a lot easier when you know the qualities of an accessible site and how these qualities help different kinds of site visitors. Sometimes it's hard to "see" where the problems are if you don't have problems seeing. To make it easier to evaluate your site without having to be an expert in accessibility, there are a number of automated testing tools you can use on your site. Some things, such as the clarity of the language on your site, will still need to be checked "by hand."

There are two main sets of Web accessibility guidelines: Web Accessibility Initiative (WAI) guidelines and, in the United States, Section 508 of the Rehabilitation Act. Although these two sets of guidelines are not mutually exclusive, building a site that complies with the highest level of accessibility using the WAI guidelines will often create a Section 508–compliant site.

The Web Content Accessibility Guidelines in the WCAG address the four principles of accessibility.

- Can the information be easily **perceived** (or "seen")?
- Can the software (Web site) be easily **operated** (or "navigated")?
- Is it easy to **understand** the content?
- Is the content **robust** enough to be interpreted by a wide range of browsers and assistive technologies?

Appendix F includes the points for each of the accessibility guidelines.

Once you've built your site (ideally while you're building your site), you will need to check to see whether you have met all the guidelines required to declare your site "accessible." You can check every point by hand using the checklists for each set of guidelines, but there are also a number of automated tests that will make testing a lot easier and a lot more accurate. Ultimately, you will need to conduct user testing with assistive devices to guarantee you have created an accessible site. Using the check lists and at least two automated test suites will find most of the problems in your site.

Accessibility Check Lists

Check lists make the world a lot easier. They allow you to quickly review the work you have done and confirm it is complete. Completing a check list does not prove conformance with Section 508 or the WCAG guidelines, but it will help you to make sure you have considered each of the points.

- Accessibility Guidelines for Drupal 7: WCAG 2.0 and ATAG 1.0 (`http://groups.drupal.org/node/18595`)
- WCAG 1.0 Checklist (`www.w3.org/TR/WCAG10/full-checklist.html`)
- WCAG 2.0 quick reference (`www.w3.org/WAI/WCAG20/quickref/`)
- WCAG 2.0 Checklist, HTML format (WebAIM) (`http://webaim.org/standards/wcag/checklist`)
- WCAG 2.0 Checklist, Microsoft Word or PDF (web usability) (`www.usability.com.au/resources/wcag2checklist.cfm`)
- Section 508 Checklist (WebAIM) (`www.webaim.org/standards/508/checklist`)

Easy to See

An image is only worth a thousand words if you can see it. In your text, describe the concept you are displaying thoroughly so that people who can't see the image can still understand what you're saying. Within the image tag itself, use an `alt` attribute to describe what the picture is showing. If you are uploading videos, provide a transcript of the video for those who can't hear or don't have the necessary plug-ins to view the video. For more information on how to make rich text accessible, take a peek at the Accessible Rich Internet Applications (ARIA) guidelines (`www.w3.org/WAI/intro/aria.php`). This applies to JavaScript-rich sites as well.

Screen readers can't guess what an image is. To make this content accessible to all of your site's visitors, you need to provide a text description for every image you upload to your site. When you upload an image, Drupal will prompt you to add alternate text (Figure 17.2). You just need to fill in the box.

If you are adding an image to a Web page without using the Image widget, you will need to remember to include an `alt` attribute that describes the image. If the image in Figure 17.2 were being added by hand, the HTML would look like this:

```
<img src="image_file.png" alt="Illustration of a male northern cardinal" />
```

Video, audio, and other "rich media" files need to have transcriptions. To make video even more accessible, you can add captions for the hearing impaired. Additional information on video captioning can be found at `www.webaim.org/techniques/captions/`. YouTube also offers specific guidelines on how to add captions to the videos you upload to its site (`www.google.com/support/youtube/bin/answer.py?hl=en&answer=100077`). Transcripts and subtitles can also be translated, making your content even more accessible to people around the world.

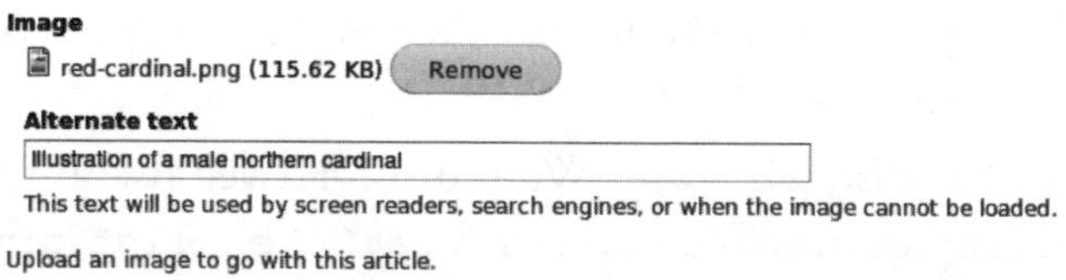

Image

red-cardinal.png (115.62 KB)   (Remove)

Alternate text

Illustration of a male northern cardinal

This text will be used by screen readers, search engines, or when the image cannot be loaded.

Upload an image to go with this article.

FIGURE 17.2 The Image upload widget will prompt you to add an alternate description of the image once it has been uploaded.

Easy to Operate

There are lots of different ways you can make your site easy to use, but the most obvious is the actual navigation system. Make sure your navigation is keyboard accessible. Navigate to a page on your Web site and press the Tab key. The first navigation element should appear highlighted or at least have a tiny dotted box around it. Wherever possible, avoid fly-out (also known as drop-down) menus that open in more than one direction. I don't have mobility issues, and it still takes me at least two swings at a menu to hit the right menu item.

Computer programs can read only the information they are provided. Web browsing software can display visual enhancements for sighted visitors, but these enhancements don't mean anything to a computer program unless the meaning is explicitly included with proper HTML tags in the Web page.

Screen readers can build in-page tables of content from the HTML heading tags that are used on the page. This allows visitors with screen readers to scan headings instead of having to listen to every single word. (Imagine if you had to read every single word of this book because there were no headings and no index. Yucky, right?) Content subsections should use heading levels h2 to h6 as appropriate. h1 is reserved for the title of the page—your theme will insert this tag for you.

Easy to Understand

Writing good content takes practice. Some people even go to school to learn how to write (we often refer to them as "authors" or "journalists"). Writing on the Web is not like writing for print. On the Web you need to write your text so that it is very easy to scan.

- Use subheadings to break a long page into multiple sections.
- Use bullet and numbered lists to break key ideas into easily digested information.
- Add illustrations, diagrams, and photos to enhance your message, but never use graphics to replace the written word.
- Add definitions for acronyms and other industry-specific jargon.
- Avoid the overuse of contractions (wouldn't, can't) and local slang or phrases (for example, "that's sik," which means "good"; "sick" is ill, which used to be good; and *sic*, which is still known to be wrong).

Read your page out loud before publishing it to the Web. This will help you spot errors. For larger Web sites, hire a professional editor. No matter how good you are, an editor will make your writing better.

Provide Help

Provide clear instructions to help users complete forms without error on their first attempt. Clearly explain what exists on the other side of a link. Don't make people guess what a ducky icon means on your site. Make people feel smart, not stupid, when they use your site. Test your site with friends and colleagues. Ask them where you could have made things a little clearer. If it makes sense, include a "help" area that answers commonly asked questions and tours people through each of the features of your site.

Testing Your Site

There are a lot of ways to test your site for accessibility. One of the easiest tricks you'll need up your sleeve is a simple one. In your Web browser, disable the CSS and the images and try navigating around your Web site. It won't find all the problems, but it will often find quite a few.

Text-Only Browsers

Computer-aided browsing (Refreshable Braille Display, screen readers) can deal only with text. They can't create meaning that isn't there. They won't describe a picture to you, and they certainly can't perform mouse actions that are used as JavaScript triggers, because there is no mouse. Use a text-only browser to test your site. Figure 17.3 shows the home page of a Drupal 7 site in Links, a text-only browser. If you can use the Web site, chances are good that it will be usable by folks who can't see your Web page.

Text-only browsers are available online from `www.delorie.com/web/lynxview.html` and `www.standards-schmandards.com/projects/fangs/`.

You can simulate a text-only browser by using the Web Developer Toolbar plug-in for Firefox. Once it's installed, use the Web Developer toolbar to disable CSS and JavaScript and turn off images. With CSS and JavaScript disabled, try browsing your Web site and see whether you can still find information and buy products.

Automated Testing Tools

After creating, or updating, Web pages, immediately check to see the page is using valid HTML markup and complies with your site's accessibility standard. Retrofitting a site will take a lot longer than ensuring only accessible pages are produced in the first place. The tools for checking Web sites for accessibility guidelines will typically return either a summary table of errors that were found or an overlay of your site showing you exactly where the errors are. Figure 17.4 shows a WAVE report for Drupal.org

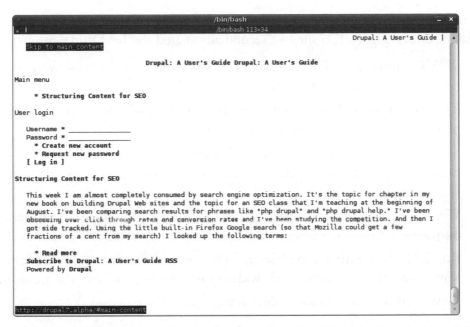

FIGURE 17.3 Drupal sites appear as a linear page of text when viewed in Links. Note the accessibility enhancement "Skip to main content" link at the top of the page.

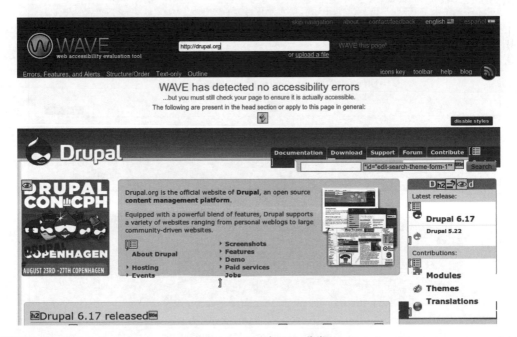

FIGURE 17.4 Drupal.org passes the WAVE automated accessibility test.

reporting no errors. Figure 17.5 shows the same report run on Microsoft.com with a few minor errors. Figure 17.6 shows a second automated test for Drupal.org

- WAVE, online accessibility checker for Web sites (`http://wave.webaim.org/` `http://fae.cita.uiuc.edu/`)
- Truwex Online, web accessibility testing tool: WCAG and Section 508 compliance (`http://checkwebsite.erigami.com/accessibility.html`)
- Stanford Online Web Accessibility Checker for Web sites (`www.stanford` `.edu/group/accessibility/cgi-bin/accessibilitychecker/checker/` `index.php`)
- Worldspace accessibility checker (includes a test for PDFs) (`http://worldspace.` `dequecloud.com/worldspace/wsservice/eval/checkCompliance.jsp`)
- Run FAE; by creating a free user account you can also test multiple pages via Web crawling and produce a sitewide report (`http://fae.cita.uiuc.edu/`)
- TAW Online also tests for mobile devices (`www.tawdis.net/`)

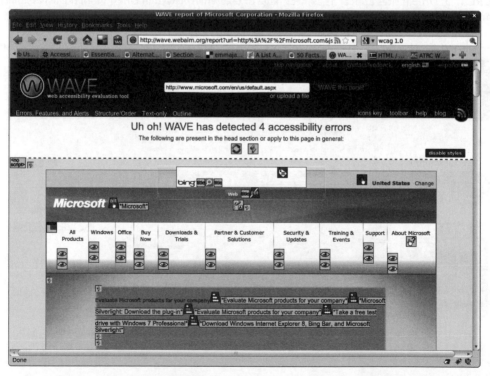

FIGURE 17.5 Microsoft.com fails the WAVE automated accessibility test with four very minor errors.

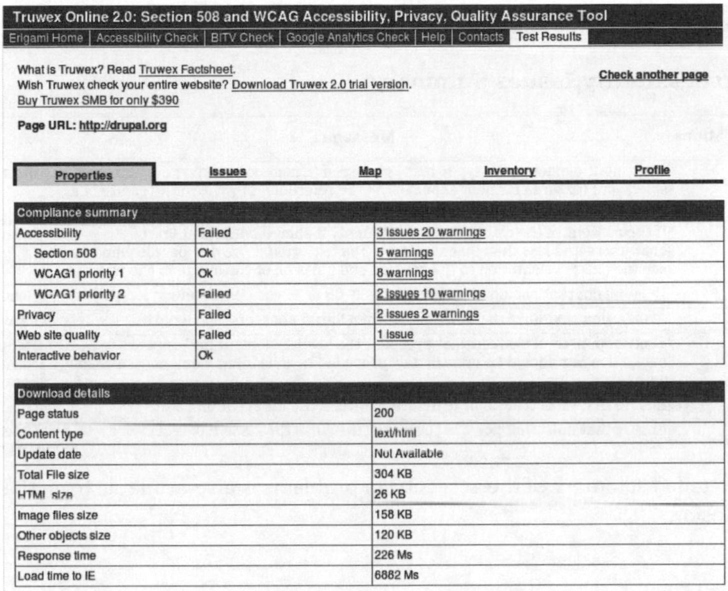

FIGURE 17.6 Drupal.org fails the WCAG 1.0, priority level 2, automated test using Truwex online.

Browser-based tools will perform checks of the page you are currently viewing. Figure 17.7 shows the pop-up window summary of the accessibility errors from one Web site, and Figure 17.8 shows the "summary" with additional information about the accessibility errors on this page.

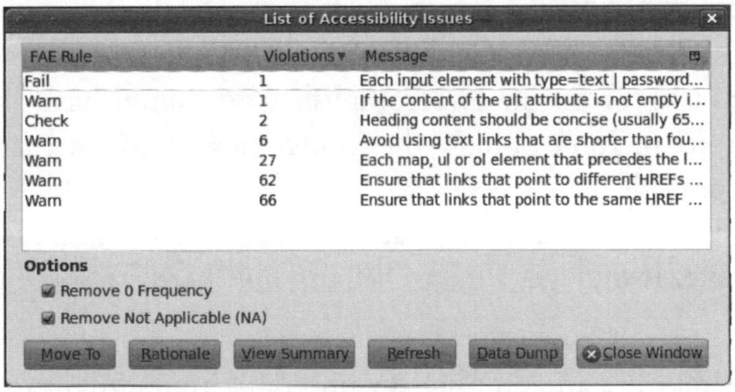

FIGURE 17.7 Firefox Accessibility Extension provides on-page summaries of potential accessibility problems.

Accessibility Extension

List of Accessibility Issues Summary

FAE Rule	Violations	Message	Class
Fail	1	Each input element with type=text | password | checkbox | radio | file and each select and textarea element should either be referenced by the for attribute of a label element via its id attribute, or have a title attribute.	Forms
Warn	1	If the content of the alt attribute is not empty it should contain at least 7 characters and less than 90 characters. The text should provide people who cannot see the image orientation to the content and purpose of the image in the website.	Images
Check	2	Heading content should be concise (usually 65 or fewer characters in length).	Headings
Warn	6	Avoid using text links that are shorter than four 4 characters in length.	Links
Warn	27	Each map, ul or ol element that precedes the last h1 element and appears to be a navigation bar should be immediately preceded by a heading element, preferably an h2.	Menu and Navigation Bars
Warn	62	Ensure that links that point to different HREFs use different link text.	Links
Warn	66	Ensure that links that point to the same HREF use the same link text.	Links

FIGURE 17.8 A detailed summary of the accessibility problems is also available from the Firefox Accessibility Extension.

- Firefox Accessibility Extension (https://addons.mozilla.org/en-US/firefox/addon/5809/)
- Firefox Colour Contrast Analyser (https://addons.mozilla.org/en-US/firefox/addon/7313/)

User Testing

Checklists are good. Automated validation tools are good. Starting with a good code base is good. But nothing beats user testing. To make a truly accessible site, you will need to find real people and get honest feedback from them about what works and what doesn't. This includes people with disabilities. When testing your site, make sure you have specific tasks for people to accomplish. You should have "most wanted outcomes" from Chapter 6. You can reuse these outcomes as tests to ensure your Web site is as accessible as possible.

Statistics suggest you probably know at least one person with a disability. Ask them to help test your site. If they get tired of helping out, here are some new ways to find helpful folks.

- My local library has an adult literacy program. Yours might too. Drop by and ask whether you can have one of the volunteers use your site in one of their upcoming lessons.

- Many communities will have outreach offices for specific disabilities. My community has an office for the Canadian National Institute for the Blind (CNIB). I bet your community has something similar. Check the yellow pages to see what resources are in your community.
- The Drupal Accessibility Working Group is filled with fabulous experts. Join the group and ask for help in reviewing your site.

Be sure to thank everyone who takes the time to test your site.

Summary

In this chapter, you met a few of my friends and learned about why it's so important to me that you build an accessible site. I showed you how a little bit of work up front would make your sites that much more accessible without a lot of extra work. You learned some of the top tips for creating accessible content and the key points used by accessibility guidelines today. Drupal makes building an accessible site easier than any other Web-based content management system. Creating an accessible site will make it easier for all visitors to use your site. Drupal has already done most of the hard work; the rest is up to you.

Appendices

Appendices

Appendix A

Sample User Survey

Seniors Advocacy and Awareness Network

These questions are designed to assess the computing power and the current level of comfort with Web sites and online communities within the Seniors Advocacy and Awareness Network (SAAN). Answers will be used to create the build plan for the new Web site. Additional questions can be added to this survey if there are specific areas you would like feedback on. These questions may specifically relate to goals outlined by the funding organization for this project.

1. How do you spend your time on the Internet each week (choose the best fit)?

   - I only check e-mails.
   - I check my e-mails and read a little bit of news (for example, *The Sun Times*, the *Globe and Mail*, or other news sites).
   - I also use the Internet to do a little research (for example, upcoming events, comparison shopping, or vacation planning).
   - I do all of the above and chat with friends online and/or participate in discussion forums.
   - Realistically? I live online.

2. How quickly did this page load for you?
   - Faster than most pages I visit
   - About the same as most pages I visit
   - Slower than most pages I visit

3. How fast is your main Internet connection?
   - Dial-up
   - High speed (cable or DSL)
   - Dial-up, but I also have access to a high-speed Internet connection

4. How old is your computer?
   - Less than a year old.
   - 1 to 2 years old.
   - 3 to 5 years old.
   - My computer is a dinosaur.

5. Has the software on your computer ever been upgraded?
   - Yes, the software on my computer is upgraded at least once a year
   - Yes, but it's been more than a year
   - No (or not sure)

6. Have you ever used any of the following online tools?
   - Subscribed to an e-mail announcement newsletters (read-only)
   - Participated in e-mail discussion groups
   - Facebook
   - Web-based discussion board (sometimes called a *forum* or a *bulletin board system*)
   - Internet "chat" (such as MSN or AIM)
   - Online events calendar
   - Gallery or photo-sharing Web site (such as Flickr or Picassa)
   - Survey and voting tools (for example, survey monkey)
   - E-commerce, eBay (purchased or sold something online)
   - Online donations (contributed to a campaign online)

7. What are your favorite Web sites and why?

   This list is important. It helps Web developers understand the kind of Web site that your community needs. Please list your favorite overall Web site as well as one that is specifically related to the work the SAAN is doing.

8. What could our Web site do for you when it's finished?

   Your answer might include a list of things that the Web site "must have" or "would be nice to have" or "I really hope this Web site doesn't."

9. What are your complaints?

   Your answer might include complaints about Web sites generally or Web sites that are specific to advocacy and/or seniors Web sites.

10. When you find a Web site that you hope you never have to use again, what is it about that Web site that you dislike?

11. What did we forget to ask?

12. About you...

    You are not required to answer these questions. You can remain anonymous if you want.

    • Your name.

    • E-mail address.

    • Community/location.

    • What is your involvement within the community that our organization supports?

Appendix B

Preparing Your Development Environment

The instructions listed here will also apply if you are setting up a Web server for use inside a company intranet. Each of these install guides includes tips on how to install an AMP stack. Depending on your operating system, you will be installing LAMP (Linux), WAMP (Windows), or MAMP (Mac OS X). The AMP stands for Apache (the Web server), MySQL (the database), and PHP (the scripting language). Drupal also supports IIS (Windows server) and Postgres (database).

The following are required to run Drupal.

- Apache 2.*x* running on Windows, Mac OS X, or Linux. IIS is also supported when correctly configured.

- MySQL 5.0.15 or greater; and requires the PDO database extension for PHP *or* Postgres 8.3 or greater.

- PHP 5.2 or greater, with a memory allocation of 64MB or more and support for the GD Image Library enabled.

The detailed list of requirements is available at `http://drupal.org/requirements`.

Full Development Environment

Acquia offers a desktop development environment. With a one-click install, you can get everything you need to run Drupal on your desktop. This is perfect for developers and folks who just want to play around with Drupal a little bit before installing it on their public Web site. The Dev Desktop is available for Mac OS X and Windows. You can download the installer from `http://network.acquia.com/downloads/7.x`.

Windows

There are a lot of different AMP options for Windows. If you like to shop around, take a look at the comparison chart on Wikipedia (`http://en.wikipedia.org/wiki/Comparison_of_WAMPs`).

If you don't like to shop around, install the XAMPP server from `www.apache-friends.org/en/xampp-windows.html`. This link includes instructions on how to install the XAMPP server for your version of Windows. Once completed, you will be able to view your Web server from a Web browser at `http://localhost`.

Mac OS X

Although Mac OS X comes with PHP and Apache installed, they are old versions of the software and will not be sufficient to run Drupal 7. Installing MAMP will ensure you are running the right version of everything you need to install Drupal on your computer. MAMP can be downloaded from `www.mamp.info/en/downloads/index.html`. The free version of the software should be sufficient for your needs.

Linux, BSD, and other *nix Variants

Most free operating systems will have a package manager that allows you to easily install a complete AMP server. I have found the most effective way to get exactly what Drupal needs is to install the software package provided by the operating system for Drupal. This will typically install all related dependencies (such as PHP, MySQL, and Apache) as well. FreeBSD, Ubuntu, and Fedora all have a Drupal package. Read the instructions carefully. You will sometimes need to install the database separately because both Postgres and MySQL are appropriate database choices. If all of that seems a little too complicated, skip to the earlier Windows section (Oh. The. Shame.) and install the Linux version of XAMPP.

Customizing Your AMP

If you want to change the location where your Web files are stored on your computer, you will need to alter the Web server's configuration file to point to a new directory. This configuration option is typically set in the file `httpd.conf`. Table B.1 lists common locations for the Apache configuration file.

Once you've located the configuration file, you will need to update two lines.

- `DocumentRoot ""`. Alter the path to match the directory where you would like to store Drupal and its related files (omit the trailing slash on the path name).

- `<Directory "">`. Alter the path to match the directory you used in the previous item.

```
#
# DocumentRoot: The directory out of which you will serve your
# documents. By default, all requests are taken from this directory, but
# symbolic links and aliases may be used to point to other locations.
#
DocumentRoot "/Users/druplicon/Sites"

[...]

#
# This should be changed to whatever you set DocumentRoot to.
#
<Directory "/Users/druplicon/Sites">
    [...]
</Directory>
```

TABLE B.1 Locating `httpd.conf`

Setup Method	Configuration File Path
Windows (XAMPP)	`C:\xampp\apache\conf\httpd.conf`
Linux	Type `locate httpd.conf` in a terminal window
Mac OS X Tiger	`/private/etc/httpd/httpd.conf`
Mac OS X Leopard	`/private/etc/apache2/httpd.conf`
Mac OS X (MAMP)	Use MAMP control panel (Preferences > Apache) or `/Applications/MAMP/conf/apache/httpd.conf`

TABLE B.2 Starting and Stopping Apache

Setup Method	Restarting Method
Windows (XAMPP)	Use the XAMPP control panel.
Linux	Type `apachectl restart` or `/etc/init.d/apache restart`.
Mac OS X	Navigate to System Preferences > Sharing, and uncheck/check "(Personal) web sharing."
Mac OS X (MAMP)	Use the MAMP control panel application (Preferences > Apache).

Once you've made these changes. you will need to restart Apache for the changes to take effect. Instructions on how to complete this step are available from Table B.2.

Revision Control

Regardless of whether you are working in an office as part of a multiperson team or alone at home with just your cat for company, you really ought to store your files in a version-control system. This approach allows you to maintain a log of all changes that are made to your files and permits you to revert to a previously saved version of your file if necessary. Several different version control systems are available. The best one for you to use is the one you are motivated to use—a choice that may be dictated by the software selected by your officemates or by your clients. Commonly used version-control systems include these packages.

- **Git.** `http://git-scm.com/`. Drupal uses Git to store revisions of its code. It is a distributed version-control system.

- **Subversion.** `http://subversion.tigris.org/`. This is the most popular centralized version-control system.

- **Bazaar.** `http://bazaar-vcs.org`. This is my version-control system of choice. It is distributed, like Git.

- **Concurrent Version System (CVS).** `www.nongnu.org/cvs/`. Drupal was stored in this system. You shouldn't ever use it, unless you must.

Appendix C

Advanced Installation of Drupal

Multisite Installations

By default Drupal allows you to run several Web sites from a single code base. There are *many* advantages to using Drupal's multisite for your projects.

- Security patches need to be applied to only one set of files.

- Several Web sites using similar (but not identical) sets of modules. You can install them into a common folder so that all Web sites controlled by that Drupal folder can easily enable modules from the shared pool. You can think of this as extending the set of modules that ships with Drupal.

- Web sites with unique requirements can have their own modules that are not available to other Web sites using the same install base.

- You can share themes between sites. For example, if you are running several department Web sites under one umbrella, they may all share the same theme but contain completely unique content.

- You have to download Drupal only once. If you want to upgrade Drupal, you need to update only one set of files.

In addition to the multisite capabilities built in to Drupal, there are two additional ways to deal with a large number of sites. The first is Aegir.

Hosting Multiple Web Sites from One Code Repository

I have traveled around the world to talk about how Drupal's multisite capabilities have benefited my business. Multisite allows you to use a single set of Drupal files (the "code base") to run multiple, completely unique Web sites. And it's available by default. You don't need to install any extra modules, set up some fancy server configuration thingy, or do anything else. You just go ahead and do it. Convinced? Great! (It is so simple you will think I've left out an important part of the instructions.) This is how you do it.

1. In the Drupal folder named `sites`, create a new folder that exactly matches your domain name. For example, if you want to install a new site for the domain name `marketside.ca`, you would make the new folder with that name. Three folders should now be present in the `sites` directory: `all`, `default`, and `marketside.ca` (no need to include the `www`; Drupal will figure it out).

2. Make sure the permissions on your new directory are correct.

3. Create a database for your new site.

4. Copy the file `default.settings.php` from the folder `default` to your new directory.

5. Rename the new file to `settings.php` and check that the permissions are set according to the install instructions earlier in this appendix.

6. Proceed with the install wizard for Drupal.

That's it! We could make it harder, but why bother?

Need Several Domain Names to Point to the Same Web Site?
Instructions on how to configure Drupal to have several domain names point to the Web site are contained in the file `sites/example.sites.php`.

Aegir Hosting System

Aegir is a complete hosting platform developed by Adrian Rousseau and sponsored by Development Seed. It is a collection of Drupal modules that allow you to deploy an entire network of Drupal Web sites. To use Aegir, you must have your own Linux or Unix server. Unlike Drupal's built-in multisite capabilities, Aegir does not work in a shared hosting environment. Unless you're planning on running a Web site hosting company, you will not need Aegir.

> **How Do You Pronounce Aegir?**
> I pronounce it with a hard *g* as in the *agar* used to grow mold in science labs. Other people use a soft *g*. The word itself is from the Norse god Ægir. I'll let the orthoepists decide whether I'm wrong.

For more information about the Aegir Hosting System, visit the project page at `http://groups.drupal.org/aegir-hosting-system`. When this chapter was first written, there was no version of Aegir available for Drupal 7.

Domain Access

This project is a suite of modules that provide tools for running a group of affiliated sites from one Drupal installation and a single shared database. It was created by Ken Rickard and is sponsored by Palantir.net. The module allows you to share users, content, and configurations across a group of sites. The module uses Drupal's Node Access system to determine what content is available on each site in the network. The Domain Access module determines user access based on the active domain that the user is viewing, rather than the group or site to which the user belongs. Unless you're planning on running a very large content network that requires precise control over publishing and syndication, you will not need Domain Access.

For more information about Domain Access, visit the project page at `http://drupal.org/project/domain`.

Appendix D

CSS Grid Frameworks

I want to make sure you understand how a CSS grid framework works. I know I said you didn't have to know HTML and CSS, but I may have lied a little bit to make you feel more confident. It's not hard, though, so stick with me!

First things first. You're going to need a copy of the 960.gs grid framework. Download the kit from `http://960.gs`. We're going to get your hands dirty and see how this stuff actually works in practice without Drupal getting in the way.

Open your HTML editor of choice. (Notepad is fine; Microsoft Word is not.) At its minimum, a Web page contains only a DOCTYPE and tags for `html`, `head`, `title`, and `body` elements. So, that's what we're going to do: make a *minimum viable Web page.*

```
<!DOCTYPE html PUBLIC "-//W3C//DTD XHTML 1.0 Transitional//EN"
"http://www.w3.org/TR/xhtml1/DTD/xhtml1-transitional.dtd">
<html xmlns="http://www.w3.org/1999/xhtml">
<head>
  <title>Conforming XHTML 1.0 Transitional Template</title>
</head>
<body>
```

```
</body>

</html>
```

To this very simple template, add the CSS grid framework files by adding the following HTML snippet on a new line, directly below the <head> tag.

```
<link rel="stylesheet" href="css/master.css" />
```

Change the file name (the bit inside that currently reads css/master.css) to match the location of your 960.gs files. Once this is complete, you are ready to start working with the grid system.

The remainder of this section will show only the HTML that needs to appear between the <body> and </body> tags.

> **Punctuation in 960.gs Differs from NineSixty in Drupal**
> The 960gs uses _underscores_ instead of Drupal's coding standard (which uses -hyphens-). You will need to adjust your class assignments accordingly when you switch to Drupal if you want to use the base theme NineSixty.

960.gs comes in two flavors: 12 column and 16 column. Before you can assign column widths in your HTML, you must first decide whether this container will be 12 columns wide or 16 columns wide. This is done as follows.

```
<div class="container_12">

  <!-- new shapes will be placed inside this container  -->

</div>
```

Assuming the whole Web site will be contained in the same shape, you will need to make this declaration only once. The rest of your <div>s will be assigned a grid width. You can also add a unique identifier to the container if you like. The following is an example.

```
<div class="container_12" id="page">
```

Working from the top-left corner of your design file, create a new <div> for each box. To the <div> add the column count as a class. For example, if you have a two-column layout where the content column uses eight columns and the sidebar uses four, you would add two new <div>s to your file like so.

```
<div class="container_12">
  <div class="grid_8"><!-- content column --></div>
  <div class="grid_4"><!-- sidebar column --></div>
</div>
```

Once the numbers in the grid classes equal the container number, a new row will automatically be created. (You can also force a new row by adding the CSS class clearfix.) Each row may be divided however you like, such as the first row as a header that stretches the full width of the page, a footer region containing four equally spaced columns, and a content area with a left sidebar (Figure D.1).

The snippet for this example would be as follows.

```
<div class="container_12">
<!-- header row  -->
  <div class="grid_12"><!-- header row --></div>

<!-- content  -->
  <div class="grid_4"><!-- sidebar column --></div>
  <div class="grid_8"><!-- content column --></div>

<!-- footer menus  -->
  <div class="grid_3"><!-- outer left footer --></div>
```

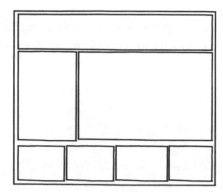

FIGURE D.1 The configuration screen for an announcement view

```
  <div class="grid_3"><!-- inner left footer --></div>
  <div class="grid_3"><!-- inner right footer --></div>
  <div class="grid_3"><!-- outer right footer --></div>
</div>
```

Using the 960.gs grid system, you can easily reorder your content so that the navigation appears after the text in the source of your document. To swap positions, you must use a push-pull technique to change the location of the page elements. For example, if you wanted the content to appear to search engines *before* the sidebar, you would need to complete the following steps.

1. Inverse the position of the content and sidebar areas in the HTML source.
2. Use CSS classes to pull the sidebar back over to the left visually and push the content away from the left.

The snippet would be as follows.

```
<!-- content  -->
<div class="grid_8 push_4"><!-- content column --></div>
<div class="grid_4 pull_8"><!-- sidebar column --></div>
```

A push-pull swap must always be performed in pairs—as one region is moved to the right, another must take its place by shifting to the left.

The previous examples assume that each row contains one page element per container. You can also have a layout where you need to nest multiple columns inside a single, larger column (Figure D.2). For example, you may want to have a two-column content area on some pages.

The easiest way to do this is to subdivide one of your regions into multiple columns. The total number of inner columns must add up to the number of columns on the parent grid. For example, 8 columns = 4 + 4 columns.

```
<!-- content  -->
<div class="grid_4"><!-- sidebar column --></div>
<div class="grid_8">
  <div class="grid_2"><!-- content column 1 --></div>
  <div class="grid_6"><!-- content column 2 --></div>
</div>
```

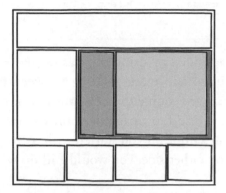

FIGURE D.2 You can also nest columns within another column.

As written, this snippet won't make a three-column Web page. The two nested columns are too fat. You also need to collapse the outer margins on the two content columns. This is accomplished by assigning the first contained element with the special class alpha and the second contained element with the special class omega. The revised snippet would be as follows.

```
<!-- content  -->
<div class="grid_4"><!-- sidebar column --></div>
<div class="grid_8">
    <div class="grid_2 alpha"><!-- content column 1 --></div>
    <div class="grid_6 omega"><!-- content column 2 --></div>
</div>
```

To remove both the left and right margins from a single element, simply assign both the alpha and the omega classes to a single element.

If there were three nested elements, the middle element would be left unchanged.

```
<!-- content  -->
<div class="grid_4"><!-- sidebar column --></div>
<div class="grid_8">
    <div class="grid_2 alpha"><!-- content column 1 --></div>
    <div class="grid_2"><!-- content column 2 --></div>
```

```
     <div class="grid_4 omega"><!-- content column 3 --></div>
</div>
```

Empty columns can be added by using the classes `prefix` and `suffix` to a grid. This is useful if you want to add more padding between columns. Like `grid`, the classes `prefix` and `suffix` are counted in columns and may be as wide as you like. For each column of space you add to a page element, you must remember to remove a column from the grid. For example, if you started with `grid_8` and wanted to make it narrower by one column on either side, you would end up with the following.

```
<div class="grid_6 suffix_1 prefix_1">
  <!-- 8 column element  -->
</div>
```

Once you have the right number of shapes on your page, displaying at the correct width, it's time to gussy up your page template using color, imagery, and type. You may need to fine-tune your layout to get everything to line up perfectly. The 960 Gridder Overlay available from http://gridder.andreehansson.se/ will help you see where things aren't quite lining up. To each page element that needs to be shuffled out of the grid framework, assign a unique ID. Create a new CSS file and style the page elements you want to shuffle.

Appendix E

Domicile Theme Files

The Domicile theme is available for download from `http://drupal.org/project/domicile`. If you would like to use this theme you are encouraged to download the theme from Drupal.org. These files are included for reference purposes only.

domicile.info

```
name = D7SBE - Domicile
description = A three-column design by Design House.
screenshot = screenshot.png
core = 7.x
engine = phptemplate
base theme = ninesixty

; Stylesheets.
stylesheets[all][] = styles.css
```

```
; To show the grid and debug your theme's layout, delete this section.
; You will be able to remove this
; when http://drupal.org/node/1032486 is rolled out
stylesheets[all][] = debug.css


; Regions
regions[nav_left] = Navigation (left)
regions[feature_middle] = Feature column (middle)
regions[content] = Content column (right)
regions[copyright_footer] = Copyright notice (footer)


; Features
features[] = logo
features[] = name
features[] = favicon


; Disabled features
; features[] = main_menu
; features[] = secondary_menu
; features[] = node_user_picture
; features[] = comment_user_picture
; features[] = search ; use the Search block instead
; features[] = slogan
```

page.tpl.php

```
<div id="page" class="container-12 clearfix">


<a href="#content" style="display: none">skip to content</a>


<div id="banner" class="grid-12 clearfix">
 <a href="<?php print $front_page; ?>"
    title="Back to <?php print $site_name; ?> home page">
```

```php
      <img src="<?php print $logo; ?>"
        alt="Back to <?php print $site_name; ?> home page." /></a>
</div>

<div id="main" class="grid-12 clearfix">
 <div id="nav" class="grid-2 alpha">
 <a href="<?php print $front_page; ?>"
    title="Back to <?php print $site_name; ?> home page">
    <h1 id="site-name">
     <img src="<?php print $base_path . $directory; ?>
       /site-name.jpg" alt="At Home" /></h1></a>
 <?php print render($page['nav_left']); ?>
 </div>

 <div id="feature" class="grid-4">
 <div class="decoration">
    <img src="<?php print $base_path . $directory; ?>
      /feature-decoration-top.jpg"
      alt="Furniture, Linen, Dishes" />
</div>
 <?php print render($page['feature_middle']); ?>
 <div class="decoration">
    <img src="<?php print $base_path . $directory; ?>
      /feature-decoration-bottom.jpg" alt=" " /></div>
 </div>

 <div id="content" class="grid-6 omega">
 <?php print render($title_prefix); ?>

 <?php if ($title): ?>
    <h1 class="title" id="page-title"><?php print $title; ?></h1>
 <?php endif; ?>

 <?php print render($title_suffix); ?>
```

```php
<?php if ($tabs): ?>
   <div class="tabs"><?php print render($tabs); ?></div>
<?php endif; ?>


<?php print $messages; ?>
 <?php print render($page['help']); ?>
 <?php print render($page['content']);?>
 <?php print $feed_icons; ?>
</div>


</div>

<div id="copyright" class="grid-12 clearfix">
  <?php print render($page['copyright_footer']); ?>
</div>


</div>
```

Appendix F

Web Accessibility Guidelines

There are two main sources of accessibility guidelines on the Internet: Web Accessibility Initiative (WAI) guidelines and, in the United States, Section 508 of the Rehabilitation Act.

Web Content Accessibility Guidelines (WCAG)

The canonical source for accessibility guidelines is produced by the World Wide Web Consortium (W3C). The latest version of the recommendations at the time this book was written was the Web Content Accessibility Guidelines (WCAG) 2.0. It is available at www.w3.org/TR/WCAG20/. The guidelines in the WCAG address the four principles of accessibility.

- Can the information be easily **perceived** (or "seen")?
- Can the software (Web site) be easily **operated** (or "navigated")?
- Is it easy to **understand** the content?
- Is the content **robust** enough to be interpreted by a wide range of browsers and assistive technologies?

These four principles are broken into 12 guidelines that a Web site must conform with to be considered "accessible." They are also rated in terms of priority indicating that a Web developer "must," "should," or "may" satisfy the checkpoint to create an "accessible" Web site. The levels of conformance (A, AA, AAA) indicate which checkpoints have been met from each priority level.

- Guideline 1.1 (Perceivable): Text Alternatives: Provide text alternatives for any non-text content so that it can be changed into other forms people need, such as large print, braille, speech, symbols, or simpler language.

- Guideline 1.2 (Perceivable): Time-based Media: Provide alternatives for time-based media.

- Guideline 1.3 (Perceivable): Adaptable: Create content that can be presented in different ways (for example simpler layout) without losing information or structure.

- Guideline 1.4 (Perceivable): Distinguishable: Make it easier for users to see and hear content including separating foreground from background.

- Guideline 2.1 (Operable): Keyboard Accessible: Make all functionality available from a keyboard.

- Guideline 2.2 (Operable): Enough Time: Provide users enough time to read and use content.

- Guideline 2.3 (Operable): Seizures: Do not design content in a way that is known to cause seizures.

- Guideline 2.4 (Operable): Navigable: Provide ways to help users navigate, find content, and determine where they are.

- Guideline 3.1 (Understandable): Readable: Make text content readable and understandable.

- Guideline 3.2 (Understandable): Predictable: Make Web pages appear and operate in predictable ways.

- Guideline 3.3 (Understandable): Input Assistance: Help users avoid and correct mistakes.

- Guideline 4.1 (Robust): Compatible: Maximize compatibility with current and future user agents, including assistive technologies.

These 12 guidelines are further broken down into hundreds of pages of detail that describe how you must build your Web site to be compliant with these guidelines.

> **Choose Your Level of Conformance**
> The government of Canada requires all federal Web sites to meet AA confor-
> mance and comply with all of Level 1 and Level 2 priority checkpoints of the
> WCAG 1.0 (www.tbs-sct.gc.ca/clf2-nsi2/clfs-nnsi/clfs-nnsi-2-eng.asp).
> You decide: Do you want to be as good as Canada, worse than Canada, or better
> than Canada?

The WCAG 2.0 guidelines have received criticism from many Web accessibility experts for being too long and lacking a number of the key factors from the first version of the guidelines. If you too feel overwhelmed by them, start by applying the WCAG 1.0 guidelines (www.w3.org/TR/WCAG10/) to your site. When you've mastered these guidelines, move on to WCAG 2.0.

Authoring Tool Accessibility Guidelines (ATAG)

WCAG covers what Web site *visitors* see and interact with. There is a second set of guidelines that covers the accessibility of the tools site administrators use to build Web sites. The Authoring Tools Accessibility Guidelines (ATAG) are currently in their second revision and can be read online at www.w3.org/TR/ATAG20/.

There are two parts to the ATAG guidelines: making the authoring tool user interface accessible and supporting the production of accessible content. The specific guidelines within these two areas are as follows:

- Guideline A.1.1: [For the authoring tool user interface] Ensure that web-based functionality is accessible.
- Guideline A.1.2: [For the authoring tool user interface] Ensure that non-web-based functionality is accessible.
- Guideline A.2.1: [For the authoring tool user interface] Make alternative content available to authors.
- Guideline A.2.2: [For the authoring tool user interface] Editing view presentation can be programmatically determined.
- Guideline A.2.3: [For the authoring tool user interface] Ensure the independence of authors' display preferences.
- Guideline A.3.1: [For the authoring tool user interface] Provide keyboard access to authoring features.

- Guideline A.3.2: [For the authoring tool user interface] Provide authors with enough time.
- Guideline A.3.3: [For the authoring tool user interface] Help authors avoid flashing that could cause seizures.
- Guideline A.3.4: [For the authoring tool user interface] Enhance navigation and editing via content structure.
- Guideline A.3.5: [For the authoring tool user interface] Provide text search of the content.
- Guideline A.3.6: [For the authoring tool user interface] Manage preference settings.
- Guideline A.3.7: [For the authoring tool user interface] Ensure that previews are as accessible as existing user agents.
- Guideline A.4.1: [For the authoring tool user interface] Help authors avoid and correct mistakes.
- Guideline A.4.2: [For the authoring tool user interface] Document the user interface including all accessibility features.
- Guideline B.1.1: Support web content technologies that enable the creation of content that is accessible.
- Guideline B.1.2: Ensure that the authoring tool preserves accessibility information.
- Guideline B.1.3: Ensure that automatically generated content is accessible.
- Guideline B.2.1: Guide authors to create accessible content.
- Guideline B.2.2: Assist authors in checking for accessibility problems.
- Guideline B.2.3: Assist authors in repairing accessibility problems.
- Guideline B.2.4: Assist authors with managing alternative content for non-text content.
- Guideline B.2.5: Assist authors with accessible templates and other pre-authored content.
- Guideline B.3.1: Ensure that accessible authoring actions are given prominence.
- Guideline B.3.2: Ensure that features of the authoring tool supporting the production of accessible content are available.

- Guideline B.3.3: Ensure that features of the authoring tool supporting the production of accessible content are documented.

- Guideline B.3.4: Ensure that any authoring practices demonstrated in documentation are accessible.

This book focuses on site building, not module development, so your capacity to follow these guidelines is somewhat limited. Either the module you select can be configured to follow these guidelines or it cannot. Later in this chapter, you will learn how to select modules that are accessible to content administrators.

Accessible Rich Internet Applications (WAI-ARIA)

A third set of guidelines are available to developers who are producing interactive widgets. These guidelines help developers add information about the widget to the widget itself. Adding information about the state of a widget will improve the accessibility of configuration screens where lists of items may be "collapsed" or in different "states."

More information is available from the following online resources.

- Accessible Web 2.0 Applications with WAI-ARIA (`www.alistapart.com/articles/waiaria`)

- WAI-ARIA overview (`www.w3.org/WAI/intro/aria`)

- WAI-ARIA technical specification (`www.w3.org/TR/wai-aria/`)

WAI-ARIA Is Written for Developers
The guidelines are written for application developers. They are well beyond the scope of what you will need to worry about as a site builder.

Section 508

As of 1998, federal agencies in the United States must make their electronic and information technology accessible to everyone. Section 508 of the amended Rehabilitation Act outlines the conditions that must be met to be "accessible." The act applies to all federal agencies when they develop, procure, maintain, or use electronic and information technology.

> **Section 508 Is Being Updated**
> At the time of this writing, the 1998 version of Section 508 was the most up-to-date version of the requirements; however, a new version of the guidelines were in draft format. The new guidelines will bring Section 508 in line with the WCAG. Pages that comply with WCAG 2.0 Level AA *and* the requirements outlined for Platforms, Applications, and Interactive Content; Electronic Documents; and Synchronized Media Content and Players will be deemed accessible. The draft guidelines are available at `www.access-board.gov/sec508/refresh/draft-rule.htm`. The current version of the accessibility guidelines is available from `www.access-board.gov/508.htm`.

There are 16 points that Web content must conform to in order to meet Section 508 compliance.

§ 1194.22 Web-based intranet and internet information and applications.

(a) A text equivalent for every non-text element shall be provided (e.g., via "alt", "longdesc", or in element content).

(b) Equivalent alternatives for any multimedia presentation shall be synchronized with the presentation.

(c) Web pages shall be designed so that all information conveyed with color is also available without color, for example from context or markup.

(d) Documents shall be organized so they are readable without requiring an associated style sheet.

(e) Redundant text links shall be provided for each active region of a server-side image map.

(f) Client-side image maps shall be provided instead of server-side image maps except where the regions cannot be defined with an available geometric shape.

(g) Row and column headers shall be identified for data tables.

(h) Markup shall be used to associate data cells and header cells for data tables that have two or more logical levels of row or column headers.

(i) Frames shall be titled with text that facilitates frame identification and navigation.

(j) Pages shall be designed to avoid causing the screen to flicker with a frequency greater than 2 Hz and lower than 55 Hz.

(k) A text-only page, with equivalent information or functionality, shall be provided to make a web site comply with the provisions of this part, when compliance cannot be accomplished in any other way. The content of the text-only page shall be updated whenever the primary page changes.

 (l) When pages utilize scripting languages to display content, or to create interface elements, the information provided by the script shall be identified with functional text that can be read by assistive technology.

(m) When a web page requires that an applet, plug-in or other application be present on the client system to interpret page content, the page must provide a link to a plug-in or applet that complies with §1194.21(a) through (l) [this is the section on software applications and operating systems].

(n) When electronic forms are designed to be completed on-line, the form shall allow people using assistive technology to access the information, field elements, and functionality required for completion and submission of the form, including all directions and cues.

(o) A method shall be provided that permits users to skip repetitive navigation links.

(p) When a timed response is required, the user shall be alerted and given sufficient time to indicate more time is required.

Letters (a) to (k) of the requirements are compliant with the WCAG 1.0 guidelines to Priority Level 1 accessibility. Letters (l) to (p) are not covered by the WCAG 1.0 guidelines; however, they are covered by the WCAG 2.0 guidelines.

There are an additional 12 guidelines that software and operating systems must comply with. These additional guidelines are similar to the ATAG guidelines discussed earlier. The complete text of Section 508, including the software requirements for accessibility, is available online (http://section508.gov/index.cfm?FuseAction=Content&ID=12).

> **Section 504 Compliance**
> A number of people have asked me about Section 504 compliance. This section of the Rehabilitation Act refers to the accessibility of the workplace. If a Web application is not 508 compliant and an employee of a federal agency needs to use that Web site as part of their job, the Web site is in violation of both Section 504 and Section 508. If you are compliant with Section 508, you are automatically compliant with Section 504 as well. There are no extra rules to be worried about if you are asked to produce a Web site that complies with the Rehabilitation Act.

Training for "Webmasters" is available from the Section 508 Web site. To register, you must supply your name, e-mail, phone number, and a password. No additional personal information is collected, and the course is free and should take less than a day to complete. You can register at `http://section508.gov/index.cfm?FuseAction=RegisterUniverse`.

Index

Symbols and Numbers

A

The Practical, Complete Guide to Customizing Drupal Sites with Behaviors, Themes, and Templates

"Drupal faces a common problem on the Web–the relative lack of new, high quality themes. *Front End Drupal* tackles this problem directly and is designed to help both experienced designers and rank novices get an understanding of how Drupal theming works. In fact, I'll be the first to admit I learned a lot from this book."

—Dries Buytaert, Drupal founder and project lead

ISBN-13: 9780137136698

Front End Drupal is 100% focused on issues of site design, behavior, usability, and management. Emma Jane Hogbin and Konstaintin Käfer show how to style Drupal sites, make the most of Drupal's powerful templating system, build sophisticated community sites, streamline site management, and build more portable, flexible themes. You'll also gain hands-on experience through several case studies that walk you through the customization of everything from page templates to Web site forums.

For more information and to read sample material please visit **informit.com/title/9780137136698**

Title is also available at safari.informit.com

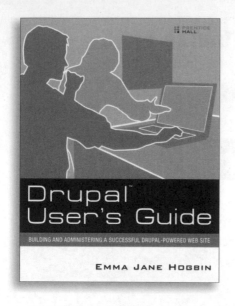